# Three Roses

# Three Roses

Living with Muscular Dystrophy and
Marrying an Exceptional Woman

## Michael S. Hudecki

**THREE ROSES**
**Living with Muscular Dystrophy and Marrying an Exceptional Woman**

iUniverse books may be ordered through booksellers or by contacting:

iUniverse
1663 Liberty Drive
Bloomington, IN 47403
www.iuniverse.com
1-800-Authors (1-800-288-4677)

ISBN: 978-1-4917-8249-1 (sc)
ISBN: 978-1-4917-8250-7 (hc)
ISBN: 978-1-4917-8262-0 (e)

Library of Congress Control Number: 2015919835

Print information available on the last page.

iUniverse rev. date: 12/10/2015

# CONTENTS

# DEDICATION

With My Eternal Gratitude, RajMohini, Veronica, Stephen, Gregory, Karen, Stephanie, and Patricia

# PREFACE

The roots of this book date back to the late 1970s. At the time I was a research fellow, a naisent scientist attempting to discover the cause as well as a viable treatment for inherited muscular dystrophy. Working with animal models, our team hit upon a number of meaningful discoveries, in fact so meaningful it looked like I might be able to garner serious funding to continue and expand our investigations. However, unknown to me at the time, certain individuals were at work to scuttle my plans by poisoning the waters of grant review with deceit and pure fabrication. It became a very traumatic time for someone like me who for the first time was putting my toe in the water for major league scientific funding. Having gone through the ordeal, and later prospered, the beginnings of this memoir was born (see Chapter 17 – High Inside Fastball). In the end, I got funding from both the National Institutes of Health and the Muscular Dystrophy Association.

Subsequently, I wrote a number of short stories, some based on diaries I had kept while traveling to Europe and India. Other topics which had piqued my interest to write included oil painting and fishing. From the time my wife Raj and I married in 1973 up to the time of my retirement in 2006, I had collected about a dozen essays. It was about this time I seriously thought of penning a memoir. In order to accomplish this to my satisfaction I needed to fill in a number of blanks and develop a chronology to my life; I needed to write additional chapters to make a cohesive memoir, one which adequately represented my life story, and most importantly, the circumstances in which I first met and later married the love of my life, RajMohini. To this end, I sincerely hope the reader will enjoy my characterization of major moments in my personal history.

In this endeavor, I am particularly grateful to Sunithi Gnanadoss and Eleanor Miles for their friendship, stimulating and encouraging discussions, as well as their valuable editorial input. In addition, I am particularly thankful to my former secretary Linda Mack who had the uncanny knack of converting my handwritten scrawl into typed works of art. Moreover, I wish to thank staff members James Reuben and Joseph Long of iUniverse.com for their encouragement, suggestions, and direction in bringing this memoir to fruition. I apologize in advance for any errors in grammar, or perceptions of style and tenor being uneven among chapters.

Michael S. Hudecki

# FOREWORD

To read this book is to recognize courage, faith and the role of community in dealing with a chronic disease. As I have been actively involved in the fight against life-threatening disease for 39 years, I have found that there are powerful "weapons" in addition to the drugs and medical therapies. These intangible factors contribute to an individual's ability to cope with a chronic disease such as limb-girdle dystrophy. The story of Mike Hudecki, my friend of 50 years, and his ability to overcome daunting obstacles confirms my own belief that "hope" is often the best medicine.

Mike and I shared laboratory benches at the State University of New York at Buffalo many years ago. During my first days with Mike I immediately realized that he is a very special person. In those early years, we shared a few scotch's, his with milk and mine with water. We lost a few golf balls together as my shoulder served as his crutch to gain access to the golf greens. I also served as a "lean to" for my friend on numerous sidelines at Buffalo Bills games. After I got married, my wife and I were fortunate to frequently welcome Mike to our home where we had many happy visits. We both were inspired by our friend's strong, positive character and his hope for his future.

Mike's strong faith has anchored him firmly in the conviction that life is a gift and should not be wasted. He has recognized the blessings of each new day and has lived with unwavering hope.

What life circumstances have created Mike's sense of hope in spite of his physical challenges and limitations? First there was his family. Mike was reared in a hard-working and loving family in which no member was allowed to focus on self-pity. Having two children with a chronic disease would be devastating for most families. In the

xi

Hudecki family it was just accepted as part of life. All the children were cherished; illness was not emphasized on. Mike's parents made sure that all the children shared the love and hope that characterized the Hudecki family spirit. The love of Mike's brother and sisters has been a precious life-long gift which still enriches his days.

The family measure of love was doubled when Mike married Raj Sabastian, also my personal friend from graduate school days. What a happy surprise it was when Mike told me that he was planning to marry Raj several years after we left Buffalo. Their love and respect for each other have enabled them to live with joy and meet every challenge together.

Mike's community has stretched far beyond the family. I have never met another person who has been admired by so many people. Friends, faculty members, undergraduate and graduate students have surrounded and uplifted Mike. He has been a role model for others with chronic disease; demonstrating that one can make life what he/she wants it to be—in Mike's case a joyous and courageous life "well-lived" each day.

Mike has always been a person who has followed his passions— golf in his younger days, his art work, and his writing. No passion has been more important to Mike than his devotion to scientific research and teaching. As readers will realize as they read these memories, Mike has inspired many undergraduate and graduate students during his teaching career. Mike's professional passion is also demonstrated by his contributions to developing animal models for the study of limb girdle dystrophy; the fight to eradicate the disease. His contributions are cited in more than 40 peer-reviewed journal articles. For years, Mike passionately pursued the goal of understanding and fighting the genetic disease which has affected his own life.

As you read this book, you will learn about a remarkable man who has met challenges of life head on, never indulging in self-pity. Here is a man who has taught so many others how to live with courage—even in the face of chronic illness.

I have been honored to be asked to write this foreword. I know readers are in for a real treat!

Robert J. Beall, Ph.D
President and CEO
Cystic Fibrosis Foundation

# Chapter 1

# O Brother Who Art Thou?

Conception likely occurred in the Sheraton Fox Hotel in Niagara Falls, Ontario, where the folks' spent their honeymoon after they were married in Hamilton, Ontario, on New Year's Eve, 1942. If I believe the math, it looks about right that the Sheraton Fox Hotel was my entry into humankind. At that time, however, unknown to my parents, I was equipped with a faulty gene – a gene which normally harbors information for making sarcoglycans, one of several proteins making up muscle. If the gene is abnormal, as it was in my case, the defective synthesis of sarcoglycans causes a domino effect gradually expressing itself as a disease called limb-girdle muscular dystrophy.

**Mom, Dad and Me (Age 1)**

Although I've seen early photos of myself taken where I was born in Fort Bragg, North Carolina where my dad was stationed during World War Two, I cannot recall a single moment there. There are pictures of me as a toddler in the arms of a nanny, standing in a cotton field, or at the nearby Pinehurst Golf course, for me the period is a total blank. I was about five when my dad and mom, along with baby Greg, resettled in Buffalo after the war. It was from this time forward that I can begin to remember things, including the not so subtle surfacing of my defective sarcoglycans. Having served as a dentist in the US Army Airborne, thankfully, dad returned to Fort Bragg safely from Europe in 1945; and in time my brother Greg was born. Due to the Hiroshima and Nagasaki bombs, WW II came to a swift end; had it not, my father had orders to deploy to the Pacific Theater. Now that the war was over, it was time to pack up and head north. The lure to be close to Canadian kin was strong, so my folks packed up their two sons, along with their golf clubs and tennis rackets, and headed to Buffalo, NY. The city was sufficiently close to Canada (close but not too close), as well as being familiar turf from Dad's dental school days.

We lived on the first floor of a modest duplex built in 1920 which was situated on the corner of Tacoma and Shoshone Streets, adjacent to a dead-end beyond which were over-grown fields and brush along with the expansive Shoshone Playground. Upstairs lived the elderly Mr. and Mrs. Augustine along with their live-in handyman/driver. For now, north Buffalo was the center of my cosmos up to 1957. From here I learned to explore, to laugh and cry, to pray and sing, to experience joy as well as pain, to study and procrastinate. In no small way, it was the place I first learned to come to grips with my genetic error; it was a mainstreaming event, much before the term was ever used in educational circles.

Growing up in North Buffalo was like breaking in a set of new shoes. With continued use the shoes became more comfortable, familiar, and safe. Shoshone Avenue near Main and Hertel Streets became my niche – an area where I was free to explore and stumble, develop self-awareness, and, not unimportantly, provided my initiation into the Natural Sciences.

Early on, Greg and I shared the largest of the three bedrooms; however, after my parents got hold of their senses, we were relegated to the smaller bedroom and a set of bunk beds. With cowboy scenes for wallpaper, the bedroom was the site where Greg and I sang carols to each other until sleep took over at Christmas.

**Greg And I**

The room had a deep narrow closet where we tucked away our earthly belongings. A small window within the closet allowed me to survey the world, in my case, the Nathans who lived across the street. As I later found out in grade school, staring out a window would be graded 'Unwise Use of Leisure Time'.

You couldn't swing a cat in our kitchen. Except for Halloween and visits by people who didn't know us very well, the front door was rarely used; in its place was a side door with a small landing leading up to the kitchen door. The kitchen was the most vibrant, welcoming room in the house, it was home-plate of the household. Within, we cooked, ate, cleaned dishes, did homework, argued, laughed, blew out birthday candles, and listened to the radio. Stumbling about to cook our meals, mom often told us, "Why don't you use your bedroom for your homework?" No matter how important or trivial, what anyone did during the day was brought to the hub at dinnertime. My vivid first memory of the kitchen was dropping a cold bottle of milk on my foot. In between tears I tried to explain, "Mom, I was only trying to help."

Periodic trips to the third floor attic were adventurous. After lumbering up one cautious step at a time to the second floor landing, and opening the door leading to the attic, I'd be met with warm, dusty, stale air. The creaky old steps were lined with stacks of worn-out paperback novels stored by mom. Once I reached the top step, the scene looked like something from a Stephen King story with a jumble of boxes and containers all cast in an eerie light from windows at opposite ends of the attic. A closer inspection yielded a snapshot of paraphernalia from a by-gone time. Impeccably encased within a dingy see-through plastic sleeve was Mom's wedding dress hanging from a ceiling hook. Next to it was my dad's olive green army uniform, pressed and ready for battle. In addition to boxes containing old clothes, there was a large steamer trunk filled with memorabilia from dad's prior life. For example, his small stamp collection affixed within a notebook, where several cartoons in India ink were interspersed among the pages. I always marveled at his handiwork. There were yearbooks and athletic certificates from his days at Cathedral High School and later Niagara University, where he incomprehensively lettered in football, hockey, track and field, tennis, and even golf. There were also biochemistry and microbiology texts from dad's Dental School days; they could have been written in Greek for all I knew. Topping off the trunk collection were black and white photos from the war years taken by a photographer friend; this collection included luminaries such as Winston Churchill, and Generals Eisenhower, Patton, and Montgomery. In the early 50's, after my parents bought a summer cottage on the Canadian shore of Lake Erie, the photos from the war found a permanent home lining a wall of the dining room. Lastly, the chest contained several trappings from dad's uniform, his Captain's cap, airborne insignia pin, belt buckle, and campaign ribbons. Each time I closed the chest, I felt I had taken a trip to a far away place and time.

At opposite ends of the attic were windows. Facing east I could see over our detached garage and the mix of wilderness and athletic fields we familiarly called 'Shoshone'. Beyond, at a distance, there were raised beds of train tracks which physically separated our neighborhood from streets radiating from Main Street and the University section of Buffalo. This vibrant stretch included Dad's dental office, our family doctor Jim Schaus, Mr. Gillette, who ran the Ben Franklin store, Walter Keller's Marine Midland bank, Jim Herzog's drugstore, Jules Klein's grocery store, hobby shop, hardware shop, the Granada Theater, and the University of Buffalo campus. For us kids, this stretch of Main Street was like a giant mall, but without the roof. Looking out the opposite west attic window, I could see the high wall enclosing the Carmelite Convent which contained a cloistered order of nuns rarely seen; however during the growing season we could spot one or two of the nuns working in a vegetable garden. Because the convent bells rang on the hour, I didn't need a watch to tell me that I was late for dinner because I was dawdling somewhere or one of our ball games ran to extra innings. My parents were always asking us when we were late – "Didn't you hear the bells!"

We kids never needed a calendar to tell us the season of the year. When the lake snows began to fly in early November, we knew it was time to put away the football and dig out the hockey sticks. Because of my immobility, I served up my body as goalie. Wearing only rubber boots, my shins were often bruised from slap shots. Sometime in April, with the snow melted and the ground softened to mud, one of the Herzog kids would show up on Saturday morning with a baseball bat, glove and ball. When we heard the familiar shout of "Oh Mike, Oh Greg!", we'd quickly scurry through the house looking for our gear lying dormant since last year. While I didn't play in the field, I was allowed to bat and have someone run for me after I had hit the ball. In fact, I became quite good at laying down short but accurate hits. Also in late spring, Greg was able to dig out the household basketball and head for the garage where dad erected a hoop and backboard. With time Greg became quite adept at shot-making from all parts of the driveway, as well as an adjacent garden bed; his early prowess boded well for the future when he later became a star in high school and college. While I tried mightily to launch the ball ten feet, the sheer weight of the ball prevented me from ever making a basket.

When grammar school ended in late June, our family packed up to spend the summer at the cottage, situated on the Canadian side of Lake Erie. Here is where I developed a passion for a more sedentary activity – fishing. When we returned home on Labor Day weekend, football was in the air. Our under-inflated football somehow appeared from a dark, moldy recess in the basement. Again, Saturday morning seemed to be the cue for the neighborhood kids to congregate, not for baseball but for a pick-up game of football. We used our narrow yard or a small clearing across the street, and sides were noisily selected. A game would begin with three or four to a side. In my case, I was the scorer, since a loud voice within shouted: "Play on – but without me!" Once, our pastor, Monsignor Duggan gave used leather football helmets to each of us; in spite of my protestations Monsignor slammed an under-sized helmet on my head and told me to go play. Moving off to the sideline somewhere, I then proceeded to spend the next hour trying to get the damn thing off my head. Ingratitude!

Born and raised in Canada, Dad had a special fondness for hockey. One weekend he was tired of getting a fuzzy reception of *Hockey Night in Canada* from his rabbit-eared equipped TV. Yearning to see games clearly from Toronto (90 miles away), he decided to erect a rotating antenna on the roof. With a twenty-five foot ladder going up the side of the house, I located myself on an adjacent sidewalk to watch his handiwork. I was mesmerized by Dad chomping on a cigar gingerly wrapping the steel bands to hold the antenna in place. Suddenly, Mom called out from the kitchen window: "Mike, where's your brother, where's Greg?" Looking up, I saw five year old Greg climbing up the ladder to nearly the top step! Dad stopped what he was doing and quite calmly encouraged Greg to keep coming to him. "That's a boy Greg, keep coming. Look at me, don't look down, that's a boy." Clumbering over the last rung of the ladder, Greg took a step or two and fell into Dad's grasp. By now, Mom had reached the attic window and took her second born to safety. My hands still get clammy every time I pictured the scene. I don't know if there is a lesson here – but perhaps there is something to say about parents who were capable of surviving the war years, as well being athletically competitive; but at my tender age, Stephen and Veronica seemed to possess the "right stuff" in dealing with life's curve balls.

My early education of the natural world took on many forms. The seasons of the year certainly had their imprint. Winter was hallmarked with lots of snow which as I got a bit older, I learned to shovel. Slowly but methodically I'd start on the sidewalk, and I would eventually reach the driveway area with its ruts and mounds created by city plows. Working with physical properties of snow and ice, I soon learned what 32 degrees meant. I also learned that slushy snow was a heck of a lot heavier than the fluffy stuff skiers liked. Going to school in the winter months became a bit of challenge, especially for Mom, who had to navigate our Buick through the icy streets in her daily round-trips to and from school. Once we arrived at school, I quickly learned what a wind-chill factor was as I embarked on my solo journey through the frozen arctic tundra, aka, walkway to the Boy's Entrance. As I gritted my teeth, bending into the prevailing northwest winds, I counted off the steps to the safety of the school entrance. The experience gave me a profound appreciation of Jack London's *Call of the Wild*. There were many snowy mornings when I had my ears glued to Clint Buelmann on the radio, hoping he'd tell us the Buffalo schools were closed for the day. However, this rarely occurred.

Our small front yard was ideal for snow forts which we used to shelter us from omnipresent snowball fights. One day I had my chin cut open by a shovel of a neighborhood kid helping in the fort construction. As she cried from seeing all the blood, Mom called our physician, Jim Schaus, who came over and sewed me up. Not missing a beat, we finished the fort by nightfall. Regarding snowball fights, we kids developed great accuracy with our tosses. Whether it was a passing car or some poor soul who previously pissed someone off, our prowess at baseball spilled into the winter months.

Fall brought on the onslaught of fallen leaves which we would rake and then rake some more into huge piles perfect for kids to run through and bury themselves in. The wet leaves were great for plugging up the sewers in the street and creating an impromptu lake. Halloween was the big hit of the neighborhood. Each year we descended upon our neighbors dressed up in costumes, such as: a tiger, hobo, or once one of mom's old dresses. Equipped with brown paper bags, we'd go house to house with our "trick or treat" refrain. One particular Halloween it rained, and by the time we were nearly coming to the end of our soggy adventure, our wet bags were nearly at their breaking point. We made one last stop in a duplex, and a kindly old lady warmly greeted us with a bowl of fresh apples. Before we could intercept the round missiles, the deed was done – our candies exploded through the damp bags covering every inch of the landing. Autumn also brought Thanksgiving time, which we shared as a family at home or with my Aunt Pauline and her husband Ray. Regardless of the venue, we feasted on turkey and all the trimmings, including oceans of brown gravy which soaked everything I ate.

There always seemed to be something to do in the neighborhood. There were overgrown fields to explore. Maybe this would be the day I'd find an arrowhead left behind by some early Iroquois. There were cowboys and Indians to imitate from movies we had seen; our pistol and rifle sound effects were better than dramatized. Hopalong Cassidy was my favorite. Thanks to Walt Disney, for a year or two, we were enamored with Davy Crockett and his band of Kentuckians, right up to the end where he bought it at the Alamo. Often, when we left the Granada movie theater after seeing a war film such as Alan Ladd in *The Paratrooper*, we simulated what we had just seen along Main Street on our way home. We would duck into Herzog's Drugstore or Ben Franklin's 5 & 10 for safety, where we'd quickly huddle up and prepare to go after the Germans hiding out across the street at the barber shop. As we zigzagged from storefront to storefront, we'd reach the train viaduct looking for snipers as we terrorized passerbys. When we reached Kart's Dairy at the corner of Main and Hertel, we breathed a collective sigh of relief. After continuing down Hertel to Shoshone, we ate up what was left of our movie candies, now disgustingly softened inside our jeans.

The Granada was our primary theater. Every Saturday for twenty-five cents we saw a double-bill plus a serial which never ended, but usually with a car about to go over a cliff. We particularly liked the previews which went on and on. There was one instance where I went to see *20,000 Leagues Under the Sea* on four consecutive Saturdays. There was another occasion when I actually climbed over the railroad tracks to see a movie. Urged on by classmate Bill Dixon, the two of us scaled the raised, cinder-laden tracks on our way to see *Love Me Tender* starring the country's heart-throb, Elvis Presley. While the route was dangerous to say the least, it was definitely the shorter route to Main Street considering the alternative of going around the tracks by way of Hertel Avenue; however, having seen a rescue squad come to the aid of a boy my age who had his legs amputated by a passing freight, I considered the tracks very dangerous. As I was young and stupid, and didn't want to show too much fear to Bill, I went along. It was the first and last time I'd ever navigate those tracks.

Ever since I accompanied my dad to the Crippled Children's Guild where he gave pro bono dental care to children affected by polio, I have made every effort to walk on my two legs. Seeing kids my age in iron lungs had an indelible impression on me and stimulated me to walk and take my lumps, as I fell frequently. Mom was always sewing up the knees on my pants. I rarely had a knee without some sort of scab. We were leery about going to the playground wading pool as the public in the 1950's believed that polio was transmitted at public areas like swimming pools.

My other walking itinerary involved going west on Hertel Avenue. Three blocks away was Sam Vastola's barber shop where I got my brushcut, even though I longed to have one of those stylish cuts seen pasted on the wall. It was at Vastola's one day when one of Sam's partners stopped me and asked: "Mike, do you know you walk sort of funny?" Too embarrassed to make any sense I nodded something in his direction and kept walking. From that day on, I looked at myself every time I passed a store window; and every time I was jolted by my awkward, herky jerky gait that I saw in the reflection. I knew by then that I had limited muscle strength, but now I had another thing to ponder. As a young kid growing up among family and neighbors, my physical ability (or lack of it) just blended in with everything else; however, there comes an age where one's self-esteem is wedded to one's physical ability. I was no exception as I tried to navigate through life which contained boys as well as the girls we boys hoped to impress. In this, I was certainly at a disadvantage.

9

Beyond the barber shop was the corner of Hertel and Parker. Across from each other were the drug store, which my parents frequented, and Tom Kerdot's Delicatessen, which kept me in comic books, soda pop, and penny candy. When I entered Tom's deli, I would first go to the magazine rack in search of the newest comic books. After a few minutes Tom would bellow from the back of the counter: "Are you boys going to buy those or just read them?" The next stop would be the penny candy counter where, depending on how much money I had on me, I'd peruse buttons, waxed figures with sugary water inside, jujubes, licorice, chocolate coins, and Good n' Plenty. Frequently, usually on a Sunday morning after Dad had gone to the drug store across the street, he'd give us kids ten cents each for penny candy. We searched through the counter as if we were examining jewels and fill our little brown bags to the brim. Life didn't get any better than this as we washed our candies down with either an orange or grape Nehi, or cream soda if Tom had any left. Round-trip excursions to Tom's deli were the staples of my local outings.

If I were particularly frisky, I would venture further down Hertel. There I'd pass the new A&P, which Mom went to periodically when she couldn't get everything she needed from her favorite grocer, Jules Klein. As I approached the corner of Colvin and Hertel, I'd pass the Sample Shop, which Mom went to frequently for clothes and various household items. I was always amazed at the vacuum tube connection between the counter and the office upstairs which received the money, and then doled out the receipt for payment. After I crossed Colvin, I'd arrive at Buddy Harnett's Sports Shop. Rarely having enough money to buy anything except maybe the odd baseball or two, I would content myself with lusting over what was shown in the display window. One summer there was a Hank Aaron glove on sale for twenty dollars. In spite of Greg and me pointing this out to Dad and Mom a thousand times, as well as once to Grandpa Anthony Kwolek who was visiting his daughter, my Mom, the glove remained in the window throughout the summer driving us crazy. Mick Jagger plaintively says it all: "You can't always get what you want."

Some Saturdays I took a bus downtown primarily to visit the Army/Navy Store and a coin and stamp shop. Enthralled with the ads I had seen in the newspaper, when I entered Army/Navy Store it was a trip to another world. Filled to the brim with bric-a-brac from the wars, the store was a kid's dream come true. I never bought anything there; I just browsed. In some ways the store was a much larger version of Dad's trunk up in the attic. Across Main Street was the stamp and coin shop. Here I added to the meager collection I had at home. Sometimes it might be just a Confederate dollar or a turn of the century stamp, but my visits downtown added to my cache piece by piece. It was Dad's stamp collection from childhood that got me interested in stamps in the first place. My interest in currency came from a classmate of my dad's Niagara University days, Father Don Kinney. He visited us periodically after coming home from his trips to China where he served as a Vincentian missionary, and inevitably he had a wad of Asian money to give us. Through stamps and money, I began to learn more about the other world out there, not just a territory we called the Shoshone Neighborhood. In addition to being educational, my bus trips taught me a degree of self reliance. Unable to climb up the bus steps one step at a time, I needed to ask the bus driver two important things as I contemplated getting on his bus. First, I would request that he give me time to crawl up the stairs on my hands and knees; and, once on my feet again, time to get to an available seat before he took off. Secondly, I then requested that he give me ample time to debus; basically reversing the steps that got me to my seat in the first place. Looking back, I was never disappointed in the assistance I got from the bus drivers, nor for that matter from most strangers lending me a hand in one way or another.

Closer to home there were little projects which kept us occupied. Stimulated by an empty cardboard box which contained our brand new fridge, Greg and I were hell-bent to construct a clubhouse. While our effort with the box failed miserably, there was a nearby pair of trees which we used in an attempt to construct a clubhouse. We gathered any loose lumber in the house or elsewhere and dad's hammer and nails, and began to build walls of the clubhouse using the trees; how these nail-infested trees survived to this day is a complete mystery. Since, progress on this project was hit and miss, further work was scrapped. One day, Dad discussed our desire for a clubhouse with Jerry Nathan who lived across the street. Jerry ran a company which specialized in a relatively new substance called fiberglass, and he offered to help us out. Dad purchased the lumber, etc., while Jerry hammered together our clubhouse which was situated next to the garage. With the structural work done, Jerry finally came to the area he was most interested in – overlaying the roof with sheets of waterproof fiberglass. I was amazed when the sheets of fiberglass were solidified by using some foul smelling resins. After a time waiting for the roof to set, Greg and I climbed up the rear ladder to the roof and surveyed the world as never before. Although we were only up five feet, it seems we had reached the stars.

For a time I had a best friend in a rambunctious boxer called Holiday, named by my mother after a magazine title. Before Holiday we had a black mongrel which was run over by a truck driver who appeared at our door with the dog in his hands. The man was very apologetic, but nothing really could be said as the dog lay dying on our landing. While I didn't comprehend it at the time, death and tears were natural partners. Afterwards, Dad found that our St. Rose of Lima church pastor, Monsignor Duggan, was raising boxers and would provide us with one of the puppies. From the day when Holiday came to our house, the boxer and I became inseparable, or so I thought. Because the boxer grew to be so strong, he had to be tied to a lead in the backyard where I also spent most of my time. One day, however, Holiday got loose from his lead and ran up the street to a new housing development called Parkside Court. Because the homes were adjacent to the fields of Shoshone, many of the neighbors laced their garbage cans with rat poison. Memories of watching Holiday staggering, and falling down on the street are indelibly etched in my mind. Through my bedroom window, I can still picture Dad and Greg carrying Holiday back home. I was beside myself in tears having just lost my best friend. Regardless of the ups and downs of my day, there was always Holiday tethered in the yard awaiting me. Who needed friends when you had Holiday?

**My Best Friend Holiday**

When we were young, we had many baby sitters to take care of us when my folks went out for the evening. Mostly the sitters were Dad's dental assistants who wanted to make a few extra bucks. Later, Mrs. Mertz and Mrs. Hauser took over the duties. They were fine women who provided us with meals and just enough rope to enjoy ourselves. When I got old enough, my parents relied on me to rule the roost or at least to be able to make a phone call if the sky should fall on us five kids. I soon learned that babysitting had its perks. The primary one was to stay up late and watch old movies on TV. I became a fan of *Charlie Chan*, *The Thin Man*, *The Invisible Man*, as well as a host of Hollywood detective stories and British mysteries. With my sitting experience, as well as being the eldest, the seeds were sown for my developing a care-taker attitude which has persisted throughout my life.

On one Sunday after church, Greg and I were ready to bolt outdoors after we shed our jackets and ties. Mom came to us in a solemn manner and said: "Your father wants to see you in the living room." Oh my God, what did we do now was all Greg and I could muster as a rational thought. When we reached the living room, we saw Dad on the sofa holding a small pamphlet. As we sat down, he began a 'birds and bees' lesson. As he read and did not look up at us, he threw out terms like: uterus, fallopian tubes, gestation, etc. After 20 anguishing minutes, he concluded: "Well, okay now, you can go." As Greg and I clambered out the door and freedom, we blurted to each other: "What was that all about? I don't know!" While Dad and Mom were content with their sex education efforts, it wouldn't be until I got into high school that I really got mixed up. At a spiritual retreat, I became more confused than ever. As I listened to the presiding priest, I had visions of sperm leaping from a boy's trousers and traveling hither and yon in search of a girl. Huh? Suffice to say the lecture was high on drama (and guilt) and very short on explicits.

While dad was the main mouth to feed, and he could actually cook himself, Mom on the other hand became an amazing cook. Since mom's mother died when she was quite young, my mother learned cooking pretty much on her own. Mom was constantly experimenting with new recipes, and this trait continued until she died in 1981. She collected recipes from many sources, such as the newspaper and magazines, all of which she taped within a notebook. She was a marvelous imitator. For example, Dad adored his mother's so-called "Easter soup." Made of a buttermilk base, it included generous helpings of kielbasa, ham and hard boiled eggs. Mom experimented with it for years until she got it just right to my dad's satisfaction. Once when the family was visiting friends of my parents, we kids were exposed to pizza for the first time. The host's family was devouring it while we Hudeckis looked at the slices with suspicion. What was that strange concoction of bread, tomato, cheese, pepperoni, and assorted spices. With trepidation, we tried it ourselves, and, lo and behold, a match was made. Mom, however, took it a step further, and made it at home rather than ordering take-out. Once, Mom was with Dad in New York City at a dental convention and they had Black Forest cake for dessert at one of the restaurants. It was so tempting that Mom asked to talk to the chef for the recipe. The rest is history, because from that time on she continued to make it at home for all her important dinners.

# Chapter 2

# In the Hands of the
# Nuns and Brothers

My parents wrestled with the fact that I was not a normal fellow. I was weaker and slower than my playmates. I fell frequently and I got up and down stairs by taking one step at a time. I was awkward getting out of a chair or up from the floor. What does Michael have? Answers were slow in coming and at times conflicting, depending upon whom my parents spoke to. The common refrain was: "Mrs. Hudecki, we think Michael has muscular dystrophy and his chances of living…" This verdict was heard by my parents over and over again. Whether I was examined at the Crippled Children's Guild in Buffalo or at the revered Sick Children's Hospital in Toronto, the diagnosis was the same: "Your son has a progressive disease of the muscle which will weaken him. We don't know how long he has to live." Initially, I heard my parents soft-pedal the diagnosis when I overheard them talking to friends, but with time Mom and Dad were more candid, paraphrasing the descriptions heard from the specialists. I often cried myself to sleep.

I was 5 years old going on 6 when Mom took me to PS 22 a few blocks from home to enter kindergarten. Located half a flight of stairs up to the first floor, the classroom was run by a kindly woman who oversaw our activities, including how we should roll up our mats after napping on the floor. From the beginning I was terrified going down the stairs at the same time that the bell rang to end the school day, and the hordes of giggling, screaming kids came pouring out from the classrooms. I clung for dear life to the banister until the tempest passed. Fortunately, my mother had a chat with the teacher, who was more than agreeable to let me leave a bit early each day. Once outside,

I looked forward to seeing my mother who either drove or walked me home.

When it came time for me to enter first grade, my kindergarten teacher suggested that we visit the nearby parochial school, St. Rose of Lima. Because the classrooms were located on the third floor of the building, the Grey Nuns who taught there suggested that we would do better to look elsewhere. A better situation might be available at a distant private school called Mount St. Joseph's, and, in 1949, I became a first grader in Sister Mary William's class. Because the classroom was located on the first floor, and the nuns adhered to discipline in all forms, the 'Little Mount' seemed like a good fit for me. Run by Sisters of St. Joseph, the school shared the campus with a nearby high school for girls (The "Big Mount"). Fortunately, The Little Mount contained an elevator, which I was given permission to use throughout my grade school years.

It never occurred to me that I could be graded for staring out a window; at Shoshone it was an "art form". For nearly every grading period I got an "F" for "Wise Use of Leisure Time." My parents also took a shot at getting the nuns to teach me a musical instrument. First, it was the French Horn patiently taught by Sister Mary Raymond. Without serious lung capacity, all I did in these sessions was to accumulate spit within the brass innards. Later, I took on the piano, when Sister used her delicate fingers to teach mine to navigate classical melodies. Progress was slow to put it mildly; however, by eighth grade, I learned enough of Gilbert and Sullivan's *Poor Little Buttercup* to team up with classmate Jane Kelly for a duet played at the school's annual spring concert.

In addition to weekly sessions with Sister Raymond, I was expected to practice on my own. A room on the second floor was sub-divided into a warren of glass-walled cubicles, each one containing an aging upright not tuned since the days of Mozart. Each week I tried to get one of the inner cubicles containing an outside facing window. Practicing in the outer cubicles was unimaginable to me, because you could easily be spotted by Warden Sister Esther making her regular rounds. While frail looking, Sister Esther could move swiftly through the hallway ready to pounce on unsuspecting students. As in *Stalag 17*, where a guard entered the prison quarters unannounced, Sister smacked her pointer against the cubicle glass if you were caught not practicing. My heart skips a beat even today thinking how Sister could rattle your bones with her sharp-pitched "Practice!" While I passed the time staring out the window, I was always attuned to the tell-tale footsteps of Sister Esther, which to a youthful ear could be heard from the next county. Once she appeared on my auditory radar, I quickly made attempts to simulate practice. Once Sister was out of range, I was back at the window. Didn't Albert Einstein "begin" his illustrious career by peering out the window of his Swiss Patent Office?

While we quickly learned that the catechism would be our best friend in first grade, it was also a time I got my first experience sitting in the corner because I blurted out "gobble, gobble" during quiet time. At school the nuns were always putting on assemblies where each class had a musical role to play. At Thanksgiving time when I was in first grade, Sister Mary William had us sing a little ditty which concluded with a "gobble, gobble" after each refrain. However, when the school assembly was over, we went back to our classroom to study. I felt this was strange because we kids were really getting into the spirit of things. So during the quiet of the classroom with each at his desk, I impulsively began to utter "gobble, gobble." Since it was loud enough to catch Sister's attention, I was ordered to haul my chair to the corner and take a seat. Feeling embarrassed, my ardor was quickly dampened as I stared at the wall all by myself. To this day I'm still confused about how an otherwise excellent teacher misjudged the moment and throttled our enthusiasm for Thanksgiving, including its sound effects courtesy of "moi."

One winter, I was waiting with a classmate for my mother to pick me up after school. Feeling antsy from waiting, my friend and I got into a snowball fight. Putting distance between us, it didn't take us too long to really get into it. We couldn't make snowballs fast enough. In the middle of our skirmish, my classmate stopped and yelled out,

"My ride's here!" Turning tails, he began to run up the front steps to retrieve his book bag. Just as he neared the front entrance door, he slammed on the brakes when our school principal Sister Mary Walter came out. Unfortunate for me, I couldn't recall my perfectly-timed snowball which was already on route. Bam! Rather than nailing my classmate, Sister got it directly on her large white bib. At that time, I felt my formal education was now officially over! Meeting Sister the next day, my classmate and I were punished by spending the next 6 weeks of luncheon recess memorizing the preamble to the U.S. Constitution. To this day I still know what comes after – "We the people of the United States in order to form a more perfect union..." Who said snowballs aren't educational?

I ventured briefly into athletics while I was at the Mount. During the last weeks of eighth grade, our class played intramural baseball games at lunchtime to while away the days before we officially ended our elementary education. As at Shoshone, I had my regular at-bats and someone ran for me. It irritated me that opposing infielders moved quite close, expecting a weakly hit ball from me; however, with Shoshone experience under my belt, I was able to hit between the gathering infielders. They eventually backed up a bit, but not much. Playing defense was another matter. Over the objections of my teammates, I pleaded to play the infield; however, after a botched play from third base and my inability to make the toss to first base in time, I was sentenced to deep centerfield.

In the last game of the year, my side was ahead by one run in the last inning. Situated a thousand yards from home-plate, I had busied myself by picking dandelions and periodically squinting to see if anyone was at bat. Lo and behold, our class's best athlete, Joe Gainey, came up and hit a towering fly-ball – toward me! As I saw the tiny dot getting bigger and bigger, I realized that the ball was coming directly at me. While trying not to stumble, the ball smacked the sweet spot of my open mitt. It was the third out and, because of my catch, we won the game. Afterwards, Joe kept asking me: "Mike, that was a lucky catch, right?" I replied nervously that it was an easy catch; however, the truth was, it was the luckiest catch ever made. What were the chances of my holding my breath, not falling down in a panic, the earth's orbit around the sun not deviating an iota, AND the fact that Joe's sky-rocket ball hit the bulls-eye of my open mitt? Joe did it all. Heart-of-hearts, Joe knew it already, but he wanted (needed) some concession from me. As much as I might wish that a memorial marker existed where I made my heroic catch, today there is a parking lot covering the entire diamond at Mount Saint Joseph's (now part of Medaille College). Sorry Cooperstown!

When my classmates took on other Catholic schools, I was their intrepid cheerleader attending all of the games played at nearby Delaware Park. The park and the adjacent zoo were integral parts of the urban landscaping efforts of the reknown Frederick Law Ohmsted. At the game I was there to cheer our team win or lose. At our final school assembly, I was presented with a baseball signed by each of my classmates, with the inscription, "Most Enthusiastic Supporter." Interestingly, the Greek derivation of 'enthusiasm' means – the divine appreciation for the gift of life. It was a label I was proud of then, and one which I happily accepted again in high school. Maybe there is more to life than having a defective muscle protein after all.

Still reveling from my cheerleading work, my brother Greg and his sixth grade class asked me if I'd umpire their final intramural game of the year. As I stood behind the pitcher, it was my responsibility to call balls and strikes, as well as umping the bases. Early in the game, Greg's team batted first. After the first batter flied out, Greg came to the plate and blasted a line drive up the middle. Rather than catch the stupid ball, the pitcher ducked, and I got smacked in the face. Amid stars, I fell to the ground. Fortunately, nothing was broken or cracked (I think), and I resumed what seemed to be my call in life – on the sidelines as a spectator with an ice bag over my face. As I would say to myself for years to come: "Life goes stumblin, bumblin on."

Back in the 1950s, baseball was our country's "national pastime," and our nuns were its biggest fans. It is incomprehensible now, but the Mount was closed the afternoon our Buffalo Bisons had their opening game of the season. Often taken by my Dad, Greg and I went to Offermann Stadium to see our Bisons, cheering on our major league wannabes such as local hero Luke Easter. On a rebound I once caught one of his towering foul balls which subsequently became one of my prized possessions (along of course with memories of Joe Gainey's fly out at centerfield). During the World Series, the nuns even put a TV in the central atrium so we could get glimpses of the nun's favorite team, the New York Yankees, play my favorite team of all time, the Brooklyn Dodgers. I still haven't reconciled the later move of the Dodgers to Los Angeles. Like most kids in the neighborhood, my jeans were stuffed with baseball cards. It's a wonder we could still walk with our jeans stretched to the limit with bubble gum-depleted cards.

While the classroom was our primary venue of learning (in nearly every class we heard "Yes, spelling counts, as does penmanship"), there were regular trips to locations within Ohmsted's urban landscaping handiwork: the Zoo, the Science Museum, the Historical Society, and the Albright-Knox Art Gallery. On these occasions we were enthralled by everything from elephants, bears and sleeping pythons, minerals of every description, early American Indian artifacts, as well as a range of artwork. Also we made visits to nearby St. Mary's School for the Deaf where we, with guidance, were taught how we could communicate with deaf people. We were struck by an amazing student who was deaf, and, blind. On the religious side, we made pilgrimages: to Canisius High School for their student rendition of the Passion Play during Lent, and to downtown theaters to see movies such as *The Robe, The Ten Commandments,* and *The Song of Bernadette.* Closer to home we took part in annual Christmas productions for parents and friends, and May Day celebrations of the Coronation of the Blessed Virgin Mary which was held outside weather permitting. I am still reminded each spring when our garden is full of scents of lilac and lily of the valley which festooned the altar erected for the May Day celebration.

Our most significant event came each June with an extravagant stage show with a varying central theme. The shows had a patriotic, historical emphasis, such as the American Revolution and Civil Wars. All in makeup and costumes, we would sing, dance, or march to tunes of

Stephen Foster. The rehearsals for the two weekend performances kept the Mount hopping for over a month. As an eighth grader, I became one of the ushers helping with programs and seating. Once I got an early ride to the show, and as I entered the solitude and quiet of the school, I heard girlish giggling coming from an open window. Looking out I saw our nuns taking part in an impromptu track meet, where each was in full habit running with her crucifix and conspicuous bib swinging wildly from side to side. It was fun to see these hard-working souls letting their hair down, literally and figuratively. Interestingly, much later I gave the commencement address to my nephew Jim's graduation class in the same auditorium as our spring show. My topic centered around the headlines of the morning *Buffalo Courier-Express* and how the nuns prepared us for contemporary life within moral and ethical boundaries. Lessons passed from one generation (me) to another (Jimmy).

Reaching the last year at the Mount presented me with new responsibilities. For one, a classmate and I ceremoniously raised the American flag each morning at a tall pole in front of the school. Another duty was to become a crossing guard when a couple of times a week, I led lower level students across the busy intersection of Humboldt Parkway and Parkside Avenue – arteries planned long ago by Ohmsted. Armed with only a small "stop" sign, a white belt folded across my chest with a silvery badge, and two gimpy legs, I brazenly led the kids holding hands double-file across the very busy intersection! What was I thinking? What were the nuns thinking?

When it came time to graduate, I felt I was about to leave something familiar and safe, a "safe harbor" not too much different from my North Buffalo existence. To mark the occasion our class dressed in our Sunday best for a group picture in the foyer of the school, where subsequently each of us were given a certificate in front of our family and friends. After good-byes to my teachers and classmates, our family made a stop at the Parkside Candies for hot fudge sundaes, a favorite haunt of our family since my First Communion eight years ago. Incidentally, many years later, Parkside Candies was one of the venues used for *The Natural* starring Robert Redford.

**At the Mount Graduation, My Eighth
Grade Teacher Sister Bibiana**

I already knew I was going to suburban St. Joseph's Collegiate Institute for high school having passed their entrance exam a month earlier. I elected not to go to Canisius High even though the school was the choice of my male classmates as well as the nuns, who thought the Jesuit-taught school was more in line with their own Jesuit-inspired order of Sisters of St. Joseph. At St. Joe's I would be taught by the Christian Brothers an order founded many years ago by St. Francis de LaSalle for the expressed purpose of training young men. In four years time my graduation class at St. Joe's would be the focus of the school's centennial celebration. Going to St. Joe's, I would be joined by two Mount classmates Bill Dixon and Charlie Bainbridge, as well as my neighborhood friends Bob Herzog and Eric Weber. While I knew a little about the school, my mind was filled with questions – would I develop the same degree of familiarity and growth that I enjoyed at the Mount?

Before the family established itself at the cottage for the summer, Mom and Dad decided to take us on a pilgrimage to Quebec, Canada, to see the Sainte Anne de Beaupre shrine. My parents felt that the family, I in particular, would benefit from the healing waters and oils from the shrine and its history of fostering miracles. Thoughts of my dystrophy were always under the surface

22

of the daily lives of my parents. Since parts of the New York State Thruway were still under construction in 1957, Dad and Mom along with Greg, Karen, and me, one of our favorite aunts, Sister St. Catherine, decided to drive through Rochester, on to Rome, north to the Oswego area and the Eisenhower Locks of the newly opened St. Lawrence Seaway, and eventually to Plattsburgh, the home of my dad's classmate Roger Boulet from his UB Dental School days. After a brief stay, we would embark first to Montreal and visit the revered St. Joseph's Oratory and subsequently follow the St. Lawrence River eastward to Ste. Anne's shrine. Sounds simple enough.

No sooner had we pulled into the driveway of the Boulet home when we were greeted by the family, kids and all. As I saw one of the young boys about Greg's age, I extended my arm to shake his hand when all of a sudden he quickly twisted my arm behind my back breaking it! With that distinctive snap sound that only a freshly broken arm could make, I quickly found myself surrounded by my parents and Roger Boulet and his wife applying pressure on the arm and stuffing me back into the car for a trip to the emergency room. After an X-ray and subsequent casting, I was released. Later when I returned to the Boulet's, I found out two things. There would be a change in travel plans and I would stay behind with my mother to recuperate, and I learned that Greg had nearly killed my assailant with his bare hands. Apparently, it took all the energy of Sister Catherine to pry Greg's hands away from the kid's neck (or something like that).

Aside from the Plattsburgh hiccup, the trip went relatively well. Dad got the rest of the party to the oratory and shrine without a hitch and came back with holy water, holy oils, and a variety of saintly relics to keep us Hudecki's on the good side of the Lord. Greg told me later that he remembers seeing lots of discarded crutches at the two healing venues. I guess I missed my chance to spiritually do something about my nagging genetic error. Many years later in 1978, I finally got a chance to visit Montreal (with both arms intact I might add) as a research fellow participating in the World Congress of Neuromuscular Disease.

Once September rolled around and my cast was now but a distant memory, I left my childhood innocence at the door to Room 104 and entered the realm of my homeroom teacher, Brother Jerome. Amidst the chaos of meeting new faces and stowing books in our desks and hallway lockers, Brother soon brought the class to order with a roll call. He gave us an introduction to what life at St Joes was all about: what was expected of us, and how we might make the best of our opportunities here. What stood out was his plea for us not to join the "2:30 club." He went on to tell us that our dedication to our coursework was a given, but in an equally important way, what we did after school, after 2:30, became part two of our education at St. Joe's. Listing various examples of extra-curricular activities, he eventually came to the subject of athletics and stressed the relevance of sports in shaping us for the future. Subsequently, Brother made a strong pitch for joining his freshman cross-country track team. A few days later as I was about to leave for the day, Brother asked me if I'd be interested in joining his team as a student manager. Mainly, I would be responsible for keeping records, supplying safety pins to affix numbers on team jerseys, and, m ore importantly, keeping times at practice and at competitive meets. I was very pleased to be asked and readily agreed to Brother's offer. Unknown to me at the time, this occasion marked the beginning of a long string of managerial responsibilities at St. Joe's culminating in track and field and basketball championships.

Vice Principal Brother Joseph arranged my schedule so that I could stay on the ground floor for my day-to-day activities; only rarely did I have to navigate the stairs to the second floor with the help of my neighborhood buddy Bob Herzog. Back then, I only recall one handicapped student at the school, a fellow who was quite nimble in spite of being affected by an early bout of polio (ironically, he also was the manager of the football team). The layout of St. Joe's was user-friendly for someone handicapped like myself. At the rear were two large athletic fields – a football field encircled with a loose cinder track and a baseball diamond. For a student of the 1960's (including the handicapped), St. Joe's had it all.

While Fall was filled with the sights and sounds of football, it was also a time for the cross-country teams to get into action. Practicing took place during the weekdays, and the weekends were reserved for meets which took place at a circuit around Delaware Park Lake (another of Olmsted's creations), or, on occasion, at a competitor's school. Once in October, 1957, our teams met early on a Saturday morning to bus to Rochester to compete with Bishop Aquinas. After all were seated in the school's aging, cranky maroon and white bus, our driver, Charlie, who was the school's all-around handyman, revved up the engine to get us on our way. As we left the parking lot, all interest centered upon the morning *Buffalo Courier Express* with the headline: "Russians Put Artificial Moon in Orbit." We were dumbfounded and amazed at the story of Sputnik rocketing into space and achieving an orbit circling the globe at an unheard of velocity. The bus was awash with chatter as we digested and speculated on the what and the how, as well as the ramifications for us in the United States. One of the spin-offs of the Sputnik launch at the national level was the development of NASA and a concerted effort to not only equal the Russian accomplishment but surpass it. On the local level, we high school students saw a renewed emphasis on science, as seen in a steady stream of visiting scientists from corporations like General Electric and Dupont who did their best to wow as well as educate us. In many respects we students were stimulated further for a future life in the sciences. The movie *October Sky* based on NASA scientist Homer H. Hickam's memoir *Rocket Boys* captured the human drama going within the minds of budding scientists our age. Thank Sputnik!

The Christian Brothers annually ran a fund drive to support the training of young men interested in becoming Brothers. Each year we students were given books of two dollar tickets to sell, with the homeroom winner given a day off from classes. The first year I teamed up with neighbor Bob Herzog because we felt we could divide up the neighborhood more efficiently if we joined forces. Individually, by Friday afternoon we had canvassed most of the neighborhood, so we decided to go together and hit some remaining blocks we had yet to visit. After a couple of empty knocks, we came to a house with a driveway packed with cars. With no luck at the side door, we knocked on the front door. From the rustling of furniture and hushed tones, we knew people were at home, but no one answered. As we were a bit frustrated, we purposely slammed the outer door on our way outside. As we reached the driveway, we saw a face or two at the window behind some curtains watching us leave. We went next door and were greeted by a kindly lady who was happy to part with two dollars to support our fund drive. Pleased with ourselves, Bob and I headed home for dinner. The next day the morning newspaper ran a front page headline of arrests made at a major mafia meeting that was held in Appalachin, New York. The accompanying story gave details of a Buffalo contingent which was also at the meeting, including a fellow whose home address was Starin Avenue! I immediately called Bob on the phone and we both concluded that the home with all the cars and mysterious goings on must have been owned by the man cited in the paper. We looked at our receipts from the day before, and, sure enough, the lady who bought our last ticket lived right next door. As a result we both stayed indoors that weekend peering out the window looking for any suspicious cars driving by our houses looking for two naïve freshmen.

On another occasion, the corner of Tacoma and Starin again became memorable. During basketball season, Greg and I were dropped off at the intersection by the St. Joe's basketball team bus after we were clobbered by a cross-town rival, Bishop Ryan. Even though my freshman basketball team was not playing, we were invited by Coach Frank Schiavone to come along and cheer on our varsity team. Reaching the east side of Buffalo and its large Polish contingent, we encountered hostility by nearly everyone. The gym had the guise of the Roman Forum as we valiantly struggled against all odds. First of all, the refs were eager to foul out as many of our players as they could (and did, as we only had four players left to finish the game), the Ryan players also used playground rough-necking not usually seen on a basketball court, and lastly the behavior of the fans. Parents, walk-ins, vandals, you name it – they were all there to scream insults and epithets throughout the game. Even the school priest contributed to the melee by tossing a can of talc on the court, as well as opening the gym door to the outside letting in frost-laden air — both actions which coated the basketball court with an untenable slippery surface. The game was highly intimidating, if not scandalous, made more so for Greg and me as the majority of the supporters were Polish-Americans. After the game, all were relieved to get back on our wretched old bus for the ride home. About a mile from St. Joe's, the team bus let Greg and me off at Tacoma and Starin for our spirited walk home. We spent the time agonizing over how incensed we were to be Polish and the outlandish behavior we had seen. We got the last laugh a month later when the visiting Bishop Ryan team was routed in our own gym. Later we beat them again at the Buffalo Memorial Auditorium where we won the Manhattan Cup and over-all League Championship. Three years later when I was a senior, we won the Cup again and my childhood friends, Bob Herzog and Eric Weber, led the way.


There was a road trip where things weren't quite as dire as our trip to Bishop Ryan. This was a trip to St. Bonaventure University to take part in "Journalism Day" where high schools were in competition for awards for the best newspapers and yearbooks in Western New York. We entered our newspaper *Student Prints*, and yearbook *The Star* in the competition. I traveled with Bob Summers, who was also co-editor with me in the sports sections of the two publications. After arriving on campus a bit late, we scrambled to find the site of the competition. After a few false steps we found the right building but the wrong floor. As we reached the elevator, the door rattled open upon which we were greeted by none other than the event's illustrious keynote speaker — Pierre Salinger, President John F. Kennedy's Press Secretary. While smoking a huge cigar, he proclaimed, "Hi boys, going my way?" The rest of the day was all downhill. We won medals for our publications, didn't get lost on our way home, and heard a rousing speech from our elevator companion. I should add that Bob Summers later became a professional journalist and wrote a popular horse racing column called the *Happy Handicapper* which regularly appeared in the *Buffalo News*.

When I compare the class instruction I received at St. Joe's, it seems that the education I received at the Mount was more content-based. Each nun taught a particular grade and covered a variety of subjects each day. While I still recall individual teachers, it seems that each nun was capable enough to substitute in one grade or another. The goal of my eight years at the Mount focused on covering a certain amount of content each year leading up to graduation. All content was taught within a strict moral and ethical framework. Now that I had a wealth of facts and figures at my finger-tips, the question was what to do with this information. This is where St. Joe's took over the educational baton that was handed them.

At St. Joe's I had teachers who were very good if not inspirational, as well as some who were quite terrible. Regarding the former category, Brother Anthony, who coached our track and field team and had appointed me to be his manager, taught me plane and solid geometry. His talent and enthusiasm actually got me thinking of a career as an architect. He was very pleased when I aced both plane and solid geometry on New York State Regents exams. Yes, content was certainly within Brother Anthony's classroom, but he went far in motivating us to think outside the box and look for the beauty and application of these math disciplines. On the other hand, I had teachers who were "turnoffs" to higher learning. For example, an older teacher who was long past his prime taught American History. His method in class was to reminisce about his growing up in the textile belts of Massachusetts, and he kept attention by literally knocking heads of a few students against the blackboard. Thank God, we had a textbook from which we could learn American History. Most of my other teachers fell between the two extremes. Some were work-a-day types, who were content to cover the syllabus, but not much more. This was true for most courses: Religion, English, Math, History, Health, and Chemistry. One could say we were exposed to a liberal education as seen in some colleges. We had a smattering of the arts and humanities as well as the sciences. At St. Joe's and the Mount, however, the common denominator of both was to provide a curriculum in and out of the classroom with moral values which would last a life time.

There was a teacher, Brother Mark, who intimidated me as a freshman by slapping my face when he took our class to the school library. After we were given a tour, I complimented Brother Mark on the eyeglasses he was wearing. The black frames looked great and I made it known to him. Thinking that I was a wise guy, he looked at me and slapped my face! From that moment on, I kept him at a distance, and we continued our separate lives at St. Joe's as if we had secrets to hide - Brother Mark's out-of-bound behavior and my all-knowing view that he had stepped over the line. There was one redeeming feature in my being in Brother's literature class – by hook or by crook, he got me interested in reading books. One of our assignments was to read and critique a book from a list he made available to the class. My contribution to the assignment was to procrastinate for as long as I could from reading A.J. Cronin's, *The Keys to the Kingdom*. Carrying the book everywhere for a couple of weeks, I finally broke down and cracked the binding on a bus ride to and from Dunkirk, NY. Our track team had an "away meet" with Cardinal Mindzenty High School, and on the way home I finally bit the bullet and actually started to read about the Catholic priest who was going through the best and worst of being a missionary in China. The next day Brother Mark had each of us come to his desk and discuss the book we had read. I was a nervous wreck at having given superficial treatment to Cronin's novel. As I stood next to Brother, I began to answer his general questioning of the novel; however, he quickly waved me off saying, "That's enough, you read it." I was flabbergasted and returned to my seat thinking I had just missed a bullet. In another sense, I felt empowered. From what I DID read, the novel was very interesting, and I should have carved out the time to actually read and appreciate the book in its entirety. A big off-shoot of my encounter with Cronin was to regularly visit a nearby bookstore. Back in the 1950's, paperbacks were relatively inexpensive with many costing as little as 50 cents. Soon I developed a small library consisting of works like: *The Gun, Moby Dick, Battle Cry, Tom Sawyer, The Citadel*, and irony of ironies, a biography of architect Frank Lloyd Wright. In spite of Brother Mark and me, he did light the spark to get me reading, not only for educational value, but for what it is - mankind's primary vehicle of lasting communication.

Coincidentally with my managerial roles at St. Joe's, I began to appreciate track and field statistics at the local and national level. Thanks to the mentoring Brothers Anthony and Jerome, and the "big" and "little" Brother Augustines (all coming from Manhattan College with its tradition of excellence in track and field), St. Joe's excelled in winning numerous championships. Going the *Walter Mitty* route, I also became a track star. At home I marked off distances inside and outside the house. Walking as fast as I could, I'd made attempts to break records in the 100 and 220 yard dashes and so forth. Equipped with my handy stopwatch, I could tell whether I'd made a dent on a world's record, and, probably more importantly, how I was doing physically burdened with my little genetic defect. In a similar vein, I became a basketball star as well. For this I have to give Greg credit. In the Shoshone house Greg and I shot hoops using our parents' ice bucket and some tennis balls. More than a few lamps were broken during our living room scrimmages. When we moved to our Kenmore house, the metal ring of the ice bucket was screwed to a cabinet over Mom's washer and dryer. I'd like to think that Greg's later court successes all began with a tennis ball and an ice bucket!

Preliminary to my graduation from St. Joe's, I went to our senior prom with long-standing friend Sue Grace, who was the oldest daughter of my parents' close friends Jerry and "Stevie" Grace. Afterwards, because the late hour, Dad wanted me to invite my classmates home for an early breakfast. With a buffet ready composed of toast, bacon, eggs, donuts, coffee, and juice, classmates started to trickle in after midnight. During the second or third serving of breakfast, Dad and I heard some giggling commotion on the front lawn. When I reached the side door, I saw a classmate with his date making whoopee, as if our front lawn was a king-sized bed. When Dad asked me what was going on, I replied: "Nothing, Dad!"

**My Date For St. Joe's junior prom,
Mary Ellen Gallagher)**

Our graduation took place at Kleinhans Hall with its spacious auditorium. Thankfully, my walk across the stage went without a hitch, as I always feared that I would trip and fall. The rousing applause I got when my name was called still rings in my ears. Now I was on my way to college! It would be Niagara, not Manhattan. Ironically, 50 years later during our class reunion, I was on stage again at the same venue. With me in my electric scooter, and Class President Joe Ryan in his wheelchair, we were backstage waiting to receive a 50th certificate during the actual Commencement Exercises. Much water had passed under the bridge for both of us. Joe, who was a decorated Vietnam vet injured in a motorcycle accident, and I smiled at each other, as we were about to go on stage. In harmony, we said to each other, "Well, see you on the other side!"

# Chapter 3

# Canada By Way of
# St. Rose of Lima

My mind often wanders to long ago memories of Christmas. While some are bittersweet, even disturbing, most of my recollections remain comforting and reassuring. There is one scenario which keeps bubbling forth and readily brings a smile to my face; it is a scene taking me back to our home on Shoshone. In the mid 1950's, I was about 11 years old, brother Greg around 8 or 9, and sister Karen who picked up the rear at 6 years of age. At Christmas time we typically had a brightly if not garishly decorated tree in the front living room so all who passed from the street could get a good look. We kids, of course, frequently went outside at night so we could see for ourselves the decorating handiwork. The fresh smell from the tree still lingers, as does the sight of the hand blown bulbs, a few of which were broken each year, and the string of lights which became longer each passing year. I particularly liked the lights shaped like candles, which when heated an audible stream of bubbles would appear. Of course the tree would be festooned with yards and yards of tinsel. One year we tried the so-called angel hair but quickly gave it up as it cut into our hands. Over our brick fireplace (never used) was a large mirror upon which my dad would paint a Christmas scene he had seen the year before in a Christmas card – a choir of singing angels, wisemen with their camels, or a nativity tableau with a prominent star in the upper corner. Regardless of the scene, Dad would spray with a can of white paint and add clouds everywhere as a final touch. With a fresh wreath over the front door, stockings tacked over the fireplace and Christmas cards taped on any available surface in the front room, we Hudeckis on Shoshone were ready for the approaching big day.

Yuletide and all its religious significance were reinforced by the nuns at the Mount who took pains in getting us prepared for our annual Christmas assembly. Whether it was Karen's first grade class, Greg's fifth or my seventh, we all had roles to play in the extravaganza. My mother-in-law Olivia, a school teacher and an administrator herself, would dearly have approved of our nun's rehearsal efforts to dress us up for nativity scenes and with shouts and pounding on the piano to get the fledgling choirs to sing on key. The nuns were so proud of their efforts that they took the show on the road and got us to sing on live television. In one program I wore a monk's robe and beard and read the biblical story of the birth of Jesus (afterward I was told I did a great job). Greg and I were so energized from the school activities that we often sang carols before nodding off at night. He would be in the upper bunk and I below in the lower, and we would alternate carols til we exhausted each other's memory. It never occurred to us to bring a songbook to bed which would have kept us up all night.

We kids sensed that the great day got nearer because our parents often whispered a lot and spoke in a sort of a code. While Karen still had Santa Claus on her mind, one Christmas Eve Greg and I discovered who the real Santa was. In bed and having exhausted our litany of carols, we heard murmuring, giggling, and the rustling of paper from the living room. Very quietly we sleuths tip-toed down the hall to a strategic corner off the kitchen and craned our necks to see our parents busily wrapping gifts and setting them under the tree. For a time we had had our suspicions, but this discovery nailed it – Santa Claus does exist but not as advertised. From then on, we decided to leave Karen in the dark and go along with her yearly habit of putting out milk and cookies for Santa near the fireplace. The previous year Greg and I did some measurements of the fireplace and concluded that Santa would need to be the size of a toy poodle to fit through it – myths die hard on Shoshone Street.

Subsequently, we brothers discovered in the basement where *Santa's* gifts were stored prior to Christmas. Before conversion to gas, our home was heated by a coal burning furnace. The unused coal bin had been cleaned out and converted to a storeroom, but with Christmas approaching a padlock mysteriously appeared on the door. Hmmm. Thankfully it was ajar one day, and Greg and I seized the opportunity to investigate. Lifting a large tarp in the corner we came upon neatly stacked gifts all wrapped in their Hallmark finest. Of course this discovery was only the beginning. With the deft hands of a burglar we explored, felt, shook, rattled, and in the end carefully triaged which gifts could be unwrapped and rewrapped with no one being the wiser. To this day I still have the knack to remove cellotape enclosing a package and not tear the whole thing up. Ah the early traditions Greg and I share!

Christmas Eve became electric to say the least. Last minute gifts to our parents would be wrapped and put under the tree. It's interesting in retrospect that our parents were always gracious and thankful for any gift we gave them, yet they very rarely wore or used anything we painstakingly bought for them. A kid's vision of what parents like or need or what their size was never really meshed in our household. With Christmas music coming from the hi-fi or radio with very little choice in TV programs or stations in the 1950's, we eventually settled into dinner. Most times Dad joined us for dinner, but frequently he'd be late coming home from the office. Being a young dentist working to establish his own practice, he'd do most of his own lab work as a way of cutting costs. With the kitchen cleaned up (Greg and I interchanged washing and drying duties back then), we'd try to catch a peek of some black and white TV program usually containing a Christmas theme. A favorite program of mine was *I Remember Mama* in which a Norwegian immigrant family lived in turn of the century San Francisco. In an episode shown each Christmas, the eldest son is duped by burglars hiding behind some cows housed in a backyard shed. Out of sight and feigning voices intended from the cows, the burglars cajole the son to rob his own home so that poor people will have something for Christmas. However, the jig is up when the son fumbles the goods with a loud noise waking everyone up. Even though the burglars are found out and arrested, the story ends on a high note. In spite of the son being outwitted, he is soon praised (especially by Mama played by the venerable actress Peggy Wood). Together the family goes on to extol the virtue of giving to others at Christmas. Hokey as it was, it does seem we are at a loss to see more stories like this.

With our teeth brushed, snug in our bunks, carol singing exhausted, now came the hard part – trying to sleep thinking of all the excitement the next day will bring. What gifts hadn't we surreptitiously opened? Will Mom like my juice glass set? I'm hopeful my imitation leather gloves will fit Dad, or will they? The mind rolls over and over waiting for sleep to come. There was, however, a particular Christmas Eve I'll never forget. I was a little older then, because Greg and I had outgrown our bunk beds which had been disassembled into two single beds. Mine was sideways in front of the back door leading to a small yard. Very late and in darkness I heard the slow crunch, crunch of someone walking through the six inches of snow in our backyard. Next the visitor came up our porch steps and carefully tested the knob to our back door. The knob was no more than a foot from my nose. I froze in fear. I have no saliva to shout to my parents asleep in the adjacent room. After what seemed like an eternity, the potential intruder turned and left. I may have slept that night but not likely. The next morning at the breakfast table I told everyone what had happened that night. With skepticism filling the air we all marched to the bedroom and peered through the blinds covering the backdoor window. There they were. See! Fresh footprints in the snow all the way to the door! It didn't take too long for my dad to install a dead bolt to the door. The movie *Straw Dogs* comes to mind where Dustin Hoffman is in a life and death struggle defending home and family from intruders. My story is not as dramatic as Dustin's but much more frightening for a kid who was already on tender hooks waiting for Christmas dawn to arrive.

At the time, our neighborhood church was St. Rose of Lima located a few blocks from home. The pastor was Monsignor Duggan: a large cigar-smoking man, a World War Two vet, and as tough as nails. He could be quite gruff, raised boxer puppies in his spare time, and he hated anyone being late to Mass. With fanfare and derision, he often stopped a service waiting for some poor late soul to find his or her seat. It was not a pretty scene and quite effective in getting everyone into their pews before bells signaled the start of Mass. In our case, Greg and I, along with Karen, always made an extra effort to be on time for the 7 o'clock Mass Christmas morning. While mom and dad were still slumbering after doing the Santa thing last night, we brothers rousted Karen and we all got quickly dressed. Our immediate aim was to go to Mass, come home and open gifts, have breakfast, dress again, and try as we could to get into the car before Dad started shouting to us. You see, on Christmas day we traditionally drove 60 miles to Dad's hometown, Hamilton, Ontario, Canada, and visited his parents and the families of his two brothers, Leon and Stan, and sister Helen.

Our trek to St. Rose on those dark, cold and snowy mornings would include a sweater, outer jacket, mittens, a scarf, earmuffs, and, lastly, buckled boots with pant legs tucked in. Like a scene out of Jack London's *Call of the Wild*, Greg sat me down on our American Flyer sled. Firmly grabbing the towrope Greg lit off with Karen shuffling close behind. We made our way through newly fallen snow, and immediately reached our corner of Shoshone and Tacoma. Without hesitation we trotted up Tacoma along the forbidding high wall of the Carmelite Convent. After going half a block, we'd take Groveland to Parkside for the two remaining blocks to St. Rose.

Those childhood expeditions still hold me in wonder – cold and dark, the neighborhood shrouded in silence, we heard only our breath, boots crunching, and the rhythmic crusted sound of the sled blades. Conversation was limited, each one engulfed with the thought that this was a very special morn. Maybe the most special day of the year, and here we were on our pilgrimage to celebrate the birth of our savior Jesus Christ. It was pretty heady stuff even for us young ones. When we turn the corner at Parkside, we could see a distant light emanating from the stained glass windows of St. Rose. On this day the corner of Parkside and Parker became our Bethlehem. Metaphorically, we were the *three kings* coming to adore the Christ child. Except in our case we had to pass muster with Monsignor Duggan who was at the stable gates.

With the altar festooned in a sea of poinsettias and a Nativity scene to the side, our devotion at Mass went without a hitch. Even a few carols were sung by those in attendance. Under the watchful eye of the good monsignor, we counted the seconds til the final blessing. We were like sprinters waiting for the starting gun. Finally with the reprieve from Monsignor, we scooted down the stairs and out the door to our waiting sled. Retracing our route we headed for home – Parkside, Groveland, Tacoma, each segment seemed shorter now. Flooded with anticipation and adrenaline, we reached home. We went up the half flight of stairs and shed our arctic gear in a heap at the landing. With coffee in hand Mom and Dad were up and joined us in the living room for the fun. Without much prodding, we tore into the gifts surrounding the base of the tree. Excitement reigned as we opened one gift then another. Karen had her dolls and scaled-down tea sets. For Greg and me – guns, holsters, and cowboy hats! It was time for Hopalong Cassidy and his sidekick to ride the range and save the county from bandits and rustlers! Even Karen got into the swing with her Dale Evans outfit complete with frilled chaps, holster, and hat, and, of course, her very own cap pistol. Somewhere buried among the loot were clothes (ignored for now), the odd book or two (wonderfully illustrated by Andrew Wyeth's father), and usually something educational like an Erector set or Lincoln Logs. Once, I got a toy microscope which I used to magnify everything from the letter "e" in newspaper print to a drop of pond water. Back then toys didn't need batteries (except for a crystal set I got one year). In the end the living room was awash with crumpled paper made more so by the playful antics of our boxer Holiday.

In a while the spotlight shifted to our parents who had yet to open their gifts. This became a special time for us kids with each one seeking some degree of approval for our purchases. There was Mom with boxes of sweet smelling things, a couple of hand-made items, and clothes mainly bought by Dad. One year I contributed an ill-fitting polka dot dress worn maybe once. Then there was the infamous orange juice pitcher with 6 matching glasses (after fifty or so years I believe a glass or two still remain). Dad was busy taking pictures from one of his many cameras. He seemed to get the same things each year – tools, some cigars, gloves, aftershave, and gadgets which seemed to get sillier (and more costly) each year. As the years went on, the rallying cry each Christmas was – "What to get father?" It was only after many years that I realized he loved a particular brand of shirt (Countess Mara), and he was pleased each time he was given one for Christmas (as well as for Father's Day and his birthday). With that discovery, part of my life became infinitely simplified.

Breakfast was next and had to be eaten quickly since we needed to get on the road for our trip to Hamilton. After wolfing down eggs and toast, we shed our cowboy gear and reluctantly climbed into our school attire of jacket and tie, which would be buried under our winter wear.

**Family Picture Before Leaving For Canada)**

Dad would be the first to reach our outside garage to warm up the Buick which was idling in the driveway. The car trunk was packed with gifts for our Canadian relatives. With the house at the mercy of an anxious boxer dog and kids fighting for a window seat in the back, we were soon navigating the treacherous north Buffalo streets. Back then, we had very little idea of *lake effect* snow. We only knew that after Thanksgiving we got regular bouts of snow while our Canadian friends to the north got relatively little. The lack of snow became more pronounced as we wound our way through the Tonawanda suburbs, and to River Road which took us to the first major leg of our journey, the City of Niagara Falls. Eventually we'd reach the chemical plants lining both sides of Buffalo Avenue. Even the foul smelling Hooker and DuPont plants were regaled with festive lights, trees, and seasonal greetings. After a few miles we reached the Rainbow Bridge, which took us into Canada; however, if traffic was heavy or, more likely, on a whim, Dad frequently liked to go over the wooden planked Lower Arch or even the rickety Queenston Bridge further down the Niagara River. The latter was particularly scary because of its narrow winding approach along the steep banks of the gorge, and, once on the rough-hewn bridge, you could actually see the swift river currents not too far below. Much later a major steel spanned bridge would be constructed offering a safer, faster crossing but it certainly was not as interesting as the original span.

Once we were on the Canadian side of the river, Dad got out to open the trunk exposing our booty of Christmas gifts. Usually Dad had more than a chat with the customs agents because of his familial roots to Canada. Invigorated with the knowledge that one customs agent or another had some far flung connection to the Hudecki clan, Dad got us under way again through the City of Niagara Falls (Ontario) and onto the much-traveled QEW (aka, Queen Elizabeth Way). While things are much different now with four lanes and no stoplights, the QEW back then was an erratic lonely stretch through farm country complete with tractors and wagons crossing often bringing you from 60 mph to a screeching halt. I recall one time that we had a blowout and Dad did all he could to wrestle the car safely to the shoulder. At the time Dad was listening to the radio while his alma mater, Niagara University, was playing a basketball game against some eastern powerhouse like Seton Hall or St. John's. Here we were in the middle of a dormant apple orchard, car jacked up with doors wide open to hear the game, and Dad changing a flat tire. If incidents like this didn't delay us, the lift bridge over the Welland Canal sure did. While boat traffic on the canal was reduced in winter, there always seemed to be a boat or two just waiting for our Christmas crossing. As a result, traffic would be backed up for many miles, long enough to get out of the car to a nearby diner for a cup of hot coffee or chocolate. On the other hand, we kids enjoyed the sight of those monstrous lakers passing before us and wondering aloud where they were going and where they came from. We got clues from the flags they were flying astern. After leaving the canal area and the surrounding City of St. Catherine's we continued on the QEW. By now the QEW became flat, tedious and boring. As we glanced out the window, we encountered row upon row of grapevines interspersed with leafless orchards. In the spring these same fields would be ablaze with gorgeous blossoms, but now the fields were gloomy almost to the point where even Van Gogh couldn't enhance their winter drab. As we tired of listing out of state license plates or counting red colored cars, we became numb from the journey – would this trip ever end!

We felt like the Pilgrims who sighted the New England coast after an arduous Atlantic crossing when we finally reached the suburban Stony Creek traffic round-a-bout. As only the British can do with their infamous round-a-bouts, we entered the asphalt pinwheel and quickly are spun off in the direction of Hamilton. With Stelco Steel as our companion for a few miles, we wound our way though now quiet streets. Each one resurrecting images of Canada's close relationship with Britain (King St, Queen St, and so on). We reached our grandparent's corner house on Sherman around midday where we piled out and headed for the front door where we were warmly hugged and greeted with a mixture of Polish and English. Affectionately called babshia and dhadshu, our grandparents led the non-stop chatter and accompanied us to the dining room table which was over-flowing with breads, colored eggs, sausages, ham, and pastries in many shapes and sizes all having one thing in common – powdered sugar. Let's eat! Steaming hot chicken soup was put out soon accompanied by sandwiches made of kielbasa and sour rye bread. The scene was not for meek appetites. Later cookies appeared with milk for us kids and strong coffee for the adults. After gifts were exchanged, we kids become the center of attention – conversation jumped from school to impromptu Polish lessons. In the kitchen we were entertained by our grandparent's parakeets who could repeat words in Polish, as well as nipping at food held in ones mouth. After an hour or so Dad declared "Ok kids, get our coats, we're going to your Aunt Helen's." Throughout our stay Dad had been busy on the phone talking up an itinerary with his sister Helen and brothers Leon and Stan. "All aboard, next stop Belmont Avenue."

Under cold, yet sunny skies, a short ride took us to the Muldoon home where Helen and Jack greeted us along with cousins John and Maureen (Paul and Mark have yet to be born). In the Muldoon house, the focus quickly became their affable but stupid black mongrel named Gus. One story after another was told as we petted Gus and engorged him with Christmas cookies on the sly. Soon Gus was put out into the small fenced-in yard to howl to his heart's delight. One interesting thing I remember in Helen's house was a small windowed alcove filled with small figurines and Christmas memorabilia. The Christmas tree was situated adjacent to the alcove which made for a postcard-like scene. By the time it took Uncle Jack to refill his omnipresent pipe, it was time to stuff us back into the car for a ride to the West Side of town and the Stan Hudecki clan.

When Uncle Stan first put down roots after the war and married Leona, they lived in a small house in a new development not too far from suburban Stony Creek; however, after Stan's orthopedic residency, he and Leona in order to accommodate their growing family bought a large tudor-style house in the fashionable West End of Hamilton. When we pulled into the driveway of the Carolina St. home, excitement reigned as we were quickly engulfed by our cousins Bern, John and Mary Ann (eventually Helen, Peter, Stephen, Cathy, Stan Jr., and Ricky would be added in succession). Amidst all the clamor, both Dad and Uncle Stan quickly had their cameras out for stills and 8mm movies; the latter involved draping a bed sheet as a curtain over an archway separating the living and dining rooms so each of us kids could be introduced on camera. While corny at the time, these moments proved to be nostalgic ones for each of us.

**At Stan Hudecki Home: From Right – Me, Bern, Greg, John, Mary Ann, Karen, and Helen)**

The Caroline house was huge by Shoshone standards with plenty of nooks and crannies to explore and play hide and seek. There are photos of Karen and Mary Ann in grownup makeup 'playing house' inside the first floor lavatory; they outfitted the small room with tea settings, small chairs, and anything else they could get their hands on. For Greg and me the basement offered the greatest challenges with its rabbit warren configuration. There was even an old wine cellar room equipped with a large heavy door to keep all the cobwebs back. Like a scene from the Hardy Boys, we envisioned the room hiding treasure of some kind. On the second floor, Stan had a study where he kept his medical books and files, plus things that fascinated me like framed maps, a human skull, and an old shiny brass microscope. Compared to his siblings, Uncle Stan was the nerdiest of them all. Always with a tie and jacket he came across as the studious one and always asked questions a school-teacher would ask. As I got to know him better and he me, I identified with my godfather more and more as the years went on. It is a close relationship I'll always treasure with Stan and his loving wife Leona. Through them I got to know and love their family as if they were my own. After snacks and an impromptu carol singing session, we were soon set to get packing again for our last stop – to visit the oldest and most garrulous of them all, Uncle Leon.

Uncle Leon's home on Park Row South was a modest-sized, single family structure; however, in Leon's case he also had an adjoining lot which was used for every conceivable sport. Leon was the "hail fellow well met" member of the Hudecki clan forever telling stories and openly affectionate. While he had previously operated a tavern and played semi-pro football, he currently ran a bowling alley called Central Park Lanes located in the heart of the city. Time might be tight for our travels, but on one or two occasions we took up Leon's offer to come down to the alleys for a game or two. On one trip I got my finger smashed from a ball returning to the rack. In a twist of fate, the bowling alley was later torn down to make room for what is now the current site of City Hall.

**At Leon Hudecki Home; Bottom Left,
Steph, Dennis, Margaret, Leon; Top
Left, Greg, Judy, Me, and Barbara)**

The atmosphere at Leon's was always lively. Aunt Rose, together with cousins Judy, Barbara, and Dennis (later joined by Margaret and Leon, Jr.) were quick to feed us and even entertain us. For example, Barbara would haul out her saxophone for notes she learned in the school band. If Christmas fell on a Sunday, we were always entertained by the Ed Sullivan Show on television. The first time I actually saw Elvis Presley was on my Uncle Leon's black and white set (no color or high definition back then). With more food and drinks passed around and lively toasts to all, the bewitching hour for our departure began to creep in. Most of the time the goodbyes were started in the kitchen, and later with more stories the adieus continued into the living room. Eventually, while getting our coats on, the farewells extended onto the outside porch and into the cold of the night. Looking back these goodbyes were always rousing and quite satisfactory for all.

Into the darkness we went, regardless of the weather, the lateness of the hour, or the weariness of the moment. The happenings of the day kept my dad alert at the wheel for a good part of the trip home on the QEW; but, like him, I was also consumed by the pitch darkness of the highway which was periodically jolted by the bright beams of opposing traffic. With Greg and Karen asleep, I'd keep vigil with Mom keeping Dad awake as we headed farther and farther east. More often than not our journey home was accompanied by a cast of highly entertaining radio programs. Some of our favorites at the time were: *Fibber Magee and Molly*, the cantankerous *Bickersons*, the lovable *Amos and Andy*, and the sinister *The Shadow* (…Knows!). If these shows didn't keep our attention, we'd always have the blaring sirens going off in *Crimestoppers*, or the horsy clippety clop effects dramatized in some of the Westerns. Radio back then fed into each one's imagination as little else could, as well as being a constant companion – especially on a long lonely drive.

Just when you thought the trip would never end, the sky lightens as we reached the outskirts of Niagara Falls. by the time we reached the US border we could usually depend on some form of snow activity to accompany our last 20 miles home. With things now more familiar, we ticked off passing landmarks which would get us safely back to Shoshone.- the Rainbow Bridge overlooking the brightly illuminated Falls (mystical even at this late hour). The succession of chemical plants along Buffalo Avenue, back to River Road along the Niagara River, Sheridan Drive deserted for all except us holiday travelers, and the last leg taking us serpentine through North Buffalo to our final destination – the garage now illuminated by our bright beams. Without much coaxing, we trekked through the snow-covered sidewalk to the side door and took the dog out for a brief run. Satisfied that the mutt had taken care of business, the house and all in it quickly headed to bed. And to all a good night!

# Chapter 4

# Catching the Fishing Bug

My love affair started at an idyllic little spot along Ellicott Creek. Just above the dam where the creek ambles under Main Street in suburban Williamsville, Greg, Dad, and I situated ourselves on a grassy bank. The creek has its source east of Buffalo, and, long before it empties into the mighty Niagara River, the creek meanders through a mix of residential and recreational properties of suburban Cheektowaga, Amherst, and lastly the Tonawandas. This watershed meant nothing to Greg and me. All we knew was that Dad kept to his promise and took us fishing.

In the early 1950's, we were given matching fishing rods and reels, and tackle boxes filled with leads, weights, hooks and lures. It would be an astronomical understatement to say we were excited at the prospect of hooking a fish. Nearly every day we'd open and shut our boxes and rearranged our lures, as if this practice might get us to the day that we actually went fishing. Dad and his Canadian kin ventured annually on excursions that took them to various parts of Ontario, such as the lake-filled areas of Peterborough and Muskoka, with even a trip or two to the Georgian Bay area. Kodachromes and 8mm movies from these trips made our mouths water. There were pictures of smallmouths, muskies, northerns, and walleyes. All we got at the time were promises and more promises. Only later would I realize that Dad's fledging dental practice kept the family afloat and that his long work hours took precedence over repeated promises to go fishing with a couple of young brats.

In the meantime, Greg and I (mainly I) kept the angling fire alive by trolling for leaves from the curb at home. Greg would rather ride his bike through the leaves. For me, I'd attach a string to a wood stick and drag the end among the leaves hoping to snare a big one. In today's world of electronic gadgetry, this might sound utterly pathetic, but this was the 1950's, and kids simply improvised when and where we could. When we'd tire from freaking out the neighbors with our curb-side antics, we'd haul out our actual fishing gear.

At first we'd be tentative, striving to cast in a small, lead sinker measured direction and distance. However, it didn't take too long before we'd get into the spirit and fling the line hither and yon – and in the process, snarling bikes, flower beds, bushes, tree limbs, and our overly curious mutt. It was a dangerous time to be near us. It was also a time when we boy geniuses discovered the backlash, and the care needed to unravel it. There were no books on the subject, and only with experience did we learn to avoid it. You see, when a line is cast, the reel is generating an RPM – when the rate exceeds the RPM of the line being cast, voila! The reel looks like a nest made by a bird on happy pills. As neophytes, we'd first holler and scream, but with time (several years I might add), we learned to sigh and take our fate like men. Unraveling a backlash takes dexterity and patience. Nothing more, nothing less will ever do.

After dinner one summer evening, Mom called from the open kitchen window, "Your father will be home in a few minutes to take you boys fishing." As he was only six or seven, Greg has only a faint memory of the outing to Ellicott Creek; however, I clearly recall staring interminably at our red and white plastic bobbers. Each one was fitted with a worm and hook. We waited and waited for something to happen – anything. We even implored the Almighty for some kind of help. It was only after we began to lose daylight and time to reel, that something unexpected happened. After peeling back a fistful of weeds from Greg's hook, we discovered a three inch bluegill. The little fellow must have been hooked early on and subsequently spent the next hour or so entangling itself further. We couldn't believe our eyes. We were so happy. We tried to sustain this epic event and pleaded with Dad to allow us to take the confused critter home in a bucket of water to show Mom. Once home, part two of our pleading began, which was to draw a bath for the fish. Taking pity on us, Mom relented, and for a day or two the family couldn't take a bath. This was the best of all possible worlds for two grungy brothers. By inadvertently hooking our first fish, a new chapter in our lives began which signaled the beginning of a lifetime pursuit of fishing. Around 1950 my parents bought a summer cottage located on the Canadian shore of Lake Erie; it represented a huge commitment of time and energy. From the beginning a routine was set up and adhered to for many years to come. While the USA was celebrating a Memorial Day weekend, it was time for us to 'open up' the cottage. There would be cleaning to do, lawn to cut, shutters to take down, and toilets to be drained of their protective antifreeze. Later, as the family grew to five children, we kids were able to take more active roles in the spring overhaul.

I recall two particular trips in early May. One involved me as a senior in high school when I needed to study for the up-coming New York State Regents exams. I spent most of the time at the lake in the family car studying. I was paying the price of getting older. On the other hand, when I was around nine or ten, only Dad and I went to the cottage, ostensibly to ready things for the family's arrival at the end of June. I was thrilled to accompany him as he loaded the car with all sorts of household stuff. There were, however, a couple of items which raised some suspicions. Somehow Dad managed to squeeze a Johnson & Johnson 10 horse outboard motor into the trunk, along with miscellaneous fishing equipment (including my time-tested backlash outfit). Waiting for us at the cottage was Dad's pride and joy – a 15-foot heavily varnished Peterborough boat safely secured for the winter on a cradle resting on a track high above the waterline. Once we arrived, Dad got the boat packed and readied for our first fishing excursion of the season – if only Dad could nudge the boat down the tracks to the water's edge!

It was at this time that I learned my first expletive – shit! With perfect diction Dad vocalized his feelings as he struggled to coax the boat down the track without killing himself. I was no help of course. The best I could do was hit the power switch of the winch when dad yelled out and pray that the boat reached the Lake Erie shore with Dad in one piece. Eventually, the deed was done and, with a few hefty pulls of the ripcord and me in my lifejacket, we were on our way to Mohawk Point a mile away.

The weather was crisp and sunny, and the water was clear and blue with a small chop. What else could one ask for? A lesson in fishing from Dad, that's what. His approach to lake fishing was to troll deeply with lures like spoons or rigs containing brightly feathered Yellow Sallies with a big juicy worm dangling behind. Going after deep-water loving Blue and Yellow Pike required panning line out for a considerable distance while the boat chugged away at trolling speed. I was never really good at deep water trolling, because holding the rod stiff required something I didn't have – strength and endurance. Dad would frequently yell out: "Mike, hold your line up, let out more line!" He on the other hand was quite sturdy (and fearless I might add) and made it a regular practice to get out into the open waters about a mile or so from shore and troll for the big guys. While no fish were caught on this trip, I'll always remember this one-on-one outing with him. With a cigar poking out of his mouth and a bottle of Labatts Blue nearby, he was in his heaven. A place in the sun that I was happy to have savored and shared.

There was one jaunt where Dad caught onto a 6-pound yellow pike. Fishing with my uncle, Jack Muldoon, Dad didn't think he'd ever catch a yellow this big again; so he had it mounted and proudly hung it over the fireplace. Many years later when the cottage was eventually sold in the 1980's, although dusty and discolored, the pike was as much a fixture as the cottage's plumbing, and it went with the sale price.

Dad's preoccupation with boating extended well into the snowy winter months. One grey February morning in 1953, he took Greg and me to New York City to see the boat show. We were accompanied by Jim Herzog who ran the drugstore near Dad's dental office. Flying for the first time, I was enthralled looking out the window from our American Airlines DC-3 and seeing the frozen landscape passing below from ten thousand feet. After arriving at LaGuardia, we detoured first to the Waldorf Astoria Hotel for the annual car show and a glimpse of the showcased "Hope Diamond". Afterwards, we headed to an immense armory for the boat show. The cavernous structure was filled with smell of marine varnish and other familiar scents one associates with new boats. We went up and down immense aisles and we ogled boat after boat. Most were quite large and beyond anything we might imagine ourselves in. After hours of browsing and with dozen of brochures tucked in a sample bag, we flew back to Buffalo. Exhausted, but alert, I sat in my window seat and gazed out into the darkness which was periodically interrupted by flames spraying from the engine. New cars and boats, even a light show, all in one day!

Not many weeks after our return from New York City, a rather large carton arrived through UPS. The outside of the package had Dad's name and address, as well as the name of the sender – *Chris Craft*

Lo and behold, Dad had ordered a do-it-yourself kit at the boat show! With Herculean effort (and luck) he and Greg somehow got the heavy, bulky carton to the basement. As on Christmas morning, the carton was quickly taken apart revealing wood pieces of every length and description, as well as an assortment of metal parts like screws and washers. The last item out was a set of instructions, including a diagram of the finished product – an 8-foot pram. My pulse raced as Greg and I encouraged Dad to get started, but he explained that the boat had to be constructed in stages. "First, there is the frame; this is followed by the…" Accustomed to gluing together a battleship in an afternoon, Greg and I couldn't understand why we couldn't have this rowboat on the water by sundown.

For several weeks a routine took over. After dinner, Dad would trundle down to the basement with his cigar and work on the boat. The early stages were consumed with lots of measuring, sawing, drilling and screwing. This went on and on until one day a skeletal outline of the boat was revealed; however, we were disheartened to learn that this was only the frame, and it later would be discarded. More days went by until it was time to use the plywood sheets to construct the sides and floor of the boat. Unlike Norm in PBS's New Yankee Workshop and his first-class tools and clamps, Dad shaped and glued the plywood to the frame with spit and grit. No tool was safe from his determination and will. Straight pieces of plywood were bent and kept in place with a surplus of adhesive, an army of screws, and a few miles of rope just to be sure. Finally, exhausted from this exercise in wills, Dad's admonition to us was: "Boys, we need to let the glue set for a few days." With relief he switched off the light and we went upstairs for the night.

Amidst sawdust and bits of wood everywhere, the boat was finally finished. During the weeks of construction, Mom's laundry efforts were confined to a tiny corner in the basement. Next in line was a trip to Niagara Street to purchase marine-grade paint and a set of oars and oarlocks. Running along the river in the Black Rock section of Buffalo, Niagara Street was lined with marinas and shops catering to erstwhile mariners like ourselves. The street was also famous for summer time clam bars, which we frequently visited going and coming from our Canadian cottage. Moreover, at the foot of Ferry Street, after it crossed Niagara Street, and near remnants of the Erie Canal, now referred to as the Black Rock Canal, was a restaurant called Sargent's. Famous for its Friday Fish Fry, Dad and Mom frequently took us there to feast upon freshly-caught yellow and blue pike mounded on a huge platter sitting in the middle of the table. As we sipped our birch beers, Greg and I would be hypnotized by the nearby boat traffic and fishermen plying the canal and river. While Sargent's deep fried pike is now long gone, its memory fondly persists for baby boomers who are still alive in the Buffalo area.

Back in the basement, the pram was rescued from its skeletal frame and given several coasts of paint. A few days later, the boat was equipped with oarlocks and brass fittings. Wow! What started out as a barely manageable carton of components, was transformed into a proud little craft currently moored between hanging laundry and the furnace. Now the fun really began.

Getting the carton to the basement was one thing, but now the hurdle was to navigate the boat outside. Casual measurements made a window escape impossible. The only exit available was to retrace its entry up the stairs and a short zig-zag through the landing to the side door. After some cleaver twists and turns around the furnace, laundry lines, and a short knotty pine-lined hall, the pram rested on the stairs with its bow touching the door of the landing. I can't be too certain, but I think at this stalemate Dad decided to have a lunch. How to extricate the pram would be contemplated over a ham sandwich.

In retrospect, Dad found the answer to be quite simple. Satisfied by his impromptu lunch he ferreted around his workbench and found the tool he was looking for – a crowbar. After carefully removing the landing door from its hinges, he deftly pried away the doorframe. In no time the pram was soon on its way to freedom, repairable scrapes and all. While I forget how the pram eventually got to the cottage, suffice to say that it got there tethered to some part of the family car. While the pram was built to be a rowboat, one day Dad brought home a tiny 1.7 horsepower outboard motor. To make things interesting, dad decided to give the motor a test run in the garage. Tethered to a wooden horse with the prop submerged in a bucket of water, Dad gave a tug on the rip cord – whoosh! Everyone including our nosy dog got very wet.

The end of June signaled the end of our school year and the annual trek to the cottage for the summer. For the most part, Dad would commute to work 4 days a week. On his return, if time and conditions permitted, he'd grab a sandwich and try his luck at fishing. Early one evening when conditions were extremely calm, Dad and I took the pram and headed toward nearby Morgan's Point. With a shallow, rocky bottom, the point offered great opportunities for bass. Because there had been little wind for the last few days and the lake surface was like glass, baitfish moved close to the shore. Also, the clarity of the water allowed us to see clearly to the bottom allowing us to actually see a few fish passing below us.

We were only a hundred feet from shore when Dad hooked his first smallmouth. By using his favorite red and white flatfish, he quickly reeled in a two-pounder. While he struggled to take out the lure, I got a hit with the same result. Dad cast again and bang - another one. This cycle continued again and again. We were catching bass at such a rate that there was no time to put the fish through a stringer and throw it over the side of the boat. Preoccupied with our repeated strikes, our boat drifted onto a shallow sand bar. While he was still playing with a fish on his line, he got out of the boat and pushed us into a little deeper water. It was the most amazing hour we had ever spent together. It soon reached a point where all we could do was laugh uncontrollably at our stroke of luck.

After Mom died many years later in 1981, Greg and I were in roughly the same area where Dad and I had hit the bass bonanza. While we didn't catch nearly as many fish as dad and I had years earlier, spending the July 4th afternoon together was priceless. We were kids again worming our hooks, telling short and tall tales, and wishing this day would never end. Some time later I recaptured this scene in a painting from a photo I took. With the cottage in the background, I had particular pleasure trying to recapture that lovely day. Ironically, this occasion would prove to be my last venture out into the lake as growing disability was taking its toll preventing me from getting in and out of a beached boat.

Wind conditions dictated whether you could launch a boat from shore. Facing the southwest, the cottage bore the brunt of the prevailing winds. Seeking a solution, Dad decided to moor our boat within the sheltered harbor of Port Colborne. If conditions were unsatisfactory at the cottage, we could drive the four miles and fish within the protection of the Port Colborne breakwater. However, Greg and I discovered the true value of the boat livery. Called Scholfield's, the livery was the homeport for our succession of boats. Thanks to Dad's inability to say no to the sales people on Niagara Street, our boats grew longer and more powerful with each passing year. Connected to the livery, fronting the harbor, was a small backwater creek which snaked its way under a road and into an adjacent field. It was here that Greg and I really learned and appreciated the fine art of light tackle fishing.

For Greg and me, just the name 'Scholfield's' conjures up distant memories of growing up, or better still, the sheer joy of childhood wonder. While Dad commuted to work in Buffalo, Greg and I asked Mom to drive us to Scholfield's to fish from the docks. Dropped off in the morning with a pocketful of change, we would head out to one of the empty docks and begin rigging up our poles. Using a red and white bobber, we'd construct a lead with a very small hook and dangling worm. Tossing out our rig, we waited for the fun to begin, which usually didn't take too long. Soon the nibbling would begin with the telltale bobber movements on the water surface. Oh the fun when the bobber dove beneath the water and we could feel the wiggling from the taut line! Most times we were hauling in small sunfish, bluegill, and crappie, and sometimes the odd bass.

Initially, we had gear more accommodating toward catching much larger fish. We had large lures, hooks, and a line strong enough to moor one of the passing lakers entering the Welland Canal. We soon learned to scale down our hook sizes and worm chunks suitable for hooking very small fish. In addition, our repertoire was to keep our thumbnail unclipped so we could pinch a bit of the worm as we needed it. While I usually worked in one spot, Greg would be busy working every conceivable spot in the tributary. He'd go dock to dock, bank to bank, go bobber fishing then to casting and then back again. He reminded me of a springer spaniel racing through an open field in search of elusive quarry. By mid-afternoon it would be time to head back to the cottage – hot, dusty, and reeking of fish and bait odors. Returning to the cottage, Greg and I pestered Mom when we might be able to return again.

When Dad returned from work, we brothers sounded a lot like author Robert Smith's kids when asked what they had done that day. In *Where did you go? Out. What did you do? Nothing*, Smith recounts coming home from work only to be met by his youngsters who shared with him basically nothing from their day. This recurring pattern got Smith to thinking of his own childhood. His youth was filled with wonder and awe, lessons learned for a lifetime – experiences not to be shared because he perceived them insignificant. Like boy-child Smith, and his kids after him, Greg and I admitted nothing to Dad – just that we had spent the day fishing. On the other hand, we could have shared some of our lessons of the day. Depending on the season, these may have included witnessing the healing power of spit on a dirty cut, or learning not to pick a fight with someone bigger than yourself. Little Greg frequently forgot the latter and often went headlong into combat with folks his senior. One time the 'big kids' in the neighborhood came to our Saturday morning pickup baseball game and wrestled our Mickey Mantle *Louisville Slugger* away from Greg. Like a terrier with a bone, Greg chased the guys down until, in utter futility, they tossed the bat into deep brush rather than mess with a half-crazed kid. They got the hell out of harm's way. How do you share such experiences with parents who want you to be safe, and to learn things which are constructive. We didn't think sharing our daily yarns would do much for our standing at home with our parents (and we didn't).


One summer Dad relented and took the family to a fishing camp he and his Canadian kin frequented. We drove to Pigeon Lake not far from Peterborough, Ontario. Nestled within pine trees was a cabin complex called Thurston's Fishing Camp. After we were settled in, Greg and I were ready to catch one of the whoppers we had seen countless times in Dad's photos and movies. Assigned to our own boat, Greg and I motored out into the lake among its many inlets bordered by bulrushes and surface weeds. At first, we tried to troll the channels using sizable lures we had used in Lake Erie. However, after getting our lines tangled with weeds every few minutes, we quit trolling and threw an anchor overboard. Changing tackle, we fished with big juicy worms among the weeds. The nibbles began immediately. Repeatedly, we'd bring a fish to the surface only to see it scamper away. At the height of our frustration a light bulb went on in both our brains – "Schofield Rules!" In no time, we scurried through our tackle boxes for the much smaller hooks we normally used back at Scholfield's. Carefully slicing and dicing our worms, we re-baited our gear and over the side it went. Bang! "I got one!" Then another and another. We were in paradise.

Every couple of minutes we'd pull in a panfish, a perch, or one of the many kinds of bass. The fish weren't big but frequent.

Later in the day, we got back to the dock and compared stories with the other campers. It was all great fun. In particular at the family-style dinner table, there were three fellows from Ohio who made everyone laugh with their humorous stories. The best tale involved two of the guys convincing the third to toss overboard his 6-pound bass, because: "Oh gee, that's a pity, because it's not a musky." Unfortunately, the poor fellow missed out on a good size pool for the biggest fish of the week. The day before we left camp, Greg added a little drama to our stay by hooking himself in the leg while casting from the dock after supper; however, all was made right when Dad in the dim of the evening was able to find the Peterborough Hospital. A year later Greg repeated this feat by snaring himself while casting into the wind from shore at the cottage; however, in this scenario it was Mom who valiantly intervened. At first, she prevented serious damage to Greg's thigh by a local physician who wanted to dislodge the treble hook by simply tugging on it. Secondly, Mom got Greg into the car and drove him to the Emergency Room at Port Colborne's General Hospital. Ironically, the hospital was located within spitting distance of our favorite haunt – Scholfield's. Mom shared most of our angling triumphs as well as the pain. Her good-nature was manifested in many ways, including allowing us to preserve our live bait in her fridge; however, we may have stretched things a bit when we heard a loud screech one day after our worms got loose and intermingled with some spaghetti leftovers.

Transfixed with the fishing bug, Greg and me owe a lot to Dad who initially planted the seed. Whether it was bobbing for carp on a Sunday afternoon in Ohmsted's Delaware Park Lake, or casting from a breakwater in Canada to celebrate a First Communion or graduation, we brothers shared something special in our early lives. As we would discover later on, our passion for fishing will reverberate with many of our contemporaries, as well as with a younger generation under our care and tutelage.

# Chapter 5

# Another Hill to Climb
# – College Snapshots

I genuinely thought of quitting. For each twist in the road of the Niagara University campus, another soon appeared, then another. Rather than a school housed in a single structure, everything was spread out with the dorm in one direction, meals in another, and up two flights of stairs for chapel, Chemistry lectures were on the third floor of a huge antiquated building, and to boot, the accompanying labs were held in a dingy basement of an adjacent building. How the hell was I going to get around and get to classes on time? Then there were the courses themselves. I cried myself to sleep the first week when I picked up my Analytical Geometry & Calculus text. I wondered what had I gotten myself into?

I knew very few people on campus. There was my roommate, Tom Meyers, whom I knew from high school. We couldn't have been more different; we could pass as a version of the odd couple; however, in some crazy way Tom had a comforting influence on me. While disquieting, his John Belushi-like antics were maybe the daily distraction I needed at the time. While I knew a few of the priests, there was one in particular who most probably saved my academic career – Father Robert Rivard. As he was the university registrar, Father Rivard had the power to oversee class scheduling. When I first came to the registration table to work out my classes, I was nearly in tears. I was carrying sixteen hours and I had classes all over the campus. I had religion in one building at 8 AM, followed by chemistry three floors up in an adjacent building. My math class was scheduled in another building across campus. If I wanted lunch, it had to be back across campus, but at least if I did make lunch, my English class was in the same building (three floors up). Chemistry lab thankfully was held only twice per week, so I could somehow muddle around it, as well as my French lectures which were held in another building three times a week. At first blush my schedule was impossible. With my pulse racing, I figured I'd give it a week or two and then bow out of Niagara as gracefully as I could, allowing me to say later: "Yeh, I'd been to college".

Then, along came a short little man with a glowing red face with a wit to match – Father Rivard, who said "Hi Mike, let me see your schedule." Just as I was about to reveal my get-away plan, he quickly concluded that my schedule would not work for me. Taking out a little red pencil, he took my schedule card and added notes here and there, along with a series of arrows going this way and that. I wondered what the hell was he doing? As if he had all the power in the world, he rescheduled *previously* scheduled classes and moved classes from one building to another. In some instances he changed class times. Wow! As a result, 'Rivard the Wonderful' adapted my schedule to my physical ability to navigate the campus. There were no back to back classes, and when possible, most classes were to be held in the same building. I couldn't believe my eyes, in ten minutes he had rescued my college career, and in the process likely pissed off hundreds of professors and students, who by then had had their schedules written in stone.

With Father Rivard's green light, I embarked upon my college career. It was an experience of a lifetime. I got to know classmates who turned out to be friends for life, I learned the value of coping and patience as never before, and I quickly learned that being a big fish in a small pond was for high school, not college. The principles and conclusions I had previously treasured were now fair game for attack. I was soon gathering the mental equipment I'd need later in life – things that I would employ as a graduate student, researcher, teacher, administrator, friend, spouse, citizen, and, importantly, as someone who professed to be a Christian.

When the time came to choose a college, I elected to go to Niagara University. In retrospect it was an easy decision to make.

Niagara was my dad's alma mater, and because of his close association with the school and its care-takers, the Vincentian Fathers, it was relatively familiar to me. In high school I had toyed with the idea of pursuing architecture. Frank Lloyd Wright's work had intrigued me greatly, and I had a natural inclination toward my geometry courses; in fact, at the suggestion of my high school teachers, I obtained an application from Manhattan College which was also run by the Christian Brothers. While Manhattan's architecture program seemed right up my alley, in the end I went for the safe route and threw my fate into the hands of Niagara and its premed program. The medical arena was familiar ground to me due to my dad's MD buddies, as well as my Uncle Stan who was an orthopedic surgeon, and my godfather to whom I felt quite close.

It was through Niagara's athletic teams where I first developed a comfort zone on campus. With my high school experience with athletics under my hat, along with my dad's close interest in Niagara basketball over the years, it was natural for me to get to know several coaches (including the legendary Taps Gallagher) and players prowling the campus. I came to Niagara with well-experienced cheerleading skills from my grade and high school days, and it was time to put them to the test. Initially, I spent time watching the basketball teams practice, including the freshman team coached by the affable Chet Pryzlucki. After I got to know Chet fairly well during the basketball season, he approached me one day – "Hi Mike, do you think you might be interested in giving me a hand with my baseball team?" And as the saying goes the rest is history. For four years, I was the official scorekeeper of the varsity baseball team. I kept the statistics, and afterwards dutifully phoned in the results to the *Niagara Falls Gazette*. The experience was fun, as I got a first-hand appreciation of NU at the intercollegiate level, as well as a wealth of banter and camaraderie with classmates to last a lifetime.

While Niagara was mediocre at best, we seemed to enjoy our usual role of underdog. One particular road-trip highlighted our entire season. We traveled to the University of Rochester for a double-header. Rochester's field was manicured like nothing we had ever seen, and if that weren't intimidating enough, their pressed uniforms looked as though they had just come back from the dry cleaners. Moreover, our Rochester opponent was composed of several blue chip athletes on scholarship. For our part, we were a ragamuffin band of non-scholarship walk-ons content to have the opportunity to just compete. Regardless of whom or where we played we were ecstatic to get $6.75 after each game for meal money. Most of the time we headed to a dive called the Meeting House in the Italian section of Niagara Falls where large steak dinners were less than four bucks.

In the first game, we were treated to a predictable show of talent and lost 10-0. In the second game, things were a little different as we tightened up our defense and held on to 0-0 tie going into the last inning. The lithe Artie Coleman (a starter on the varsity basketball team) got us going by cracking a single. Subsequently, Artie got to second on a fielder's choice and later to third on a sacrifice fly. Now it was two outs and Artie alone at third. At this dramatic moment, Chet signaled to Artie to *steal* home, yes steal home! You see, Artie was as quick as the wind. If Artie could time it right and take advantage of the Rochester pitcher's long and lanky windup, he would be home free, and that is exactly what happened. Artie stole home before the pitch even hit the catcher's glove. With the score 1-0 NU, Rochester kept the suspense going with their batters swinging for the fences, only to fall short each time with long fly outs. Afterwards you would have thought we had won the World Series. Off to the Meeting House for grub and a celebration!

There were other games which were notable, but for differing reasons. For one, there was a double-header in May played at St. Bonaventure in Olean. It snowed all afternoon long, and only with difficulty was I able to keep the scorebook dry under my coat. Then there as a double-header with Canisius College played near my old grammar school haunt – Delaware Park in Buffalo. While I don't recall how we did against Canisius, I do remember sitting on the same bench that I used to sit at when I cheered my Mount Saint Joseph's team when we played other parochial schools. A few other road trips stick in my mind, including visits to Brockport State and the University at

Buffalo, where we hormonally-maladjusted males rubber-necked at the coeds every chance we could. Even our coach couldn't conceal his enjoyment of this perk of road travel.

During my junior year I turned twenty. At the time I thought it would be interesting to record what my last day as a teenager was like. Tucked into my lower bunk around lights out time, I reflected on the day's events. I picked up my biology notebook, which I had just put down, and located a few vacant pages to write a short journal. What follows in **bold italics** are notes made the night of November 6, 1963. I have inserted explanatory notes within parentheses.

***Well, here it was Wednesday, November 6, 1963, and it was Mass Day at O'D.*** (Niagara's O'Donohue Hall was a sophomore dorm and because O'D was closer to the academic core, I stayed behind rather than dorm at distant Timon Hall along with my junior class.) ***I knew the night before I needed to set the alarm at 6 even though I gave 6 haircuts the night before and I was dead.*** (Throughout my NU years, I gave haircuts and trims using pet clippers from home.) ***I never heard my alarm but I did pick up Eddie's at quarter to 7*** (Eddie Yamashiro was an older foreign student from Guam and my roommate.) ***He woke me up but I know I couldn't get ready in 15 minutes, so I stayed in bed half asleep until Eddie came back around 8:05. I asked him to turn the radio on, he did and I listened until about 9:20. I got up, Eddie went to class. I was still tired, flipped onto the chair, regained myself and slowly got my socks, sneakers, pants on. Put my keys, rosary, and wallet in my pocket, gathered my soap, washcloth and towel and headed for the john. Things were quiet there. I washed up. Gathered things up and back to the room.*** (I got out of bed by transferring from bed to chair, and used the nearby desk to get to my feet.)

***I felt a little better, used Trig and turned on WEBR for music. Got my shaver and shaved off my 2 day shadow. Took out some English Leather after some mental debate, but what the hell, my last day as a teenager. Put a lot on and it felt and smelled great. Put on my blue tab collar shirt and good-looking blue tie; put on brown tweed sport coat***

*and looked in the mirror, and boy, I looked real good. Saw it was 9:47 and I'd better hustle. Grabbed glasses, dull pencil, pen, notebook, text, and assignment book – all set now. Made Sign of the Cross and talked to Our Lord, and offered myself for His honor and glory. Shut radio, light and locked door.*

*Commotion out in hall, said good morning to Art, the janitor, and went outside O'D and walked slowly along sidewalk – the air was cool and clean and it felt good to be alive, from there I knew this day would be special (it was). Passed a freshman, he paid attention to my right foot (tightened heel cord), it didn't bother me, I turned the corner into the cool refreshing breeze and down the sidewalk. I stopped at the end, rested, and gained energy. 3 sophs passed as I started across towards DePaul Hall.* (DePaul was the new science building 100 yards from O'D, and was connected by a walkway going through two roadways and a seldomly used set of railroad tracks). *Walked across first roadway to the tree, around the bush to the walk, on to the railroad tracks where I rested for a second. I knew I was being followed – it was a soph and he offered me his hand which I took and off we went. We talked about the weather, classes, and general bull. We reached the sidewalk and I said "thank you very much." He asked if I was going to DePaul and I said yes and he gladly took me there.* (Most times I needed assistance in stepping up curbs, walking long distances, getting up and down stairs, as well as assistance in getting up from my classroom seat.) *On way we passed Father Rivard. He was busy talking. I wanted to talk to him about his bet with Greg, but I figured I'd see him later.* (My brother Greg was a first year pre-dent student and a starter on the freshman basketball team on an athletic scholarship.)

*We got to the door of DePaul where Miss Kimmel held it for us.* (Betty Kimmel was a Math professor with a quick smile which masked the fact she had an often-concealed withered arm). *Got down the stairs and waited til class of Father Sullivan's was through. After general bull from Bob Winzinger and Charlie* (Charlie Janiewski was a classmate from Connecticut who was my Physics lab partner year earlier, and whose wedding I later attended with another classmate, Ed Kampf. He was the catcher on our baseball team, and subsequently, attended

Tufts Dental School) *Word was out that Father McGlynn might not make the scene – he did and class got started.* (McGlynn taught English Literature and for his amusement I think, often called upon me to read passages in class). *Father borrowed my dull pencil, he gave us a little quiz, 10 things from what we read. Afterwards he spent the whole period on history and background of the 16th century – it was boring.*

*After class got helped up by Turgot (good man).* (I was indebted to a large number of classmates who assisted me throughout my college days –some names I can still recall, but most not.) *I got my dull pencil back from Father and went out into the hall. Waited for Frank, he helped me up the stairs against traffic, we reached outside and he nicely took me to the sidewalk of O'D. Saw Rick, he was busy, no lift, so around to the front door I went. The door was ajar, great!* (The back door to O'D had a very big step, while the front entrance had only a small step; however, this door was very heavy and difficult to open if not ajar.) *Forgot, Mohney passed me at tracks and gave me 9 letters, I was thrilled.* (John Mohney was a classmate and a very good friend who played shortstop for our ball team; during my senior year we roomed together along Del Presowitz in the seniors-only Varsity Village) *Got through door and to room, Eddie was in john, I grabbed a knife and spent 15 minutes reading the cards and letters. It was great.*

*Left the room for lunch, met Steve in hall, Biology test talk, went to cafeteria with him, got there and found we were going to have steak, wow, what a day. Met my good lady friends there, treated me real good. Sat at table with Phil, Rabbit, and Phil Penny – they were busy mocking everybody out, I just laughed. The meat was tender and delicious, salad with lots of oil and vinegar. The lunch was superb and I felt great. I got up and said so long to Phil and proceeded down the hall* (For 4 years the ladies in the cafeteria food line made me a tray and took it to my table; they treated me and most of the others as their own sons.)

*Felt tired in the legs, got to the outer hall and rested awhile. Started out the door to see Colaprite in an old MG surrounded with 3 guys saying what a great car it was.* (Classmate John Colaprite was now rooming with Tom Meyers; their room was known around campus as the "Animal House;' before we could have TV in our rooms, Tom provided all the entertainment one could ask – from lighting farts after a night on the town, to his uncanny ability at a drop of a hat to trash a room; Tom later joined the SeeBees in Vietnam, and after the conflict bought a yacht with some friends and wandered the Pacific. He eventually married and settled down in the mining business in Australia.) *I felt good and walked pretty quickly, reached the drain pipe in 60 seconds. Good time. Rested at the laundry, started again, said hello to a passing freshman, reached the street, crossed it, and walked along St. Vinnies* (St. Vincent's Hall was one of the original buildings on campus; top floor dormed by dad in early 40's. Because I had my freshman chemistry class on the third floor, I got to know many physically strong students sufficient to get me up the two extensive flights of stairs.) *Rested, then got going again, and reached the room tired. Got inside and took off my good clothes and put on my HIS pants and shirt, good sneakers. Al came in room, borrowed banjo, got my stuff together for Chem and off I went at 12:10.* (Organic chemistry was taught by Joe Forrester who two weeks later would tearfully announce in class the assassination of President John F. Kennedy.)

*Got outside of room, told Al to take care of the banjo* (While I couldn't play a lick, I enjoyed picking at the inexpensive instrument, at the time, folk singing was all the rage on campus*) Got outside the building and some soph took me all the way to DePaul, for which I was very grateful (said Hail Mary going up the steps). Fixed my shirt, gathered strength, off I went down the hall to call Dad.* (My favorite places to make phone calls from campus were from booths located in O'D and DePaul.) *Met Sharon Fucella and exchanged a few works. Got to booth, and got Dad on the phone and talked about the Bills, letters, and that I'd see him Friday. He told me that Mom was at a Holy Angels luncheon.* (My sister Karen attended Holy Angels High School back in Buffalo.)

*After the call I gathered by books and things, hoped to say hello to Sharon again but she was down the hall studying while I studied her derriere. Placed key in elevator, we were in business, up to the second floor.* (DePaul was the newest building on campus and was equipped with an elevator which I was allowed to use.) *First person I met was the older lady who was the lab technician under doc Hubbard* (Hubbard was Chemistry professor who was fond of saying that 'if it doesn't work get a bigger hammer!') *She asked me about my leg. I told her that it wasn't just my leg affected but all of me – it is called muscular dystrophy, and I wanted research on the disease. She wished me well, and I felt good inside. I whistled my way into the john. Got out and proceeded to the empty Freshman Chemistry Lab to study 'Aldehydes and Ketones.' Looked things over quickly and was satisfied. Walked over to the window and watched the digging for the new library building with Mr. Napoleon* (My freshman Chemistry professor, who like the other chemistry teachers had previously worked in industry in Niagara Falls*). He was in a comical mood – good man. It takes 3 scoops to fill a truck! I was joined by Ed and Larry* (Ed Kampf previously mentioned, and Larry Downs from Philadelphia who sported a repaired cleft palate and who was a very good basketball player*). We talked about the gash on Ed's forehead and had a couple of laughs. It was 1:07 and we took off for class.*

*Got to class, missed Terry.* (Classmate Terry Francowiak from Niagara Falls frequently gave me assistance, Terry unable to get into med school settled for a teaching career.) *I was relieved when Mr. Forrester covered the chapter in the book he had gone over previously. After reviewing the difficult chapter, I asked Forrester after class a quick question. Got answer and proceeded toward Organic Chemistry Lab. Met Jack Heywood for couple of laughs together. Took off jacket and into the lab for 3 hours. I didn't do much except spill my cyclohexene all over my bench, books, and everywhere except into the beaker. Forrester checked results, 'bromine water' and gave my poor 7% yield effort a suitable grade. He and I both laughed. My lab neighbor Tony blew up his equipment for Exercise 22. I felt good.* (Classmate Tony was a chemistry major from Philadelphia and always had 2 or 3 experiments going on simultaneously; he and the other chem majors usually made us pre-med types look like simpletons.) *After much time, I finally set up my apparatus for exercise 22; it was ridiculous. Forrester announced that there was a 4:30 deadline for yearbook pictures. I got a little panicky as I wanted mine taken. I cruised around the lab a little after I got my equipment put away. After a bit I saw Tim at the balance.* (Classmate Tim Siepel later because a physician graduating from the University at Buffalo; he later encouraged me to apply to Med school after my Master's degree from NU in 1967. During the Vietnam War era Tim deferred to the US Public Health System in lieu of active military service, and provided medical care to Native Americans in South Dakota. Ed Kampf enrolled in the same deferral program by providing dental care to the Appalachian region.)

*Tim was great as he said he'd take me over. I went out in the hall to wait for him, saw and talked to Forrester and shared a couple of laughs. Sprague gave me a hand down the steps to the outside of the building. He had a football game and it was getting late for him as well.* (Classmate Dick Sprague from Rochester played third base for our baseball team, and later obtained a dental degree from Georgetown, as did fellow classmates Paul Capacci and Les Abamonte; another friend and classmate, Dick Gangemi, entered Georgetown Medical School.) *Meanwhile I was getting worried about time myself. Just then Tim blew out the door and we were off. We made good time by piggy-back and we finally made it to House 4.* (Seniors had the option of dorming in Varsity Village composed of six two-story houses.) *When we arrived for the photos our classmates were all dressed up except for Tim and me. Somewhere in House 3 Tim found ties and sport coats for us and we had our pictures taken along with the others. Afterwards with coolness setting in we went back to House 3 to collect my jacket. Tim was going to take me back, but in meantime saw Ed Haley who offered to take me to the refectory.* (Classmate Ed Haley was a rotund, happy-go-lucky Chemistry major who had fun concocting and testing recipes for explosives in the lab.) *Met Ed at the road. Tim left and I was grateful to him. Ed asked for 10 cents and gladly gave it to him.*

*At the refectory, went to the john, then to the senior-junior cafeteria. Met my lady friends. We talked about the future, weather, my career, the band in the hallway, and Mr. Clarkson* (Clarkson Food Service ran campus food catering, "mystery meat" was the favorite response to the campus-wide question of the day – 'What's for dinner?'). *I got the newspaper boy to bring me the daily paper. I read it til 5:30 along with a Biology lab exercise on pigeon dissection. I had a veal cutlet and ice cream, etc. for dinner. Was real good. Joe and friends sat at the table with me, to be later joined by Ned Stanton and Steve. We had good laughs about Ned's 66-0 loss in football. Later Ned was kind enough to take me clear back to O'D. What a great guy. I gave him my College Zoology textbook til 9:00. He left and I read the newspaper. Afterwards I played hockey with Al til 6:50.* (Al and I would sit in chairs in front of our respective doorways and act as both goalies and wingers; the previous year my favorite after dinner activity was gin rummy with Bob Scheilein and Jim Hay. Bob from Albany later graduated with a PhD in Physics, and Jim from Brooklyn married an NU coed before going overseas to Vietnam. Sadly, Jim along with another classmate John Bobo died in combat in the Vietnam War – I twice visited them at Washington's Vietnam Memorial Wall, and each time my eyes flooded over with tears as I penciled etchings of their names from the Wall.)

*Read biology text and took notes during study time till 9:00. Ned and Bob came over to eat my chocolates. Together they spanked me 20 times, and my cloaca hurt. They left and Al and I played hockey til 9:30. I made coffee, read a little Bio, at 10:30 played hockey with Al. Lost. Played Hectus and lost. Played Al again and lost. Bell rang at 11:00 and that was end of hockey. Gathered book, new tube of Crest, toothbrush, soap, washcloth, and towel. Eddie? 15 minutes? He agreed. Off I went to the john. Studied Bio a little while on the throne, Eddie came later* (Throughout college I needed someone to assist me from the toilet.) *Washed and brushed teeth. Gathered stuff up. got into bed. My toe hurt. Set alarm for 7:50 and studied Bio and the pigeon exercise.*

*I began to think about November 6, 1963, the last day of my days as a teenager. Those years were a ball, felt good thinking about those years. Before hitting the pillow, I wrote this passage of the day's events. Good Nite, Mike.*

Reflecting upon my 'last day' after several years, I was amazed at the writing – sophomoric and naïve at best; however, reading the passage reminded me of my unvarnished self and in a bigger scheme, what lessons took root during college. For one, I learned that our primary goal in college is to learn about ourselves – who we are, our strengths as well as short-comings. As I used to tell my students at UB, the most important course you'll take here is YOU 101. Whether you are a science major or any of the countless disciplines, the process of your growth and development is on view for all to see and appreciate. At Niagara, YOU 101 was of immense value to me. Ironically, if it weren't for the intercession of Father Rivard, I wouldn't have enrolled in YOU 101 in the first place. Once on board, however, my learning of self began in earnest.

In retrospect, there are some lessons which I exported from NU to the next levels of my life. For example, I seemed to have had a talent for dissection and drawing in biology lab; in fact, I shortly became the 'go to' person in many exercises where preserved specimens are ripped apart and subsequently drawn and labeled. These early lessons proved invaluable in my later research studies, where I commonly used live animal models for my PhD thesis, as well as my muscular dystrophy studies (and I may add my lifelong passion of oil painting).

There were genuinely kind and caring people to go along with the 24 carat 'shits' that I came across on campus. One such shit threatened to toss me down the stairs from the Chapel entrance because he wanted to cut Chapel and I was in his way. However, since I depended on all types to cope with the physical barriers of the NU campus, I needed to develop a knack for getting along with everyone. Drowning was not an option if someone, anyone, was there to assist me. Hence, I developed a fathomless ability for small talk. Dwelling on trivia helped greatly when traversing the ups and downs of graduate school where I needed to 'reinvent the wheel' again and seek out those who could help me navigate another tier of scholastic life. My cadre of helpful buddies continued to include fellow students (mostly unknown), delivery people, and janitors – you name it, I needed them all. Much later when I served as Executive Officer of biology at UB, my 'bullshit' was honed to the point where I could always be counted on "to put lipstick on a pig" when the situation needed it.

At NU I was exposed to a range of teaching prowess – while many professors were not very good at holding a class's attention, there were a few who were gifted and able to transform a class into deeply learning moments. A prime example was Professor Daniel McGuire, who taught American History, a required course we science majors needed to graduate. Three days per week he would enter the classroom with little scraps of paper – in essence these were the notes for the day's class. Rather than give stand-up lectures, Professor McGuire would quickly get into a Q and A session with the class, soliciting our opinions on a variety of issues at hand. For example, one day he had us "role play" as farmers to discuss what was at stake before the Civil War, such as: What were the differences if you were a farmer from Ohio rather than a farmer from Dixie? In this manner, we as a class dissected out the salient events and causative issues of the Civil War. His teaching approach was not unlike what today is commonly called Case Studies. For several years in my own classrooms at UB, I would frequently use Case Studies as a learning tool – a tool I witnessed early on from Professor McGuire at NU.

Another professor of note was Wayne Gallagher who taught a newly established Biochemistry course. Professor Gallagher's interest and enthusiasm for the material was infectious. As he knew that most of us in his class were health-related majors, he drummed into us the many applications of what we were learning to our future careers. Whether it was metabolic pathways or the DNA structure, his common refrain was: "Isn't this stuff neat!" Of course, he was dead on. Nearly every breakthrough in biomedical research over the past 40 years has been dependent on our understanding of how molecules work within living tissues. Because of the subject matter and his unvarnished enthusiasm, Professor Gallagher provided us with the foundation we needed to proceed with our budding biomedical careers.

While not quite up to the level of Professors McGuire and Gallagher, I also recall several NU teachers who in one way or the other made a lasting impression on me. There was Father Gagne who taught me French III. Rather than repeat what my previous French teachers had done, Gagne from day one got us to actually speak French in class. His common refrain was, "If you speak in class, you get a grade. If not, no grade." I immediately took him seriously and hacked my way through the semester with a B grade. Many of my fellow students (most were brighter than I) barely passed the course because they simply decided that they wouldn't play Gagne's little game and not speak up in class.

Thomas Morton was the distinquished Chair of the Biology Department. With his angular physique and white hair, he looked as if he could have stepped out of a Norman Rockwell painting.

He taught us Introductory Biology, and, later, Histology, Embryology, and Biological Photography. His quiet unassuming manner, coupled with the dignity he bestowed upon the material he was teaching, made him a favorite of mine as well as my classmates. As the years progressed at NU, we became very good friends up to and through graduation, as well as later when I became a graduate teaching assistant within the Department. Because his daughter was handicapped, we developed a special bond. My other biology professors included: Larry Kiely, Jack Reedy, Ed McKeegan, and later Bryan Britten. Each of them was enthusiastic about the courses he taught, and we students who were under their care. With a keen wit Professor Kiely shared with us the mysteries of human anatomy and physiology. Always confrontational, Jack Reedy challenged us with the minutiae of comparative anatomy, and, later, the relatively new area of radiation biology. The soft-spoken and modest McKeegan introduced us to bacteria making up the microbiological world, and, lastly, Bryan Britten who was fresh from his own PhD studies at the University of Wyoming, opened up the rest of biology to us. Through Britten and his unbridled enthusiasm for field studies, we learned statistics, taxonomy, ecology, as well as an immense appreciation for why we chose a life sciences career. Through these men, we neophytes began to think as biologists - if not as real scientists. We began to think on our feet. It was an exhilarating experience for all of us – whether one went on to medical or dental school or, in my case, to graduate school. The men of NU Biology

Department succeeded in equipping our quiver with arrows meant to last a lifetime.

Lastly, rereading "last day" reminded me of the value of my faith in carrying me through NU. Early on at NU, I recognized the steep hill I needed to climb; it was a hill I could not do by myself. Each day became a challenge as I navigated my academic pursuit through an uncompromising campus. Travel to and from classes and meals (over curbs, up and down stairs, in any kind of weather) – what was I to do? I needed help, a shoulder here, a lift there, even a sprinkling of piggy back rides thrown in. Who would provide these to me? As I noted earlier, fellow students came to my rescue, as did Father Rivard who made it a 'fair' fight from the beginning. In the grand scheme, however, it was God Almighty who I had relied upon and who delivered. Whether it was someone to catch a door for me or assistance from the toilet, it was Our Lord's assistance I had solicited. For four years, my morning prayers were critical for me; my intimate conversation with Our Lord as I gathered myself for the day's classes allowed me to form a mind-set that all would be possible. Without missing a beat, God provided me with help every step of my day.

# Chapter 6

# With Peter and Bob –
# So This Is Graduate School?

As my months at Niagara University were winding down, it became clear I was developing an irreversible case of cold feet about applying to med school. During the spring of 1965, while most of my classmates were busy with interviews, I sat on the sidelines. While I thought I had an academic record to be competitive (if not very competitive), in the end I was listening more and more to the nuances of my body, and whether or not I could handle the physical rigors of running around a hospital, much less the med school corridors.

One day in May I had a chance to talk with Professor Tom Morton about my immediate future or lack of it. As Chair of Biology, Morton had a particular closeness to each of his graduating seniors. In most cases his recommendation letters would make or break one's application to med or dent school. Over the past four years we had developed a rather close relationship, and he was all ears as I spun my tale about the uncertainties I had about my future. Having digested the gravity of my dilemma, Dr. Morton suggested another avenue. "Mike, what do you think of entering our Masters program and be one of our graduate teaching assistants?" The rest as they say is history. I acquired an application, took the GREs, and just before graduation, was informed that I was now a full-fledged graduate student at NU, and to boot would receive a yearly stipend of $4500! With a spring in my step knowing where I'd be in the fall, I was ready to face the summer.

As my classmates (and now me) were eager to jump into our respective post-graduate challenges, I myself was quite content to enjoy the last of my undergraduate days – senior dinner dance, chilly weekends at my parents' cottage, concerts featuring The Kingston Trio, The Brothers Four, and The Limelighters, and last but least, our remaining baseball games.

Before one of our last baseball games played at nearby Hyde Park, I sat on the bench and opened mail I brought from campus. One piece of mail was a large envelope containing dozens of letters from students taught by my cousin Judy in a poor section of Hamilton, Ontario. Unknown to me, Judy had talked up the idea in her class that I was a budding scientist who some day would find a cure for muscular dystrophy. I was so overwhelmed by the letters, I distributed them to my teammates who got a big kick reading the simple but sincerely written notes. I was flattered by the kids' kudos, but I knew I was a long way from making any mark in science, much less in the dystrophy field. With medicine excluded from my immediate plans, the hopes and dreams of Judy's kids would likely come to naught.

While I enjoyed watching Dr. Kildare and Ben Casey on TV, a medical career path seemed far away now. In addition, I had very little understanding of what it might take to research a disease like dystrophy. How would you research a cure? I hadn't a clue. I did however, have some insight from Uncle Stan as well as a fourth year med student from UB. One day Uncle Stan gave me a large volume on muscle disease authored by a leading expert in the field, Professor Denny-Brown. Paging through the book, I quickly found out I was ill-equipped to understand its contents, much less the section describing my own Limb-Girdle dystrophy. Moreover in 1961, I ran into a UB med student while I got out of my car en route to our high school track meet held on the UB campus. Politely he asked me if he could ask me some questions, including: whether I had muscular dystrophy, when did it started, and so on. After he was satisfied, I reversed gears and quizzed him about what was he learning about the disease. He replied: "Not much, what was known about muscle disease only took a fraction of a single lecture."

While many would think my parents would have been a fount of knowledge on the disease, they weren't, only happy that I was still breathing and kicking. As it were, Judy's students would have to fend for themselves and learn about the disease themselves later in life. I was no hope.

My graduation gift from my parents was a significant contribution for the purchase of a new Buick Skylark. Without much ado, I soon put the new wheels to use: chauffeuring my younger sisters to school, attending classmate weddings throughout New York and Connecticut, and regular commutes to our summer cottage as well as to Hamilton to visit my Uncle Stan and his brood. In addition, accompanied by my sister Karen, I attended the Canadian Open Golf Championship played outside Toronto. Here I was able to enjoy seeing my golfing heroes in the flesh – Arnold Palmer, Jack Nicklaus, Tony Lema, and Gary Player. Pretty heady stuff for a duffer like me.

Summer wound down, and equipped with a well-earned summer tan, I was ready to make my inaugural twenty mile trip to the NU campus to register for my grad classes, I also needed to check in with the Biology Department to receive my teaching assistantship assignments. I parked my car on the road adjacent to DePaul (a road I had traversed countless times on foot over the last four years), and I started my approach to the building. Hailing a passing student for assistance, I got to the building and up the short flight of stairs to the main floor. All of this was familiar ground, or was it? What was in store for me as I hobbled down the corridor to the Biology wing of the building? When I reached Dr. Morton's office, I heard familiar and not so familiar voices. After brief introductions, I found the alien voices belonged to the other two in-coming graduate assistants – Peter Gunther from the north shore of Long Island and Bob Sheehan from Springfield, Massachusetts. After eyeing each other for a few minutes, the three of us broke for lunch intending to get to know each other better. Little did I know at the time, that the three of us would grow to become as close as any three fellows in 1965 America could possibly become.

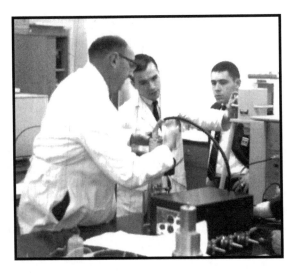

**Dr. Jack Reedy along With Bob Sheehan and Pete Gunther In Radiation Biology Course)**

On the way to the student center, both Peter and Bob offered me assistance by way of their shoulders. In no time, like putting on a comfortable pair of shoes, we sauntered down the hall chatting as if we had known each other all our lives. It is hard to put my finger on it, but in some way we seemed like three lost souls. While each of us had just graduated from college, our futures were up for grabs. In an unspoken way, the three of us recognized this and clung to each other as if maybe one of us has the answer for the other two. Over lunch, I found that Peter finished at St. John's University where he had spent his summers working a variety of jobs ranging from a bakery delivery man to the non-cursing member of a highway road crew. He was pure New York – quick witted, clever, with an accent to boot. Bob, on the other hand, completed his degree at a small Catholic college on the Maine coast, and had spent a good deal of free time honing his soccer skills, a sport he had excelled at in college. In certain respects, Bob embodied what I knew of New England - a mixture of ability, intolerance, and a wry sense of humor. You were never quite sure which head might peep out in conversation. One thing was certain however, I came away from our lunch buoyed by the prospect of working with these guys. Now was the time for us to get our act together.

The three of us shared the same courses. On the biology side, we took Morton's Biological Photography tutorial in which Morton enthusiastically reveled in explaining the intricacies of the camera, as well as its applications to microscopy. One day, Morton showed me his private collection of behind the scene photos of Marilyn Monroe which he took during the filming of the movie *Niagara*. Lessons from Morton would come in handy not only recreationally, but notably to my later research work. Learning how to attach a camera to a microscope provided me with the tool I needed for chromosome analyses which became the focus of my Masters project. Moreover, I used photomicrography in my subsequent PhD research at the University at Buffalo. Thanks Mort!

There was also Jack Reedy's new course, Radiation Biology. Equipped with monitoring instruments, we systemically learned alpha from beta from gamma rays. Our first exploratory exercise involved injected radio-labeled iodine and the time-sequence involved in concentrating the isotope in the thyroid of a cute little bunny rabbit. Unknown to me at the time, we were learning from Reedy what would be of value in my post-doctoral research. For instance, I used radioactive tracers to characterize protein synthesis in cultured muscle with Jim Florini at Syracuse University., and later on in the Biochemistry and Biology Departments at UB. What we three neophytes learned seemed to be only the tip of the iceberg of the expanding role of radioactivity in the biomedical sciences.

The other biology course we took was taught by newcomer Bryan Britten. With the ink not yet dry on his PhD thesis, Britten attempted to teach us everything he knew (which was considerable). Starting with Community Ecology, he systematically introduced us to the totality of the biological world. Beginning with taxonomy and a host of ecological terms, Britten passionately took us on a journey the likes of which we had never seen before. By the end of each class, my right hand ached from my extensive note-taking. While self-absorbed much of the time, Britten stimulated in us a fathomless desire to learn, for our sakes as well as his. The lab component took us out into the field. Our first outing was to a rural area to characterize a decaying log. Here we were, all 8 of us, staring at a God-forsaken log on the ground. However, it didn't take us long to get busy collecting samples to bring back to DePaul: wood chips and bark, mushrooms, plants, insects, etc. I made a rough diagram of the site, which appeared to please Britten. Off to the side I mentioned to Bob, "Can you imagine if some rod and gun type came by in his pickup and asked us what the hell we were doing!" We could only guess how the thin skinned Britten might have reacted. In another field exercise, we attempted to census the rodent population. Here we were equipped with live traps for catch and release. Interestingly, each of these two studies became the focus of research projects of Peter (decaying log) and Bob (rodent census). I was still a long way off from choosing my project.

In addition to filling our heads with the marvels of the natural world and all its ecological complexities, Britten regaled the three of us with a weekly statistics tutorial. Selecting examples from published biomedical studies, we systemically learned and applied the rubrics of statistics. Back in the 60s, there were no software short-cuts to hammering out tests of statistical significance; each one was laboriously acquired using a slow, noisy mechanical calculator. Despite the inconvenience, the three of us obtained a working knowledge of statistics which would keep us afloat down the road as we later entered our respective doctoral programs.

In order to satisfy the necessary credit hours we needed for our degree, we took a few courses outside of the biology curriculum: Geology taught by a chemistry professor whose pet interest was the effect of glaciation upon our local land masses including Niagara Falls, Crystallography instructed by a physics professor who reveled in explaining the inner intricacies of minerals, as well as biologically important compounds like DNA and protein, and Astronomy taught by a senior UB graduate student whose lack of enthusiasm put us promptly to sleep.

As TAs, the three of us set up and taught the undergraduate labs. My main responsibilities were Dr. Morton's Histology and Embryology courses and Dr. Kiely's Human Anatomy and Physiology which was geared toward NU's note nursing program. Peter and Bob handled the remaining courses: Comparative Anatomy, Microbiology, and the entry-level General Biology. Dressed in our uniform for the next two years, the white lab coat, we not only supervised each lab, but we proctored and graded the exams. Frequently, the three of us would bundle up our exams and head for our favorite watering hole – "The 'Hitching Post". Once inside, our regular waitress Rosie would set us up with meatball sandwiches and beers, and we'd be ready to red pencil everything in sight. And so it went, the three of us navigating our way through our first exposure to grad school.

The three of us grew in ways we might not have expected when we first joined the department. For one, we got along famously, reveling in each other's company. Coming from separate backgrounds, fate threw the three of us together into circumstances which allowed us time to figure out what we were going to do in life. I for one was full of uncertainty. Was this grad school stint merely a stop on my way to med school? This I did not know. As for Bob and Peter, they were in the same fix.

Bob was extremely resourceful, as having an avid interest in athletics, especially soccer. One day I saw Bob dribbling a soccer ball outside and marveled at his strong set of legs as he adroitly navigated the ball to and fro. A few months later, I really got a taste just how strong those legs really were. During one snowy evening after evening class, and as I was about to drive the 20 miles home, Bob asked me, "Why not spend the night here at my dorm?" Without flinching I welcomed Bob's offer; he quickly piggy-backed me half across campus, and clear up the stairs to the 5th floor of the dorm, Reaching the final set of stairs, holding on to me, Bob precariously dug into his pockets for keys which let us into his room for the night. Needless to say, I was taken aback by Bob's strength and will power. Eventually, Bob got to meet my family, especially my dad who was not only a dentist, but the dentist for the Buffalo Bills football team. Through him, we were able to see some games together from the sidelines. For Bob, it was a great opportunity to not only see a game up close and personal, but for Bob and my dad to discuss dentistry. As it turned out, a match was made, and Bob soon started to apply to a number of dental schools, including Tufts where he eventually enrolled after graduation. One career path settled, with two more to go!

Peter, on the other hand, was quite different from Bob. Peter wouldn't know nor care what end of a hockey stick one used to play the game. It really didn't matter. Earnest in all things, he was blessed with a mischievous grin. It was infectious. One look at him, and I'd grin myself, but it never ended there. Subsequently he'd say something like, "How's your face? Do you like your face?" I'd bite by saying something perfunctory like, "Oh it's great, I just shaved it this morning." In the end, we'd go off in some silly tangent discussing the quality of our faces and what they had to offer the world. Not your ordinary banter. This repartee however eventually became our signature, whether we were alone or in public. As stupid as it sounds, our close friendship grew out of this quirkiness. Like a Dick Van Dyke or a John Cleese, Peter was a bit awkward physically, but, in a graceful sort of way. Whether it was inadvertently busting one of Britten's favorite (and expensive) BOD bottles during a limnology study, or crashing through a parking gate with a boat and trailer in tow, Peter had a knack for creating impromptu humor wherever he went. With Peter, "The other" shoe dropping was always around the corner.

I got to know Peter even better during our second year when we shared a rundown apartment in Niagara Falls. On the weekends, I would head home, and Peter would seek refuge at the home of his fiancée, Paula Scanio. Peter met Paula on campus our second year and romance soon blossomed. Ironically, Paula and I were classmates in grammar school, and, after losing touch for several years, we met up again when she enrolled at NU as an undergraduate. Together, Peter and Paula had a mutual interest in drama, especially with the NU theatrical group. Things were on the upswing for Peter, not only did future marital life look promising, but he had a career goal to pursue a PhD in plant ecology at Penn State. His decaying log project with Britten was paying immense dividends. Two down and now one to go.

After my first year, I needed a change in scenery, a desire I shared with my Uncle Stan. The result of my little chat with Stan ended up with me getting a summer job in the Pathology Department of St. Joseph's Hospital in Hamilton, Ontario. At the time there was a need for an assistant in their newly operational chromosome lab. The timing couldn't have been better for me, as I greatly needed a Master's project, and, on the surface, the chromosome work seemed an ideal project. Working with an energetic soul by the name of Ken Stiles, I constructed karyotypes of patients who were suspected of chromosomal anomalies, such as Down's Syndrome. Moreover, through our test procedure, we were able to identify the gender of the unborn from amniotic tissue samples.

Very soon I began to frame a project which I could carry on at NU – my plan would be to duplicate the karyotype procedure, but as an added wrinkle, I would test the effect of caffeine on my growing cells. My rationale was to picking something commonly buffeting our body such as caffeinated beverages like coffee and tea; in the oft-chance I might be able to quantitate a dose-dependent effect of chromosomal aberrations with caffeine. I was beginning to feel pretty good about my chances of finishing my Masters.

By day, I was a white-coated lab tech dropped off in the morning at the hospital by my cousin John and his best friend and future brother-in-law, Paul Thompson. By night, I lived with my Uncle Stan and his family. I initially I stayed in their spacious Caroline St. home, and later when school was over for the kids, I stayed at their summer cottage situated nearby on Lake Ontario. At the Caroline home, my Aunt Leona earmarked the spacious living room as my bedroom. Without pretense whatsoever, Leona had me bed down on their sofa; from here I greeted school friends, guests, delivery people, clergy, you name it. In addition, the living room became the primary venue for the 'Contels' to practice. The Contels were a rock and roll band, ala The Beatles. With John on guitar, Bern on bass, Peter on drums, and Paul on piano, the Contels would fire away. Later, Uncle Stan constructed a sound room on the second floor of the cottage, where subsequently Stephen and Cathy also got into the act. While Stan would give his eyeteeth for a budding physician in the family, he settled for, and encouraged his musically-inclined brood of Beatles wannabes.

As the summer wore on, I got to know my cousins as never before. In some sense my aunt and uncle felt that my presence would have a positive influence on each of my cousins' preparation for college and maybe a career. I quickly found out that each cousin listened to his or her own drum beat. Beginning with the eldest, Bern was the extrovert, always seeming to get on the wrong side of Stan. Besides frequently locking horns with Stan, Bern had quite a serious side which later blossomed into being a highly successful educator of children as well as artist. On the other hand, John was even-keeled, frequently displaying his engaging sense of humor; as well as his passionate interest in photography and cinema. In much as I may have been a peace-maker in the Steve Hudecki household, John was the go to person for the siblings to work out their problems with their parents. Mary Ann was my sister Karen's age, and she played the role of the older sister for the younger ones to a tee. Equipped with an engaging sense of humor and natural curiosity of the contemporary world, she was a joy to be around. Batting clean up, Peter was the wild man of the Contels – drumming away until his hands bled. Artistic to the core, he later became an animator, as well as educator of cinema. Next came Helen, who even at a young age, was a spitting image of Diane Keaton in manner and dress. Of all the siblings, I think it was Helen who displayed most of the wonderful Irish tendencies exemplified by her mother Leona. Cathy was a very sincere and striking young girl. With her long and pure brown hair, and piercing brown eyes, Cathy became one of my favorite photographic targets. Named after my father, Stephen was an exuberant lad, quick with a smile and laugh, and ready to jump into any or all. He later became a major cog in the Contels playing the organ and synthesizer. The second youngest, Stan Jr., was most interested in the mechanical side of life. Whether it was how things worked or how to build a better mouse trap, Stan Jr. could be seen frequently in his own little world, dreaming and calculating. He later joined the Canadian Armed Forces. The youngest, Ricky, was in many respects just what my uncle wanted me to be – a businessman. Even at a very young age, Ricky had an assortment of real and imagined money-making schemes. As fate would have it, he later became quite successful in the Toronto business community. As it were, my nine 'roommates' described above, provided me with a summer I would not soon forget; seven years later when Raj and I married, they and their parents were the first to be included in our guest list.


Today, as I look back at those summer days in Hamilton, I recall them with gratitude, wonder, and a smile on my face. It was then when I witnessed my first surgery. One day Stan asked me to join him as he implanted a pin into the leg of a young girl with polio. Fortunately for me, an understanding nurse grabbed me before I fainted when I saw Stan make a clean, crisp cut into the skin of the patient. On another occasion, I was examined by an orthopedic surgeon who concluded that he could surgically slice into my right foot heel cord so I wouldn't have to walk on my toes. Fortunately, Stan agreed with me when I told his colleague that I could not afford to be immobilized during the rehab process, as I would lose too much muscle. Frequently in the hospital, I shared cups of coffee with my cousin Barbara. Being constantly under the gun as an emergency room nurse, she welcomed our reprieves within the relative calm of the snack bar.


Outside the hospital, I led an eclectic life surrounded by my cousins. One particular escapade involved John and Paul. Over a late night poker game, they decided to take me golfing at a nearby course: "Don't worry Mike, we'll take you up and down the fairways on piggy back." On a course situated on an escarpment better suited for a mountain goat, all seemed to go okay on the first few holes which were all downhill; going back up the incline however was a different matter. As we were about to make our ascent, we were met by a Scottish foursome who were shocked and not a little unhappy as I precariously balanced myself to hit a tee shot. Nonplused, the three of us carried on as we had before – John shanking a shot immediately to the right, Paul snap hooking a drive to the next county, and me, accurately hitting a tee shot fifty yards down the fairway. With Paul gathering up our clubs, and John hoisting me up onto his back, the three of us continued on hoping the Scotsmen were not armed.

As Labor Day weekend approached it was time to pick up stakes in Hamilton and get back to my NU reality. This time I'd come equipped with a Masters project, and rejuvenation from my stay with Stan and Leona and the cousins. As I got down to business, I enlisted Peter to be my daily source of fresh blood for my project. After I incubated Peter's cells for a few days in a culture medium, a chemical was added to stop the growth of the cells so photos could be taken for karyotyping of the chromosomes. All went according to plan except I couldn't get the damn cells to grow. Day after day, week after week, and Peter willingly serving as my guinea pig, something terribly had gone wrong. What step did I leave out? Were the samples contaminated? Did I use enough blood? After months of work, I was nearing the deadline for submission of my project for faculty review. Panic was just below the surface as I stared at my trash can full of discarded tubes (and of course, no data).

Back in our apartment over coffee, I discussed my dilemma with Peter - on the one hand, I had reams of data from my hospital work which I could easily use as if it was acquired at NU; or, call a spade a spade and deal honestly with the trials and tribulations over the past months to get Peter's cells to reveal their chromosome configuration. What to do? As if we were on the same wave length, Peter opted as I had for the straightforward approach - This is what I did and why, and this is what I found. Period! Not pretty or sexy, but scientifically revealing. Hence, my writing went quickly as I spun out the tale of "The *attempted* induction of chromosome anomalies with caffeine." As with Bob and Peter's dissertations, my project with accepted with flying colors.

While Bob was set to enter Tufts Dental School, and Peter joining Penn State's graduate program in plant ecology, I decided after all to throw my hat into the ring with the UB Med School. A month before my Masters Degree conferral, I was notified that I made the first cut academically, and now eligible for a personal interview. With Peter along for moral support, I soon entered the waiting room along with the other doctor wannabes. My first interview went as well as could be expected: "Mike, you have a good record, why do you want to enter medicine?" So it went with 20 minutes of predictable Q and A. My next interview was conducted by a physiology professor who took me down to his lab. After answering a series of standard questions from him, I had an opportunity to ask him a few. "So what is it that you actually do here at UB? What kind of work do you do?" Without blinking, Professor Hugh Van Liew jumped into a description of his respiratory studies, gas exchange and the like. The more I listened, the idea of pursuing a PhD became quite appealing. In fact, our discussion reached such a crescendo that Van Liew matter-of-factly offered: "Mike, why don't I indicate here that you decided to rescind your application in lieu of you applying to the Biology PhD program." In a flash, medicine was out, and a potential research career was now in play. At that very moment, Van Liew called the Biology Department requesting that they send me an application. Little did I know at the time that my fate was about to be sealed – a fate involving getting a PhD and subsequently pursuing a research career directed at muscular dystrophy therapy. Moreover, and most importantly, fate would be waiting for me at a graduate program where I would meet the love of my life – RajMohini Sebastian.

After graduation, Bob headed to Massachusetts now set to sink his teeth into Tufts Dental School. Interestingly, while Bob subsequently developed a highly successful private practice in his hometown of Springfield, he took great pleasure in an adjunct position at Harvard teaching dental photography. Like Peter and me in our respective graduate studies, Bob learned life-long lessons in photomicrography from our mutual guru, Professor Thomas Morton at Niagara.

As for Peter, he married Paula prior to joining Penn State and their renowned plant ecology program. However, before we parted company, Peter and I were accepted into a summer research program at Roswell Park Cancer Center. For the duration we were paired with Donald Metcalf, a noted visiting scientist from Australia - his claim to fame was the development of a test to quantitate 'serum colony stimulating factors' in blood. The value of Professor Metcalf's cutting-edge research lay in being able to identify cytokine or viral factors critical in promoting cancerous growth. Stephen Foster, a young surgeon escaping the

Vietnam War draft, made up the fourth of our team. Both Peter and I were highly impressed (if not intimidated) by Foster's surgical prowess as he trained us in the delicate art of small animal surgery – lessons that would stay with me in my own future research using animals.

All too soon, the summer neared its end for Peter, Bob, and me. Amongst our tearful goodbyes, we realized our friendship had grown to such an extent that little really needed to be spoken as we parted company. Two short years ago we were total strangers – rudderless and unsure of our respective futures, but at Niagara we grew in ways we could not have imagined. We not only learned more science, but we actually DID science asking questions and seeking out ways to answer them. It was an empowering experience. We became acutely aware as never before of the historical as well as contemporary value of the scientific literature. We appreciated that science is constantly evolving. Old ideas were replaced with newer ones, better techniques, better questions, and so on. We also appreciated from our TA work what it was to be at the other side of the classroom lecturn - experiences which would serve us well later on as instructors in our own right. In a sense, the three of us milked every conceivable drop from our graduate school experience at Niagara. While we cautiously entered DePaul through its front door, we came out the back door confidently ready to tackle any or all doors that lay ahead of us.

As of this writing, Bob is still prospering as a dentist. However, Peter died April 25, 2009, succumbing to a protracted illness. After obtaining his PhD at Penn State, Peter went on to join the faculty of a new up-start college outside of Chicago. At Governors State University, Peter went on to distinguish himself as a Professor of Environment Sciences in the noble tripartite pursuit of excellence in the classroom, research lab, and administration. His career as husband, father, colleague and mentor, is deservedly inspiring. For myself, I am envious of all those who had the good fortune of interacting with Peter (as well as Bob) over the years since we parted company forty-seven years ago.

# Chapter 7

# Year of Living Dangerously

On a Saturday in August, 1972, I went with two friends to an air show in Syracuse. After being astonished by the legendary Blue Angels, we dined at a local German restaurant. Over wiener schnitzel and cold brews, my friends from Buffalo, Saras Subbiah and Sheila Paturzo, chatted about many things, including our mutual pal RajMonhini who had been at home in India for over two years. Since I hadn't heard from her for nearly three months, I was anxious to hear news of her, *any* news.

From recent letters, Saras was insistent that Raj wanted to come back to the United States. Buoyed by this prospect, we continued our conversation back at my apartment. In her last letter Raj was upset and less than happy about her current circumstances in her university position. As she put it: "…I don't expect you to be overjoyed hearing from me but it is nearly two years since I left and much time has elapsed. I did not think you would mind. I've lost contact with most friends in Buffalo. Mainly because letter writing is one of those things that have to be worked at and one tends to postpone writing. Osmania University is in a terrible mess…How's life with you? Mine is in a nice little rut."

After Raj left Buffalo in 1970 with her PhD, we kept up a torrid writing pace for a little over a year; however, because of deep financial concerns, it was evident Raj could not return to the US anytime soon. Subsequently, our letter exchanges turned into a trickle. In the meantime I had my own struggles in Syracuse where I was getting settled into my new postdoctoral position at Syracuse University. When Saras arrived bearing recent news of Raj, I was all ears and wanted to hear more. Just before heading back to Buffalo, Saras made one last pitch: "Mike, write to her. Tell her you want her to come back to Buffalo. She can always stay with me, or, whatever. Mike, she misses you!"

As we said our farewells at the door, my mind was reeling. As soon as the apartment door closed, I had paper and pen in hand and began writing to my dear old friend living at B4F4 Vigyanpuri. The gravity of the moment was not lost on me. A huge opportunity beckoned and I needed to seize it. It would prove to be my *entre* to a year I'd never forget nor ever regret; however, four short months earlier things had been terribly different.

On a quiet, sunny afternoon in April as I was driving home from the University at Buffalo where I was finishing my PhD research, I noticed a car stopped up ahead. A Tonawanda police officer was standing by the car. As I got nearer, I noticed Dad's familiar Buick with him at the wheel. I pulled up to the policeman and identified myself. He indicated that my dad had brushed up against a parked car and apparently was too inebriated to continue home. I took one look at him and my heart sank.

When we got home, Mom dutifully tucked him into bed. With my pulse racing, I concluded that something had to be done. No more excuses, no more intimidations. It was time to do something. After we retrieved Dad's car, Mom and I in the solitude of the garage got into a spirited, frank, and nearly desperate discussion of what to do. Initially, Mom was reticent to rock the boat. She believed that he would be okay with a little rest, and that things would take their course in due time. This is not what I wanted to hear. I pleaded for action. How much longer could the whole family go on like this? His drinking had to stop, as he might kill himself or maybe others some day. Eventually, after much discussion, she gave her approval to set a new course for our lives. Later I called my brother Greg who was in his final year of Dental School. After a brief recap of events and my emotional discussion with Mom, we both agreed that the person who had the most clout with Papa was Fran Hornung. We needed a stubborn, persuasive, yet familiar intermediary, and Fran was the man.

From the time of their Dental School days together, Dad and Fran had shared all there was to share between long-time buddies – classmates, the war, golfing, bowling, summer cottages, and families tied together by birthdays, baptisms and graduations. The lives of Steve and Fran were intimately intertwined; however, now we needed Fran to step up to the plate and courageously put this friendship on the line. Without any coaxing, Fran agreed to be the sacrificial lamb.

The plan was to have Fran come to the house the next day and take Dad to the office of Dr. Armand DeFrancisco, a local psychiatrist who was an old chum from Dad's Canadian youth. With all of us treading on pins and needles (except for Dad), Fran came unannounced through the garage door and into the kitchen with the simple greeting of "Hi, Steve!"

At this moment, Dad was offered a singular opportunity to soberly re-chart his life (if not save it). It was a situation foisted upon him by family, circumstance, and a dear old friend. Fran's intercession jeopardized a long-standing relationship which took months, if not years, before their close friendship could be renewed. While they still played golf together or were seen together at various outings, Dad had feelings of betrayal, and he kept Fran at arm's length. When Fran's name came up in conversation, Dad couldn't help himself and would throw out a disparaging remark or two; however, for the rest of the family, Fran's stature was inestimable. He was a man of character and not dismissed easily.

I loved my dad, but in many circumstances he truly tested that bond. It seemed that over the past dozen years, Dad's ability to drink and not be confrontational lessened. Basically Dad was a hard-working, caring man – a man devoted to his family, his dental profession, as well as a host of institutions and people. Not coming to Buffalo after the war with a silver spoon in his mouth, he strove very hard to earn a living and raise a family. Financial and social status would only come later on after he'd established himself in the community through his care and attention to his dentistry, his family's activities, his friends, and a growing list of altruistic organizations.

Dad was complex. Like an onion, he embodied layer upon layer of experiential history —most good, and some not so good. Never sure which layer you might poke through. Not a pretty picture, especially for someone you are close to and love so much. Thus my garage discussion with Mom had much to do with not only getting Dad's former self out of the closet, but it had the hope of reigniting the flame of love we all felt as a family for our father. When I was growing up, Dad was my knight, my protector from the dragons in my life. When I would fall to the ground, Dad was always there to encourage me to get up. Hence, Fran concluded early that his buddy's life was indeed worth rescuing. After an initial meeting with the psychiatrist, an appointment was arranged for Dad to take up residency in a six week de-tox program located in rural Pennsylvania.

As for the family, Greg was in the throes of finishing his dental studies and soon would be joining the Army. Electing the early enlistment route, Greg at least had a choice to where he might be stationed, meaning not going to Vietnam. In a few months with a DDS in hand, Greg and wife Joann, along with their baby son Jimmy, would be off to Fort Devens, Massachusetts. While Greg and Jo were married four years earlier, my dad and Jo never really hit it off. At times they resembled gasoline and a lit match in the same room. One day I asked my godfather, my uncle Stan: "What gives with my dad and women?" He told me about his mother who was strong-willed and ruled the roost at home. If young Stephen stepped out of line, which he did frequently, his mother would wait for his father to come home from work and she would demand a strapping. While I listened to Stan, I couldn't help but think of how not to raise a puppy. Slap it around and you have a pretty good guess on how the pup might behave later in life. There would be much for the Pennsylvanians to sort out.

When she was growing up, my sister Karen ran like the wind. Old 8 mm movies show her cavorting with our pet dogs, picking up earthworms from a pile of wet leaves, and generally mugging for the camera wherever it was. Karen was a true spirit. Two years after receiving her degree from Niagara University, she was busy working in the adoption division of Catholic Charities. She drove around in her low slung gold Barracuda, as her work took her all over Western New York, where she encountered the best and the worst of humanity. Because she was energetic, as well as possessing a gentle understanding temperament, Karen was immersed in the lives of would-be parents along with society's unfortunates eager to give away innocents born out of carelessness. More importantly, however, Karen was also preparing for her wedding in June, after which she would be picking up stakes and moving to Long Island to settle in with her new husband, Bob Albanesi, an ex Navy man. I'm sure Karen's wedding would also be on the list of Dad's talking points in Pennsylvania.

Stephanie the fourth oldest, she was entrenched in her senior year at Mt. St. Joseph's High School. Known as the 'Big Mount,' the school was on the same campus as the 'Little Mount' where we all went to grade school. As she wore her characteristic black uniform, Steph was busy with the academic than rather with the social side of school. A good deal of her free time, however, was filled up in assisting her younger sister, Patricia. She, like me, had limb–girdle muscular dystrophy. While Pat at the time was relatively independent, Steph seemed to be forever on call to help Pat with this or that. As a consequence, Steph's life was split up among study, housework, and listening for Pat's familiar, "Hey, Steph!" Like us older kids, Steph wondered what to do after graduation. College? Work? In Steph's case, her quick intelligence and work ethic should have made college a natural choice. Should she pursue her natural talent in art at a local college or train as a dental assistant in Dad's office? In the short run, Steph chose to do both by taking art courses as well as putting in time in Dad's dental practice. She did all of this while dancing to Pat's tune.

Much later, after mom died in 1981, Steph finally took the big step and moved out of the house to take an apartment with my former graduate student, Carol Gregorio. This decisive and long-delayed moment swung open the world for Steph. While she worked as a full-blown dental hygienist (and not for Dad), her social life grew by leaps and bounds, including meeting her husband-to-be, John Sharkey, a brash, talented chemistry PhD student from the University at Buffalo. Consequently, the fire in Steph's smile was something to truly behold. After years of living under the shadow of the whims of Pat, as well as dad, it was wonderful to see Steph flex her wings and savor life as never before.

At the time, a chapter was also coming to a close for Pat. After finishing seventh grade, she was in the hunt for a high school after graduation next year. I thought Pat had more difficulties in life than I did. While we shared cycles of frustration followed by anger, I somehow learned to cope. I developed more of the glass is half full approach to life. With Pat, she found it more difficult to get out of herself and resorted more to guile if not anger. Unfortunately, her moodiness became legend. I recall a time when I drove Pat to the Mount, and as I was driving away, I glanced in the rear view mirror and saw Pat's progress in climbing the stairs to the school. Moved by the sight, I pulled over to the curb and sketched the scene. Call it duty, call it empathy, at the time I had a proprietary interest in Pat's comings and goings.

The previous summer I scouted nearby high schools with Pat to gauge their physical accessibility. Academically-related questions would have to take a back-seat, as she more preferred a booked up social calendar. At Mount St. Mary's Academy, the nuns showed us around the school, quickly making it apparent that Pat could navigate its premises; however, Pat's grade transcripts did her in. Choice number two was a new school called Cardinal O'Hara. The visit proved fruitful as she not only could get about there, but her grades were not a hindrance. It would be here that Pat's social world really began to blossom. As we might have expected, her high school orbit did not intersect with that of the family. I could only guess at how having two handicapped kids played a part in Dad's behavior – likely another talking point with the folks in Pennsylvania.

As for myself, I was near the end of my experimental graduate work at UB. I spent most of my time writing thesis drafts and simultaneously chasing down leads for a post-doctoral position. Periodically, I'd get a letter from Raj in India. At that time, Raj was the only bread-winner in her parents' household due to the recalcitrance of the Indian bureaucracy in processing her parents' pensions. Raj's paycheck for teaching required her to look no further than Hyderabad. We didn't like the circumstances, but those were the cards dealt to us. Our future together seemed to be in limbo.

Prior to the internet, my quest for a post-doctoral position was confined to letter writing and follow-up phone calls. I sought to work with a scientist actively studying muscle disease. My post-doc quest focused on universities in Iowa City, Rochester, Syracuse, Baltimore, as well as The National Institutes of Health in Bethesda. Indeed, it was a hectic time for me as well as for my siblings; each of us trying to carry out double lives – life outside and inside the home.

What about Mom? How did she survive these mini-dramas? Part stoic, part escapist, she carried on the best way she knew how. In simple terms, she was happy when Dad was happy, and she did what she could to accomplish this end. Unlike Dad who came from an established family structure in Hamilton, Ontario, Mom was born and raised in the tiny town of Melita, Manitoba, which was situated on a small rise in the vast Canadian prairies. From the center of town you could see forever looking in any direction. Fresh air, open skies, and a wind-blown solitude comprised her early environment. Complete with out-house and earthen cooler, Mom's home enjoyed few creature comforts, and Mom and her siblings learned to do without. After her mother died soon after giving birth to the last of the seven children, Mom's father hired a housekeeper. Together with older sisters, Mary and Sophie, Mom learned to be self-sufficient and to help in looking after her younger siblings Pauline, Agnes, Vicky, and Anthony, Jr. As the girls got older, however, they set their sights (and futures) on the metropolises of Eastern Canada. After Mary and Sophie left for Toronto, Mom traveled east herself, and through family connections she met a handsome, dark-haired bachelor named Stephen Edward

Hudecki. An engagement flowered into a New Year's Eve wedding in 1942.

Soon after the nuptials, my Mom and Dad headed for the southeast United States. After his graduation from UB Dental School, Dad enlisted in the U.S. Army. His tour of duty began with basic training followed by residency at Fort Bragg, North Carolina, where Dad would receive his final Army Airborne training before sailing overseas to England. All was in preparation for Operation Overlord and the D-Day landings in Normandy. Through it all, Mom adapted, and adapted, and adapted again. While she only had a high school education, she applied her well-honed survival skills to her life in North Carolina, as well as after the war when Dad and Mom decided to carve out a life in Buffalo. Ironically, it was because of his Dental School class-mate, Fran Hornung, among others, that Dad felt at home in Buffalo.

In 1953, my parents took a sentimental journey to Melita and visited Mom's father who was still going strong as a foreman for the railroad. With the Buick loaded up, we headed across Ontario to Sarnia, through Lower Michigan to the Straits of Mackanaw. After a breezy ferry ride and a stop in Duluth, we then headed west for Minot, North Dakota. After an over-night stay, we proceeded north for the Manitoba border and a lonely immigration outpost. At the Canadian border, Mom renewed acquaintances with an old friend who was now a Canadian Immigration Officer. Twenty miles later through open country, we finally arrive in Melita. From our comings and goings in town caught on Dad's 8mm movie camera, and it was obvious that Mom was never happier. As she retraced her childhood, she played on a swing in the school grounds, walked through an overgrown park adjacent to a Red River tributary, and proudly posed for pictures with her father, as well as with all those whom she still knew in town. She was home again!

Much later in 1965 after Steph and Pat were born, the family again packed up – but this time we were loaded into our Plymouth station wagon and headed for North Carolina. Again, the trip was filled with recollections, but this time however, it would be *both* parents who would be retracing their steps. Fort Bragg, Fayetteville, and Southern Pines all occupied the thoughts of my parents, and at times we kids felt like intruders. They took us down this route and then another, visited this house and then another, and periodically introduced us to some of their buddies who decided to stay on after the war. Looking back over these trips, my parents recalled the fulfilling moments of their lives, and they did not harp upon how difficult the times had been at that time.

Now presented with a new dilemma, my mother would need to muster again her self-made skills and face Dad's crisis. In times past, Mom might have been argumentative, but not at this time. I've always wondered how things might have been for my parents and for the family if she had stood up to him more often; however, after years of employing her own brand of quiet diplomacy, she was physically and mentally tired. In spite of everything, there was no doubt of Mom's unqualified love for Dad – her husband. In the end she would be a strong and effective ally in his recovery.

Fortunately, Mom had a few escape venues which renewed her spirits and got her competitive juices flowing. Growing up with six siblings, Mom exhibited self-reliance and a competitive bent. Whether it was smacking the heck out of a golf ball or preparing a Black Forest cake, Mom threw her all into it. While she did not possess a fluid golf swing (hitches and pauses like PGA pro Jim Furyk), she somehow was able to wallop the ball out of sight. Not pretty but effective shot-making! Trophy-wise, Mom easily was the leader of the Hudecki household and gained recognition in a number of local tourneys. One time she even had her picture in the morning paper for leading a local closest-to-the-pin contest.

When the snows came, bowling became Mom's avenue to vent. Again her form was ghastly, but you had to pity the poor pins once smacked by her fast ball. She threw herself each day into chauffeuring kids to and from school, shopping, cooking, cleaning, and when the growing season was upon us, gardening, and strawberry picking. No matter what she was doing however, Mom always had her antenna up gauging the mood of the day, such as what was on Dad's agenda and what was HIS frame of mind. What survival lessons would she need to apply today? While not frequently open with their affections for one another, I did know how close they really were. After Mom died, Dad would refer to her death as "losing my right arm." Knowing him and the gut-wrenching way he spoke those words, there was no question of his love for her. Maybe the Pennsylvanians would be able to unravel the paradox of loving someone, yet cause pain through thoughtless words and behavior?

# Chapter 8

# Syracuse

A few days after Fran's ambush, Dad was scheduled to be at Chit Chat Farms located in Pennsylvania Dutch country. I made arrangements with my grad school friend, Lew Rodriquez, to go with me and share the driving. Ironically, the return trip would give me the opportunity to visit Syracuse University where I strongly considered for a postdoctoral position. In addition, the journey would give Lew a chance to see his folks in nearby New Jersey.

After we were warmly greeted by the Chit Chat staff, Lew and I quickly left Dad and headed for East Orange, New Jersey. Throughout our brief stay with Lew's parents, I ate, smiled, and listened.

With dinner finished, Lew grabbed the wheel and we lit out into heavy evening commuter traffic, on our way to Route 17 which would take us to Syracuse via the Catskills and Binghamton. En route, a light rain was gradually replaced by intermittent sleet, and then heavy, wet snow. Route 17 was wet but navigable; but, as we began to lose daylight, the road became greasy and treacherous. Continuing, the snow only worsened. With each mile, we'd pass a car which had slid off the road down an embankment with its headlights still shining. To make matters more terrifying, semi-trucks passed us creating instant blackout conditions, leaving us two ruts to hang onto ahead of us. Sitting in the passenger seat, I was terrified that we'd end up in one of the adjacent trout streams, or worse, into a dark abyss never to be found again. Lew, however, had a cool head, lightning reflexes, and an instinct for the road born from his days as a deliveryman in New York City. Thankfully, we reached Binghamton where we decided to spend the night rather than to continue on to Syracuse.

The next morning, under bright sunshine, we easily navigated the melting interstate and soon reached the hilly campus of Syracuse University. We located the stately but aging Lyman Hall and parked at the rear delivery entrance. In one of those after-thoughts of collegiate construction, the rear entrance served as both delivery and pedestrian entrances. After negotiating wooden steps down to a small landing and a hefty wooden door, we were faced with another landing which took us to an elevator accessible by two more steps. Muttering to myself, "What the hell is this?" we got the elevator clanking away to the second floor to meet my potential sponsor, Dr. Jim Florini.

**Rear Entrance to Lyman Hall)**

Hustling through the dim, high-ceilinged corridors, we reached the door to Dr. Florini's office. In contrast to Lyman's turn-of-the-century interior, Dr. Florini's lab complex was modernly equipped, noisy from the cold room compressors, and busy with activity. After apologizing to Dr. Florini for our tardiness, we got on with the business of getting to know each other and what our mutual work might entail.

While my post-grad plans were still up in the air, I did know that I wanted to learn more about muscle biochemistry. Up to now the study of muscle disease was largely descriptive, shedding little light on etiology or treatment avenues. Dr. Florini used dystrophic chickens as his research model where he found a defect in their ability to synthesize protein. Consequently, he planned to measure protein synthesis of muscle cells grown in culture. As he came from a recently held tissue culture workshop, he was gung-ho to set up a culture facility, I would be the guy who would be front and center in the project. I was impressed by his enthusiasm and with the fact that Dr. Florini would write up the project which I could use in a fellowship application to the Muscular Dystrophy Association. Hence, I told him that it all looked very appealing, and that it was a go from my standpoint.

I was also entertaining other venues for postdoc work. First, there were lukewarm responses from the University of Iowa and Johns Hopkins. On the other hand, two serious leads came from Dr. W. King Engel at the NIH and Dr. Robert Griggs at the University of Rochester. From Dr. Engel's offer letter I got the sense that he would like me at Bethesda more for my role as a guinea pig in his on-going dystrophy studies, rather than as a neophyte research scientist. The invitation from Dr. Griggs however was most enticing given that the widely-respected Neurology Department within Strong Memorial Hospital was vibrant and welcoming. Although I had a most friendly interview, I decided that their research involving muscle biopsy histopathology was too reminiscent of my prior chromosome work. I wanted to learn new things, as well as new ways of approaching muscle research problems. I had had enough of working with preserved specimens. So it came as both a pleasure and a relief when I received a lengthy letter from Dr. Florini with details of the experiments I would run if I joined him. Also in the note were instructions on how to fill in the MDA Fellowship application, which I accomplished in short order.

After mailing my fellowship application, it was back to thesis writing. Fortunately, my first two chapters represented already published material; microscopic followed by biochemical analyses of brown fat tissue of the pigmy mouse during and after cold torpor. The chapter yet-to-be-written, was to integrate these data with body temperature and oxygen consumption. In effect, I needed it for my thesis committee in preparation of my oral defense exam. However, it was quite frustrating and disheartening to sit at my desk overflowing with piles of papers, graphs, tables, and notebooks, and integrate the mess into a cohesive story. Where would I begin? Who would read it anyway? My mind drifted in and out of these inner conversations. The process was so maddening that any relief would be welcome, in any form. As it turned out, Lew and his wife Rebel had just the cure for my malaise. Over dinner one night, we planned a trip to Jamaica. Along with a Departmental secretary, Lynn Mills, the four of us lit out for Toronto and our Air Canada flight to the Caribbean. Although I'm quite a nervous flier, I trusted Lew to physically assist me whenever needed. The upshot was a temporary good-bye to the damn thesis, as well as Buffalo and Chit Chat Farms.

Touching down first at Montego Bay we were met with bright sunshine and a delicious sea breeze, and our first Red Stripe lager from a tarmac watering hole. Next we flew on to Kingston and collected our rental car. With a supply of maps and Lew at the wheel, we navigated through suburban Spanishtown searching for our cross-country route to our final destination, Ocho Rios. Spanishtown, however, proved to be quite a hurdle. It seemed street signs were either stolen or covered up as we kept going in circles. By simple luck, we eventually reached the outskirts and into the vast sugarcane fields enveloping southern Jamaica. Regretfully, the slums of Spanishtown made me think of Raj back in India. While physically far-a-way, she was still on my mind. What will be, will be, I muttered to myself.

Reaching Ocho Rios near dark, we quickly set ourselves up in adjoining bungalows. In addition to our daily beach-bum activities, the next ten days included: a boat trip to Dunn's River Falls where Sean Connery was once filmed as 007, a guided tour of a banana plantation, and a car trip to scenic Antonio Bay where native Jamaicans enjoyed the sights as much as the tourists. One evening we stopped for dinner in a nearby nightclub called *The Cave*. The food was authentic and the music pleasant, but as we were about to leave, we saw band members gradually being replaced by fellows who throttled up the volume, and tuned their instruments to a catchy, almost hypnotizing beat. In no time the stage was filled with animated, dreadlocked Jamaicans, and as if on cue, the leader of the group came on stage and took the mike. Bang! The four of us heard reggae music for the first time – live! From that moment on, Bob Marley and The Wailers became etched in our minds, and the stimulus to return to the club night after night, not at dinner time but like the local Jamaicans, *après* dinner.

Incidentally, to put our vacation in context, our earlier boat trip to Dunn's River Falls was hosted by two young, bare-chested Jamaicans at the helm. Once we toured the Falls, Lew and I returned to the anchored boat and treated ourselves to couple of ice cold Red Stripes. While Lew and I extolled the beauty of the island, one of the Jamaican lads blurted out in his best dialect: "So maan, what is it that you do?" We took the bait and jumped head-long into a description of our graduate research studies. After a tedious few minutes, the Jamaican interrupted and exclaimed with a wide toothy grin – "Why maan?" We had no answer for him.

Once home, I was saddened to read a letter from Dad where he bared a bit of his soul. While I was buoyed by his conciliatory tone, it struck me that it was himself who was the vulnerable one, not the scrawny kid with Limb-Girdle. A couple of weeks later I got a congratulatory letter from the Muscular Dystrophy Association signifying a post-doctoral fellowship for the then princely sum of $9000. In effect, I was given the green light to begin my post grad work in July with Dr. Florini in Syracuse. In June, my reborn father and I drove to Syracuse for apartment hunting. After some false leads, we found a physically accessible unit located on the first floor. The furnished apartment had all that I needed – a small kitchen area with table and chairs, raised counter area with stools, and a living room and bedroom each with a window. The ground floor windows provided me with a lovely view of license plates of tenant cars, a situation which served as my alarm clock during the winter months. The fellow who lived above me worked at a local Army recruiting office, would rise very early, jump from his balcony to his car and let it idle, all the while he performed noisy calisthenics. In the meantime, I had the choice of getting up or staying in bed and dying from carbon monoxide. Hence, during the winter months I usually got to the university quite early in the day.

Rather than use the main lab of Dr. Florini, I took up a desk in a small room 100 feet down the hall. Since most of my post-doctoral study involved cultured muscle tissue, it was a no-brainer for me to situate myself near the planned tissue culture equipment.

**My Daily Commute Bewteen Tissue Culture
Lab and Main Lab at End of Hall)**

In addition to getting acquainted with Florini's equipment, students and technicians, I spent much of the summer reading the muscle literature. It would be difficult to argue with James Watson, who, in his controversial book *The Double Helix*, reflected that clever ideas came from those who have the time to think, unencumbered by day-to-day concerns, such as punching a clock to make a living. Hence, the real value of a post-doctoral stipend.

Equally important to establishing a functional worksite, I needed to develop strategies for my day to day needs. I found a nearby grocery store which delivered all the groceries I needed for the week. Meals were simplified: eggs or cereal for breakfast, brownbag lunch of a sandwich or yogurt, and TV dinners for the end of the day. A friendly fellow at a nearby gas station took care of my Buick Skylark. I successfully tested the drive-thru features of the Marine Midland Bank situated next door. An obliging young girl with a two year old child agreed to rescue my mail each day from the second floor box, relieving me of struggling up the stairs on all fours. While a laundry room was near my apartment, it was more practical to periodically lug my soiled stuff home. The physical logistics, however, were promising to be much trickier on campus.

I soon learned that I needed to park as early as possible at the rear of Lyman Hall, otherwise I'd be competing with delivery trucks clogging my ability to get to the door. While at UB, I got to know many of the delivery and maintenance fellows and the same would be true at SU. It is no exaggeration, but without their help, I couldn't have possibly finished my PhD. If you can't attend classes nor do the research, you're plum out of luck. There were no distance learning classes back then.

Most times I used the toilet in my apartment in the morning; however, there were times when I needed to hike to the gent's lavatory located within the pipe-laden basement of Lyman While cumbersome, this trek was okay for nature's big business; however, that still left the question of what to do after I've had 2 or 3 coffees during the day. Fortunately, two understanding females in the lab, grad student Mary Nicholson and technician Linda Powers, ran interference for me as I used the Ladies Room located just across the hall from my culture room. "All clear, Mike," and off I'd go with one of them standing vigil outside the door. Adaptation again became my *modus operandi* on and off campus.

The Science Library was located on the top sixth floor of Lyman. Although Florini maintained a personal collection of current journals, I needed to go periodically to the Biology Library located on the top floor. Taking Lyman's cranky elevator and navigating a long dark hallway, I came upon a large classroom brightly illuminated by skylights. Wearing only her birthday suit, a SU coed was sitting on a stool in the middle of the room. Surrounding her were a dozen students busy sketching and painting at their easels. Acting like a fly on the wall, I thought to myself that this old codger of a building provided a compelling blend of science and the arts.

Eventually my room was set up for culture work. A new laminar-flow hood arrived, followed soon by a state of the art incubator. Next, we needed to create an enclosure to insure a sterile environment. With the lab door opening and closing all day long, we needed a protective barrier; to deal with this problem, we summoned the SU carpenters who built a wooden frame covered with strong plastic sheeting; they even cut a flap through the plastic to give us a "door" to our inner sanctum. Now that we had a room within a room, it was time to field test our facility and grow muscle cells. Bring on the chicken eggs!

The animal facility was located near Lyman's Medieval back entrance. In addition to boisterous chickens, the facility housed an incubator where fertilized chicken eggs containing embryos could grow. Using a published technique, I dissected muscle tissue from the embryos, and teased apart the tissue composed mostly of unfused cells called myoblasts. Once the myoblasts were filtered, I put them into small dishes and placed in the incubator. After a few days, the myoblasts fused into tiny straps of "mini-muscles" which I then could use for my protein synthesis experiments.

Our experimental approach allowed us to study muscle devoid of influences, such as nerves, and hormones. At the time, there were questions whether muscular dystrophy was an inherent muscle problem, or caused by other organ systems. In our case, we were in pursuit of identifying a potential error in protein metabolism; one which was inherent and specific to genetically dystrophic muscle. We hoped that a disease marker, or even a treatment avenue could be uncovered and later pursued. Once we were successful in growing muscles in culture, we were like kids again peering through a microscope and actually witnessing spontaneous twitching of our cultures. Game on!

Shortly after our little breakthrough, Jim Florini asked me to join him at a local TV studio carrying the annual Jerry Lewis Labor Day Telethon to raise donations for the MDA. With pride and a renewed sense of responsibility to the organization that funded me, I was more than happy to oblige. When the totals were tallied by Jerry Lewis and Ed McMahon on national TV, I couldn't help but think that I had been part of the fund-raising effort. It was a nice shot in the arm for this nascent scientist.

While I was carving out my niche in Syracuse, I had much yet to do at UB to prep myself for my defense-of-thesis exam. Rewrite suggestions from my committee were coming at a snail's pace. In September I took a week off from my culture work in Syracuse and returned home to finalize my thesis and take the defense exam. With Dr. Carm Privitera as my mentor, my PhD committee was composed of physiologist Dr. Kipp Herreid, biochemist Dr. Ed Massaro, and plant physiologist Dr. Jim Tavares. Thanks to Departmental Chairman, Dr. Philip Miles, the defense went relatively smoothly. He kept the exam on track in spite of volatile discussions between Professors Privitera and Herreid. Dr. Miles on the other hand, intervened and brought calm and resolution. After a positive Committee vote, I was showered with congratulatory handshakes, and cake and wine toasts back in the lab. During the festivities, Carm presented me with an engraved walking stick carved from a hickory sapling he had found camping in Allegheny State Park. "Mike, I'm so sick and tired of that damn broom handle you use; here try this!" To this day I'm still using Carm's stick for just about every imaginable purpose; I would truly be lost without it, even to this day. After an evening dinner with my parents and sisters Steph and Pat, I was finally freed up to hopefully embark on a productive science career. Moreover, maybe it was also time to put my toe in the matrimonial waters again.

Ever since Raj left in 1970, I had been haunted by her. Her letter after she safely arrived home in India distracted me no end - "You are the <u>most</u> wonderful person I know (and although you are miserable sometimes!) I would like to someday "make a team with you..." Those words lingered over the past two years up to the time Saras recently dropped with her Syracuse visit, and her insistence that I write to Raj again in the hopes of getting together. I leaped at the opportunity. In response to my return letter, Raj too, expressed her desire to renew our relationship wherever that might lead. Moreover, she added: "...Please don't think I have been mean or cruel to you. This has been the <u>most</u> unhappy year of my life. There seemed no ways out. In my letter to you, I told you that I had written not because I did not love and care for you but because circumstances were beyond my control..." From the instant I tore open her letter, I felt we were back on track, and indeed, we might 'make a team' after all!

November was full of election talk on the airways as well in everyday conversations. Passions were most evident on campus as anti-war feelings were everywhere. The candidate of choice was George McGovern for us peace-niks, while Richard Nixon represented more-or-less an anti-christ figure. On election evening, I invited folks from Florini's lab for pizza and beer and, hopefully, a victory celebration; however, the party turned out to be the shortest on record as McGovern was trounced, early and often. The results were dismal, and the party adjourned nearly as soon as it started. Little did we know at the time that the seeds for the "Watergate Scandal" had already been planted for Nixon's fall from grace the following year.

As winter set in, Raj and I exchanged letters frequently. The main topic had to do with visas. In our case, it became clear that the route to take was the K-visa. In this instance Raj would be coming as the fiancée of an American citizen, and within 90 days evidence of marriage would be needed. By the year's end, I still had not heard from the US Embassy in New Delhi about my request for the appropriate documents to get the K-visa application off the ground; however, both Raj and I agreed that we could be patient a little longer. In the meantime, Raj had broken the news to her parents and got resounding support for her future plans with me; on the other hand, I was more circumspect when spilling the news to my parents.

My mother was very approachable about such matters and quite supportive. On the other hand, it was different with Dad who was suspicious by nature. While he didn't jump up and down with a ringing endorsement, he did so none-the-less. To his credit, he only raised a number of practical questions regarding sponsorship, and "once married, how do you know Raj wouldn't just take off?" I already knew the answer to that question.

1972 ended with me saddled at home with the Hong Kong Flu. The entire family gathered for a New Year's celebration: Greg's crew from Massachusetts, and Karen and Bob from Long Island. All the while, I groped around the house with a temperature and aches and pains; however, as I wrote Raj, I had never seen my parents so happy in having the entire family around them – it was probably one of the better times for being at home.

Like icing on a cake, Raj wrote about signing off the old year, and ringing in 1973 – "…In spite of all these feverish activities there is a lot of time to think of you and miss you. I was imagining how it will be next Christmas. Of course I'll miss my home and family. The 'family' have an idea about you. A few hints have been dropped so that I won't be too much of a shock to them. Only 4-1/2 months more. I can hardly believe it. I am waiting for the papers from you. My passport ought to come by Jan. Then with the necessary documents I'll send it to Madras US Consulate. I hope the University closes early for summer because of water shortage. We are re-opening on Jan 8th, 1973. A very happy, peaceful New Year to you darling. 1973 promises to be a good year. Anything will be better than 1972. This time next year we'll be shoveling snow! I'll bring you a gold cross. Much love, Raj"

# Chapter 9

# UB Biology and the Charmer

Now that the crossroad-infested year of 1972 was behind us, Raj and me were now preparing to jump into the deep end of the pool. Raj was leaving her parents and job security, while I was consumed by questions: What was she thinking of in marrying a gangly, disabled kid from Kenmore? Were my instincts on target? Was she truly the person I thought she was when we were friends nearly three years earlier at UB? Centering me, I always harkened back to the images of the two of us – our friendly banter and the unspoken joy of simply being together.

Coming to UB in 1967 was a revelation. Having spent my formative years within the hallowed halls of Catholic schools, I was accustomed to a tidy parochial existence. Jacket and tie was the order of the day, coupled with a dutiful (if not fearful) respect for what was alleged to be the right way of doing things. My entrance into the UB campus, however, brought me into another world - a world defined by diversity and activism in all its dimensions. It was a vibrant environment in which I treaded softly at first, but one which I would soon embrace. The times themselves were turbulent. Campus life was filled with anti-war slogans and graffiti, and authority figures were labeled "pigs". The Kent State tragedy was looming around the corner, advocates such as Ralph Nader and Rachel Carson, were "must reads", and nearby Love Canal in Niagara Falls was more than a simple ditch.

In contrast to my benevolent experiences with Peter and Bob at Niagara, my fellow students were prone to bitch and moan. If it were not about courses, it was about the war, Nixon, pesticides, or global population issues. There was a topic to fit anyone's bent. You didn't

111

need to subscribe to the *New York Times* to be in the loop; all you needed to do was hang around the Departmental mailroom to quickly get up to speed on the issues of the day. Early morning bullshit in the halls was all the news you really needed to know. All interlopers were cordially and loudly invited to jump into the fray.

It was also a watershed time for the University, as well as for up and coming Departments like Biology. Touting itself as the "flagship" of the State University of New York system, UB recruited and brought in hired guns from well known universities across the country. The new faculty represented a disparate band of mercenaries eager to be conceived as the country's best and brightest, and in the bargain make UB the "Berkeley of the East." Moreover, visiting luminaries made the campus buzz with excitement. Whether it was newly-crowned Nobel Laureates like Christian DeDuve, Sir John Eccles, or James Watson, or senior awardees like Linus Pauling, we students salivated at the very thought of meeting these titans of modern-day biology. Some of our own faculty tried to feign indifference, but we students saw straight through the ruse.

Within the Department, I encountered a culture where two ends of biological thinking were prominent – faculty who were traditional or organismal in their thinking; usually older, some were entrenched with old tried and true notions – thinking 'outside the box' was not for them. Then, there were the relatively young, new faculty who were molecular in thought and practice; they were driven to catch the current wave of genes and proteins. It was a conflicting time for us entering students – some senior faculty holding on for dear life to traveled ways of doing and preaching science; and the young turks drooling and extolling the virtues of molecular biology. We students tap-danced between the two camps, impressed when and where we could, but mostly we tried to hitch our wagon to someone who would serve as our research advisor and mentor.

After much consideration, I decided to join the lab of Professor Carm Privitera and his comparative physiology students. During the first year, I had gotten to know Carm, and his PhD students, Jim Kane, Al Rotermund, and Bob Beall.

**Dr. Carm Privitera and Bob Beall)**

While I was interested in their projects, in the end it was Carm and the collegiality of his students which drew me to their lab. Carm personified the comforting experience I had at Niagara. Moreover, in his realm, the twin cultures of organismal and molecular biology were enthusiastically bridged. While my thesis project didn't set the world on fire, the work provided me the apprenticeship I needed to prosper later, as well as an important lesson in choosing an elevator companion.

Fresh out of Niagara, I first met Raj in 1967 when I joined the Department. It was pure serendipity one day when we rode the elevator together. I was thunder-struck by this smiling young woman neatly dressed in a colorful sari. She introduced herself as RajMohini. Reaching our third floor destination, she indicated that her name translated into 'Charmer of the King.' We continued down the hall together – I to my TA desk within Professor Gordon Swartz's lab and Raj to the research lab of her advisor, fungal geneticist Professor Phil Miles. During our brief encounter, I was struck by how pleasant and attractive she was and how engaging she was to talk to. I felt myself smitten. She emitted an aura of grace and confidence as she swooshed and kicked forward her sari as she walked. I was bemused by her constant fidgeting with the bangles on her wrist as she spoke. Parted on one side, her beautiful jet black hair was swept back and kept in place with a simple clip. Her disarming smile was highlighted by a small chip to a front tooth. Yes, you could say our first meeting was indelible.

UB grad student (ca 1969)

**RajMohini)**

Raj came to UB two years earlier on a prestigious Fulbright Scholarship. How she actually got to UB is a story in itself. Except for a couple of cousins, and a Peace Corps volunteer, she knew no one in the US. It was by chance that Raj ended up in Buffalo. In her mind, Buffalo couldn't be too bad as if it were within shouting distance of the well-known New York City. Upon arriving in the Big Apple along with other Indian aspirants, the Fulbright people arranged visits to sights such as: Radio City Music Hall, Times Square, and the United Nations. Next in line was a trip arranged by the State Department to Indianapolis. There she was "instructed" on the rudiments of table manners and other supposed American niceties. This training had intended to help make the transition easier for those from Third World countries like India. The crowning achievement of Raj's stay in Indianapolis was to hand out bowling trophies at a local tournament. Even today, my heart wants to cry out as I visualize my elegantly clad RajMohini presenting an array of cheap chrome-plated trophies to a boisterous crowd of beer swigging bowlers.

Arriving in Buffalo by train in the wee hours of the morning, Raj was persuaded by a fellow Indian traveler to take a cheap room at the Markeen Hotel. As it was situated in the red light district, this hotel's fame rested on hosting father-son communion breakfasts and after hour bordello activities. After a sleepless night in a room where the door could not be locked, Raj took a bus to the UB campus and eventually found the Student Union building. Since it was the weekend, no offices were open. Being the industrious sort, Raj found a bench with the intention of camping out until the International Student Office opened Monday morning. Just when Raj began to regret the "luxuries" of the five star Markeen, a Polish-American student introduced herself and invited her to stay at her home. Raj was so grateful, she emptied her luggage of the gifts she had brought from India. In due time, Raj rented a series of apartments within walking distance of the campus. In subsequent years, Raj in the bargain met an array of interesting friends.

Many of Raj's grad school contemporaries became life-long buddies, such as Sylvia Harvey, a chemistry grad student from New Zealand, and mathematician, Saras Subbiah, from India. Not surprisingly, Raj developed several friendships in the community. These included the affable George Georgantis and his circle of Greek-American pals, the effervescent Clarice Giampola, a product of the Italian west side, and Mary Ann Perry, who opened her heart and family to Raj. Interspersed among classes, lab work, and undergrad teaching, Raj scratched out money from her TA stipend to visit Atlanta to see her dear friend Rosalind Van Landingham who was formerly a Peace Corps volunteer in India. Other shoestring excursions included bus trips to Montreal and a cross-country adventure to San Diego via Chicago, St. Louis, and Phoenix. It is safe to say that Raj had seen more of the US in the short time afforded to her than most Americans would see in a lifetime.

Raj chose Dr. Phil Miles as her research advisor, not so much for his research area, but for his gentle, caring nature. Phil and his wife Eleanor were known to go out of their way to open up their home to all of their students – get-togethers were highlighted by lunches and teas, as well as 'field trips' (aka, picnics) to local parks. For Raj, as well as for her fellow graduate students, Phil's keen interest and guidance in their progress led to each student being quite comfortable in Phil's lab. This paradigm would also be true for two students who came to UB the same year I entered the biology graduate program – Wei-Li Lee from Taiwan and John Mayfield from North Carolina. During Raj's tenure at UB, it should be added that she was a hot commodity in the marriage trade; periodically at the behest of friends of Raj's parents back home in India, trips were made to San Francisco and Pittsburgh to meet potential suitors. Fortunately for me, Raj had foregone early fame and fortune and not hitched her nuptial wagon to an up and coming engineer or physician.


I knew little about India – her people, her culture, or anything substantial about the sub-continent. I had been exposed to smatterings about India, but nothing of real consequence; e.g., Kipling's *Gunga Din* and Winston Churchill's formative years spent in India to jaundice my view. We Americans all know the story line of the starving millions and the unclean masses as portrayed in so many United Nations posters. Madras shirts were popular with my preppie high school crowd. These colorful, bleeding garments were all the rage – but where is or what is "mad-drez?" Later on, I got a whiff of Indian cuisine through the unmistakable masalas infiltrating the hallway outside of an apartment of my Niagara grad student friend, Bob Sheehan. It was quite a sensory experience for me who thought black pepper on eggs or an anchovy pizza to be exotic. As for Indian mannerisms or language, all I had to go by was my college physics professor – scholarly, pleasant, but, for the life of me, I could not understand a word he said in class. Then in 1967, along came RajMohini with her colorful sari framing a warm smile. She embodied India in all of its elegance, complexity, as well as talent, grit, and pride. Back then I was indeed out of my element, but willing to learn.

Over the next two years, we exchanged pleasantries in the hallways or at seminars, but little else; mainly we were consumed with our own circle of friends. However, during the summer of 1969, I casually invited Raj (as well as anyone within earshot) to come to one of our softball games – the offer was as much a dare as it was an invitation. I was the manager of our Departmental softball team.

**Managing our Biology Softball Team)**

It was my duty to keep the peace between our more talented grad students and the faculty, who had the mistaken notion that they still could play. Dealing with a bunch of barking dogs and hissing cats, I tried to create a winning team. At one game, Professor Hal Segal, a clever if not intimidating faculty member, literally took his bat and ball and went home, after I put him in the outfield subsequent to muffing everything that came his way in the infield. When I talked to Raj about my self-made predicament, her curiosity was piqued and came to the next game. Comfortably sitting on a nearby hillside, Raj wore a neatly folded sari and flashed me a broad smile under large dark sunglasses. Looking her way, I was quite pleased she came.

Entering the 1969 autumn term, we spent more time together. Initially there were lunches at my desk; nothing fancy, cheese or cucumber sandwiches for her and cold cuts for me. It wasn't too long before our lunches became a daily ritual. Before I could wrestle change from my jeans, Raj headed for the vending machines to get milk. While eating, we discussed our research, sports achievements of the day (my contribution), our mutual love of photography and art, and, importantly, recent letters Raj received from India. Raj took pains to get at least one letter off to her parents each day, and in return she'd eagerly await hearing back from them. Aglow with a letter in hand, Raj happily dispensed tidbits; the more she read, the more animated she became. Excerpts included: visits by former students to see Raj's father incapacitated by a stroke, church and YWCA activities, and various marriages attended by Raj's mother Olivia, and her aunt Elsie. Raj would smack her lips at the mere thought of biryani and bhagara bangain served at the receptions. I'd also hear about cousins, John and Liz Elisha living in Bombay, Roy Sebastian visiting wildlife sanctuaries with his camera in tow, Uma and Tom Franklin from Madras, and several lively Hyderabadis, such as: Marie Charles, Fiaz Quader, George and Lena Stephens, Malathi Cotelingum, Usha Gideon, and Maeve Sebastian. In each case, Raj recounted their comings and goings as well as the colorful background of each person.

Sometimes Raj spoke fondly of her Peace Corps friend, Rosalind, whom Raj wanted me to meet some day. Little did I know at the time but Raj was doing a little matchmaking of her own; however, it was Raj's companionship that I had grown to enjoy. Her interests and experiences were far-flung, and without much coaxing I became her willing student. I was treated to lessons on the differences among the Urdu, Hindi, and Telugu languages as those were the most popularly spoken in Raj's locale in India. Sometimes maps would appear, and I'd be given a primer on the Mogul invasion and how present day India had been shaped. We were clearly becoming the best of friends – comfortable in our own skins, we frequently sat quietly after lunch and just read, very aware the other was nearby.

In the winter months, we shared morning coffee – nothing fancy, instant coffee prepared from an Erlenmeyer flask heated over a lab burner. We chatted about our respective research and what we planned for the day. In Raj's case she was finishing up the last of her *Schizophyllum* genetic crosses and would soon be drafting her dissertation. She targeted May, 1970, to finish her defense and to return to India. As for me, I was in the throes of getting my pigmy mice to breed during winter months; I needed dozens of the little critters for my depressed metabolism experiments. My dilemma was simple: no animals = no thesis.

One snowy morning, Raj came to the lab in tears. Without taking off her corduroy coat and scarf, she sat at my desk, head bent over, and loudly sobbed. My instinct told me to leave her alone, as I had the impression she had lost someone near and dear to her. Heating up the Erlenmeyer to make coffee, I tried not to disturb her. In a moment or two Raj regained her composure, and, through a tearfully blown nose she uttered: "It's so cold, so bloody cold!" During the time it took me to drive the wind-swept, snow-covered streets that morning, Raj had walked more than a mile from her apartment to campus. Taking her snow-encrusted boots off to warm her feet, Raj gratefully accepted a mug of hot coffee. Relieved that she had not lost anyone back home, I sat with her to commiserate on the brutalities of Buffalo winters. While brief, this heartfelt episode reinforced a growing bond between us.

As signs of spring appeared, both of us were making progress on our respective dissertations studies. In fact it reached a point when both of us needed to document segments of lab results with photomicrographs. Raj needed a record of her mutant strains of *Schizophyllum* for her thesis, and I needed pictures for a manuscript I was preparing for publication. Beating bushes with a single stick, we decided to join forces and work the darkroom together. Like an assembly line, I started to run negatives through the enlarger, and subsequently handed the exposed prints to Raj, who in turn began feeding the prints into an automated developer. Presto! Sharing the work, we thought we'd be able to process the hundreds of prints we needed in a jiffy. First print was done quickly – click, click, click. The paper hummed through the developer, appearing out the back as a finished print. "Raj, this is great, we should be finished in no time!"

However, things started to unravel, figuratively and literally. Shortly into our operation, Raj called out in an insistent tone: "Mike… Mike…Mike…" I lamely responded: "What? What's the matter?" In response, I heard something to the effect that, "My sari is caught, I can't stop it!" Perplexed, I saw that Raj's sari was slowly disappearing within the rollers of the developer. Seeing Raj turning around as her sari became unwrapped, I hit the OFF switch. "Why didn't I do that?" exclaimed Raj, who was nearly down to her petticoat. With the crisis over, we had a good laugh extricating a yard of sari from the hungry developer. Now dripping wet from the developing solution, gallantly, I offered Raj my lab coat. We left the darkroom to go to the lab sink so Raj could rinse out her sari. Giggling side-by-side, I gave Raj a fond smack on her bottom, the effect of which brought us into an immediate embrace followed by a warm kiss. From that moment, my hormonal chemistry would never be the same.

In April, anti-war activity reached fever pitch at UB and campuses around the country. Highlighting open rebellion, students were gunned down by the Ohio National Guard at Kent State University. At UB, demonstrations were rampant, graffiti desecrated buildings, and stones were thrown through windows (including one room where Raj was attending a lecture). On the afternoon of the Kent State killings, I was working in the third floor electron microscope room. Afterwards, I took the elevator to my basement lab; however, my trip down was accompanied by an eerie silence – not a soul could be seen or heard. Wondering what was going on. I made a few calls within the department, but no one answered. Apprehensively, I next called my dad whose dental office was located across the street from the campus. "Mike, where are you?" asked Dad who was obviously excited. He said a nearby bank had been attacked by students and all hell had broken loose - "Mike, I'd get out of there if I were you. Go home". I quickly told him "I'm on my way!" and hung up the phone.

Seeing no one on campus, I drove past the graffiti-festooned Student Union, on my way to the usually busy Main Street entrance. Rather than make a right turn toward the bank, I made a left turn to reach my usual Englewood Avenue cut-off. As the only car on the road, I spotted a smoke-filled barricade a couple of hundred yards ahead with police, students, and by-standers everywhere. With my pulse racing, I safely reached home. The campus was closed for a week to allow a cooling off period. Subsequently, for safety's sake, I drove to campus each morning with Greg, who was in his second year of Dental School. For the rest of the month, the campus shared a quasi calm; in turn, many faculty devoted their classes to open discussions of the war and avenues of dissension.

Fortunately, an influx of balmy spring weather caused a moratorium on all things political (and work-related). Sharing a dose of spring fever, Raj and I went for a drive. Our first stop was at my home in Kenmore to say hi to my mother, who up until now had not met Raj. After a brief but warm introduction, I went into the other end of the house and shouted: "Mom, Raj would like to go to the john!" In response, Mom told Raj: "See what happens after all those years of education." Quite pleased, Raj had a chance to see my home and especially to meet my mother. Afterwards we went to Friendly's for ice cream, followed by a visit to the picturesque grounds of the suburban Brookfield Country Club. It was a magnificent day to greet the onset of spring, especially with someone as lovely as Raj to share it with – our first public date!

In the month before Raj was to leave for India, I was terribly conflicted. On the one hand, I was happy for her and for all the expectations she had for her return to her loved ones back home, and yet I had grown increasingly fond of her. One morning I was at a gas station situated across the street from UB, and lo and behold I spotted Raj walking fifty yards in front of me. Rather than tooting my horn to get her attention, I simply stared at her parading in the morning sunshine. Her walk was regal. She was a beautiful sight. Like a moth drawn to a flame, I was not sure what to say or do.

In addition to her dissertation preparations, Raj was consumed with the wedding preparations of Wei-Li. Donned in a beautiful sari, Raj attended to everyone's needs, including yours truly. A little

later, Raj borrowed Saras's car and made a surprise visit to a party
at my home in honor of Karen who just graduated from Niagara
University. Raj later confessed she wore an old pair of shoes under
her sari, otherwise she couldn't have driven wearing her favorite pair
of sandals. As time continued to wind down, we exchanged token
gifts to each other. Raj gave me a small stained glass figurine of a bird
and a collection of Eliot Porter's photographs. In turn, I gave Raj a
whimsical set of earrings made up of little apples where a bite had
been removed. I'd like to think they were symbolic of me taking a bite
from the forbidden fruit.

When it became time for Raj to receive her PhD, I decided not
to go to the commencement exercise which was going to be held
outdoors at the football stadium. Word was out that there might be
anti-war demonstrations and likely not a good venue for a gimpy soul
like me to be present. However, I previewed Raj's cap and gown the
previous day when I took several pictures of her to take home with
her. Posing near a loading ramp area, surrounded by lilacs in bloom,
Raj radiated a smile to die for.

**Toasting Raj After Completing Her PhD)**

In mid-June, we saw each other for the last time in her lab. Just
the two of us, we quietly shared Raj's last few hours in Buffalo. On

her desk, piled high with saris, books, etc, Raj was preparing to give away just about everything she had accumulated in the US. The only exception was a reel to reel tape-recorder which she was going to lug to India. Over the years, the recorder had been a quality source of classical music for Raj. After I found out that Raj had little money for her journey, I dug into my wallet and gave her what I had – seventy dollars. I wished it were seventy thousand!

When I told Raj that I wouldn't be coming to the airport to see her off, I mumbled about having some things to do; the truth, however, was I going to miss her terribly. Not sure what my emotions would be, I didn't want my tearful good-bye to detract from the airport farewells of her dear friends, Phil and Eleanor Miles, Saras, and several others who have known Raj much longer than me. Ironically, Raj's send-off from Buffalo was a far cry from her arrival five years earlier at the desolate train station in the middle of the night. With a heavy heart, choking back tears, we bid each other adieu with an embrace and a warm kiss. "Take care of yourself, maybe we'll see each other again" was our duel refrain. "Yes, write when you can. I want to hear from you too" followed our good-byes. Teary-eyed I left her to finish packing and caught the elevator to my basement lab. Standing in front of my desk alone, I began to ponder my future without my charming Indian. I hated what I felt inside.

After a sandwich at home with Mom, I drove to Brookfield. Subdued, thinking of the void left by Raj, I fiddled with the car radio and came upon Beethoven's *Ode to Joy*. In the midst of the rousing music, I spotted Raj's jet climbing toward New York City, the first leg on her journey back home. The gravity of the moment was not lost on me – how I missed her so. Later that night while watching Johnny Carson on the kitchen TV, Karen came by and joined me. I told her how much I missed Raj, and I revealed to someone for the very first time that someday I'd like to marry her. Like pieces of a jigsaw puzzle all coming together, it was the first time I realized our friendship had grown to such a critical mass. I had a bite from the apple, and I liked it very much. Rajmohni, Charmer of the King!

# Chapter 10

# Letters from India

I wanted Raj to hear from me as soon as possible about my feelings for her. However, I knew there would be significant delay as Raj was breaking her journey in London to stay with Sylvia, who was now a Postdoc at Imperial College. Yet, I quickly fired off a letter to Hyderabad, not knowing when she might read it, nor when I might hear a reply. I wrote how much Raj had meant to me, her friendship, and how happy I was for her to finally be home. I also indicated in so many words that I had fallen in love with her, and that maybe in the future we might make a 'team together.' In only a few days I got a postcard and a short letter from Raj in London detailing her comings and goings. Carrying her letter in my shirt pocket made me feel close to her. I also received a package containing an elegant and pricey Pringle cardigan with a matching shirt. I was ecstatic with the sentiment, though I knew full well Raj blew the cash I gave her for her journey. Seeing how happy I was to get the gifts, Mom knew that something was brewing between us. For the next several days, I anxiously awaited mail from India. Did she get my letter? Was the Pringle an omen for our future? Would she reciprocate in kind my deep feelings for her I had expressed in my earlier letter?

I was not disappointed! In mid-July I received a letter from Raj which read: "Michael, I love you – Your letter made me very, very happy. I nearly took the chance of phoning you from N.Y.C. and even had the change to pay but I was sure you were out. Also I thought if you said "Don't Go" I would have stayed the whole summer. I gave you a deadline til my commencement and as you did not want to come to the party I felt I was mistaken and you did not care for me that much. Anyway it's no use talking about the past. You are the <u>most</u> wonderful person I know (and although you are miserable sometimes!) I would like to someday "make a team with you"…I tried to lean one of your photos but without a support it slips. Soon as I get a little money I'll frame it. <u>Please</u> don't apologize for being emotional. I am glad you wrote that letter. What we have between us is beautiful and NO one can take that away. Much love, Raj" Suffice to say, I was smitten all over again, just like the day I met Raj in the elevator three years earlier. The over whelming power of a simple letter! Trying to content myself with the delay of sending a letter to India and not getting a response for at least ten days, I was soon awash with return letters from Hyderabad.

One day I happened to spot an advertisement for an up-coming Indian movie called *Aradhana* which, according to the poster was the previous year's best picture in India. Filled as I was with "Rajmohini Fever", and as the film would be shown on campus, I decided to go. After I situated myself at the rear of a large Med School classroom, I was bemused as numerous Indian families one by one took their seats. Once the lights were dimmed, I was greatly entertained for the next three plus hours. The movie was a sure-fire tear jerker where the heroine raised an illegitimate son who was fathered by an Indian air force pilot later killed in the Indo-China conflict. Furthermore, the heroine was ostracized from her community, and only at the end was her dignity rescued by her now grown up son, who had become quite successful and prominent. As mother and son reunited there was not a dry eye in the room. Interspersed, there were colorful dances and loud songs to raise all spirits; yet the angst throughout the film was indeed palpable. It was great matinee material for a diehard film buff like myself. During the two intermissions, an array of exotic sweets and curry puffs were distributed to the crowd contributing to the noisy hubbub in the room. Throughout, I kept thinking of Raj – where she was and what she was doing. I was still gnawing on that apple and enjoying it more and more each time.

As summer wore on, I needed to hear Raj's voice again. Prior to satellite or internet linkages, it was a precarious process to place an international call. While my initial attempts were utter failures, I finally did get through one day. The call booked in advance with an overseas operator located in White Plains told me to hold while she attempted to call Hyderabad. Shortly, a cheerful operator in England came on the line made possible by the transatlantic cable. With the two operators discussing the best route to connect, the Englishman decided to go through Bombay. "Haven't had much success as late but let's give it a go!" Soon I heard some weird rings abruptly stopped by an excited voice who told the English chap: "Can't make the call, lines down!" Not to be deterred the Englishman begged, cajoled, and finally demanded that the call be placed. "We are all booked up. We have to get these calls through!" Just when I thought the tide may have turned, the Bombay operator quickly dealt with the dilemma and simply hung up! We in Buffalo, White Plains, and England were left with only a hum to entertain us. "Bloody hell" shrieked the Englishman who then tried to go Australia followed by Madras. He added, "In spite of the floods we've been able to get some calls through." So it went – for a love-sick bloke in the US and three phone operators who were simultaneously on the line, each attempting to bridge East and West.

Once we made the connection, the fun really started. "Hello! Can you hear me? It's Mike." Fortunately, Raj was waiting for the call, otherwise I would have had to go through domestic intermediates who neither understood me, nor I them. Raj came on the line, but we could barely hear each other, with a hollow echo ricocheting half way across the world. To circumvent this, I raised my voice as did Raj, and for the next 10 minutes or so we had to be content with: "I'm okay, how are you?", only to be answered by, "I'm okay, can you hear me?" "No I can barely hear you, what did you say?" came the reply which was followed by "I'm okay, what did you say?" Just when we thought we were breaking into a thread of a conversation, a loud train went by Raj's house drowning out both of us. After our phone misadventure, it became clear letters were the only way to go; letters would be our exclusive vehicle of expressions of unabashed love, as well as diary-like accounts of our comings and goings.

Everyone in the family except Dad knew about my true affection for Raj. They were supportive, if not bemused, of my romantic preoccupation. Breaking the news to dad required special handling; I needed the right time and circumstances. My opportunity came on November, 1970, at a restaurant in Baltimore when I accompanied the Buffalo Bills to play the Colts. Because Dad was the team dentist and a friend of the administration, I was able to make a few road trips with the team, and rub shoulders with the hometown icons. On this trip, however, I had another agenda – I was going not to see the legendary Johnny Unitas but to have a heart-to-heart with dear old Dad. After we arrived, we joined the Bills' brass and media types for dinner at the famous Chesapeake Restaurant. After the first round of drinks and cold crab appetizers, I began to think that this might be the right time to broach THE subject. Amidst the animated table conversations, I mentioned to Dad that I had been writing to a class-mate who had returned home to India. The timing was perfect. There was just enough noise in the room to keep our conversation between us and enough food and beverage to keep Dad's interest. I had gotten his ear, and I ran with it through the hot crab plate and clear into dessert. While we only tied the game 17-17, for me the trip was a win. All I needed now was Raj.


Through 1970 and into 1971, Raj and I continued to write, but as time wore on it became apparent that she needed to extend her stay in India. Our letters became less and less frequent, and I could sense the hand-writing on the wall. The other shoe did fall when I got a letter in July, 1971: Raj spelled out why she needed to stay at her university job for at least another year, maybe two. Her parents' pensions were lost within a sea of Indian bureaucratic red tape, and Raj had become the *de facto* bread-earner of the Sebastian household. While I was extremely disappointed and saddened at the time, I later came to understand Raj's excruciating predicament - her deep sense of responsibility to her family and how difficult it was to get things done in India. The passage of more time put a heavy burden on both of us. Could we ever recapture the intense feelings we both had earlier? These thoughts continued to consume both of us as we plowed through 1971 and 1972. Raj took care of her home-front while I tried to coax data from my pigmy mice in Buffalo and subsequently from my dystrophic chickens in Syracuse.

As the lake snows continued to whiten Syracuse, our letter exchange accelerated. Each letter was filled with a mixture of hope, plans, and more hope and plans. May, 1973, was targeted for our long-awaited reunion at JFK. Interspersed were concerns over the type of visa to apply for, who would act as a sponsor, and what job might be available to Raj. Our thinking was so frenetic that my letters often were signed off with: "I can hardly believe that what we've wanted for more than two years is within our grasp"; while Raj often ended with: "Your letter made me feel happy and loved and that is a wonderful feeling. I hope I can make you feel loved and wanted too." We both began to think that it was just the other day that we had last seen each other and at times it seemed so very long ago. Filled with emotions, we were constantly dissecting what was fiction and what was real. In only five months we would know for sure.


It was a bittersweet time for Raj. While she enjoyed a slew of friends and family during the holiday time, things would be much different next year when she would be away from home. In addition, she was leaving the financial security of her Osmania post, a position not easily acquired. Leaving India involved severing not only familial ties but financial security as well. On the visa front, we opted for K status, and I would sponsor her application. All of these items required a host of paperwork. Moreover, for Raj to get a passport and air tickets, she needed security clearance from Osmania. On that front, the red tape was grinding slowly.


Against this backdrop, political turmoil embroiled Hyderabad's State of Andhra Pradesh. Separatists known as the Andhras were angry at Prime Minister Indira Ghandi's police action in the State causing pockets of violence and strikes against natives known as the Telangana. No one was immune from the conflict, not even Raj who had to adjust her lecture and exam schedules because of the student rebellion. As if this weren't enough, water shortages and food costs were on the rise everywhere. It was not easy for a comfortable Westerner like me to fully comprehend what Raj was experiencing.

In the meantime, I made attempts to line up a Catholic priest to marry us. Although Raj's affiliation was with the Church of England, she readily agreed to a Catholic nuptial. After I failed in my initial efforts with Niagara University President, Father Ken Slattery, and with my former classmate, Lew Maynard, I contacted my own parish at Saint John the Baptist, and. successfully recruited the Assistant Pastor, Father Donald Trautman. He was an enthusiastic and earnest soul, and quickly booked us for a June 9th wedding. Rather than use the large main church, Trautman arranged for us to be married in an adjacent chapel. Initially constructed of logs in 1836 under the supervision of Father John Neumann, the chapel was intended to serve the pastoral needs of Catholics living in the rural region of Buffalo known as "North Bush." Father Neumann was later assigned to Philadelphia, where he became Bishop. Only recently, he was canonized as a saint. Not a bad location for us to start married life! When I discussed the wedding plans with my parents, they were eager to have the reception at home – the menu and guest list would be sorted out after Raj arrived in May. Two venues down, St. John's and 96 Doncaster, and one more to go – JFK.

With winter easing its grip on the Syracuse area, Raj and I were engaged in a bit of a contentious debate. My suggestion that we live together in Syracuse prior to the wedding didn't go over too well. I planned to meet Raj at JFK, stay with Karen in Long Island, and afterwards drive to Massachusetts and visit with Greg. In this way, I felt Raj could acclimatize to the arduous time change, and at the same time, get to meet the family. Later, we would drive to Syracuse and sort out our marriage plans and, importantly, sort out each other after our three year hiatus. Raj, however, interpreted my plan as a 'trial period,' and she was quite upset. Sensing I struck a nerve, I backed off and agreed that staying with Saras in Buffalo would be quite okay. Should things not work out between us, Raj entertained a contingency plan to return to India sometime in the summer. As the JFK touchdown neared, the matter was unresolved. Raj stated it best: "Let's not write anything too weighty."

Snapshots from some of Raj's other letters included her resignation from her voluntary work at St. George's Church, where she was becoming a rather feisty member of the lay committee. Were we to be married in India, St. George's would have been its venue. Another letter described the purchase of a crème colored wedding sari with a red, embroidered border; she reminded me that she wouldn't look like the "fruit salad" I had imagined after seeing a *National Geographic* photo showing a garishly clad Andhra bride. Traditional white is worn by Indian widows as a sign of mourning, hence, Raj avoided white for her wedding sari. Raj's mother's unresolved pension popped up in nearly every letter, in spite of numerous visits to the pension office. Financial support for her parents and household was a major concern after she left. Moreover, Raj's Aunt Elsie had cataract surgery which necessitated Raj making several medical trips, with each one interwoven with Raj's lecture schedule. Multi-tasking at its very best!

As time approached for Raj's trip to the American Consulate in Madras to get her visa, she obtained painful immunizations against smallpox, cholera and typhoid. In addition, Raj had a chest x-ray, her urine scrutinized, and her arm again "excavated" for a blood sample. Along with her medical records, police clearance, and no objection from the university, Raj had to swear to the US government that she was not a prostitute, communist, anarchist, drug user or dealer, and not a beggar. I was so glad Uncle Sam was looking out for my best interests.

Interspersed among Raj's letters were moments of pleasure. For example, she went to a Poetry Society meeting with fellow Fullbright Scholar, Isaac Sequira who spoke about Robert Frost. Frost became famous in India when it was later known that Jawaharlal Nehru left scribbled on a pad next to his death bed: "The woods are lovely, dark and deep, and I have promises to keep, And miles to go before I sleep." Through her parents Jaya and Olivia, Raj was reared in an atmosphere of prose and poetry. At age ten, Raj recited *The Cataract of Lodore* by Robert Southey at one of the Society gatherings. The alliterative poem was a good example of the Lake District poets, a specialty of Jaya, a Professor of English at Osmania University. While trained as a biologist, it was clear that Raj had a wealth of literary knowledge. Being able to bridge the "*Two Cultures*," C.P. Snow would have been very proud of her. While I enjoyed reading, I certainly didn't have

Raj's breadth. At the time my pleasure reading included popular works such as Hailey's *Airport*, Puzo's *The Godfather*, and Dickey's *Deliverance*. Notably, however, there was one book which captured my imagination – John Kenneth Galbraith's *Ambassador's Journal*. Through Galbraith's first-hand insight and witticisms while US Ambassador to India, I came to appreciate so much more about India and its people, history, and culture.

Trying to stretch my research at SU, I set in motion a collaborative project Doug Gersten, who was a fellow UB grad student, and now working as a postdoc at the University of Rochester. Talking to Doug, we came up with an idea of seeing whether a membrane abnormality might be a root cause of the muscular dystrophy. Prior to the discovery of the dystrophy gene in the 1980's, reigning hypotheses of the disorder included the notion that the genetic error was expressed in a component within the muscle itself. To tackle the problem, we used an electrical separation technique and found abnormalities in the red blood cell membranes from Duchenne patients, a neuropathologic strain of mice, as well as from my brood of dystrophic chickens. The collaborative study was submitted and accepted for publication in the reputable *Archives of Neurology*. The work reinforced the idea that dystrophy is indeed expressed in tissues other than muscle, and opened the door for a potential diagnostic test. Not a bad outcome for my round-trips to Rochester and back!

Closer to SU, I set the wheels in motion to carry on research with neurologists affiliated with the local Muscular Dystrophy Clinic. After phone calls and face-to-face meetings, a project was hatched to set up muscle cultures from biopsies obtained from Duchenne patients; in effect, we would be researching questions identical to our on-going chicken culture experiments. Because this work involved obtaining muscle from an aborted fetus, approval would be needed from the SU Human Experimentation Committee.

While the proposed work appeared straight-forward, using aborted tissues conflicted with my Catholic conscience. I aired my misgivings with both Father Slattery and Raj. Slattery's appealing opinion was to go ahead since the tissues would only go to waste if not used, and the proposed work would only enhance society's understanding of a tragic disease. In a similar way, Raj was all for the work. While she didn't condone the practice for herself, from her experiences Raj saw the positive role abortion played in over-populated countries such as India.

After we got the okay from the SU Review Committee to proceed, we were eagerly expecting fetal muscle tissue from our clinical colleagues. After I recruited three undergraduates to assist me in setting-up the cultures, we encountered one false start after another. Like an aborted NASA launch where weather windows kept shifting, we experienced one delay after another. Finally in the end, we had to call the project off. For several days in succession, I was on the phone with a rotation of neurology residents who had little or no knowledge of what we were trying to accomplish. It finally reached the stage when I had to tell my patient cadre of students to go home. Frustrating as the experience was, I learned a lesson of the nature of biomedical research where variables are involved beyond one's control. I got a taste of one of "Murphy's Laws."

Sandwiched in between the Rochester red cell and myoblast clinic studies, I initiated an investigation of blood CPK enzyme which could be used as a marker of muscle damage such as might be expected in our dystrophic chickens. In my study, I inherited a Syracuse football player who had designs to go to medical school. On our first day together, we gathered our supplies and went to the animal unit to draw blood from our chickens. Just as I broke the skin with the needle, the bird squawked loudly, which sent my six foot six assistant through the ceiling! With feathers flying everywhere, we got the bird back to its cage with its full quotient of blood. While I calmed my hyperventilating footballer, the big fellow explained how he grew up on a rural Pennsylvania farm and was routinely terrorized by the indigenous barnyard fowl. Deciding to give this project a rest for now, I outlined a library project for my gridiron assistant; in this way, I would be momentarily safe from another one of Murphy's Laws.

After the human culture and CPK studies fell through, I decided to drive into the country to clear my head. On a bright, cold Sunday afternoon after attending Mass, I went southeast into the rolling hills which surround Syracuse. Passing small towns alive with winter activities, I took a small road which meandered uphill to an area where I could see miles in all directions. Under blinding sunshine, a large expanse of Central New York was at my feet. I couldn't wait to return to the apartment and describe the remarkable sight to Raj. I liked this particular vista so much that I returned once with my sister Steph, and again with my cousin Maureen Muldoon. Steph came to Syracuse to visit the sister of a dental hygienist who was working with dad, and Maureen flew in from Kingston, Ontario, where she was currently a medical ethics student at Queen's University. Each visit was a pleasant relief of the tedium and loneliness I felt at the time from my current research efforts.

My most frequent visitor was Sam Johnson, who was a UB Dental classmate of Greg's and was currently an anesthesiology resident at Upstate Medical Center. In addition to his pleasant and engaging demeanor, Sam was an avid fisherman. After dinner one evening, Sam inspected my fishing gear, which was adapted to trolling the deep waters of Lake Erie. He couldn't believe my heavy gauge rod, reel, line and lures. As he was a light-weight enthusiast, Sam recommended that we go to a tackle shop and he get me fixed up with some "proper" equipment. No sooner had we entered the door than I had a Zebco ultra-light combination in my hands. Immediately, I was hooked. From that moment on, I became a life-long user of ultra-light equipment, and like Sam, I began to enjoy the sensitive side to fishing. Not only was light tackle conducive to fishing in the local waters, it was easier on my tender muscles. It was a win-win situation.

My other frequent visitor was Pete Kuhn, who was a military cop at the local US Air Force base. I got to know Pete through patients of my dad's, and because we both had a penchant for loud, up-beat music, he joined me one evening to a local stereo shop. After tying up the clerk's time for an hour, I proclaimed: "I'll take that Pioneer receiver and those two Marantz speakers." Pete told me the clerk nearly fell on the floor, he was so used to people listening to the demos and never buying anything. Raj was overjoyed with my purchase; she had a love affair with good music, most of which we had in common. In addition to classics, we shared a fondness for the likes of Peter, Paul and Mary and their *I'm Leaving on a Jet Plane,* as well as tunes by the seductive Judy Collins. With Judy serenading in the background, my writing to India very much became a sensuous exercise.

Now that Raj was only a short time away from cutting the cord, I was getting to know much more about her close circle of friends and family. In addition to her fathomless love and respect for her parents, and her sparring partner, Aunt Elsie, Raj had immense fondness for several relatives and friends. Notable examples included her cousin Roy, who worked for an agricultural supply company which took him to many rural areas. Roy's travels allowed him to dip into his favorite pastimes of hunting, fishing, birding and wildlife photography. Then there was Raj's soul mate – Renulka Naidu. As a measure of her intellectual appeal for Raj, 'Renu' had completed the vigorous Cambridge tripost in the UK, and afterward she nearly became a research scholar with Francis Crick of *The Double-Helix* fame. As duty called, however, she returned to India to marry a man chosen by her mother, P.M. Naidu. Dr. Naidu was an eminent and strong-willed OB/GYN physician who broke the early mold for women in India who were excluded from medicine as a career option. During a recent visit from Madras, Renu came to see Raj to get caught up on all the news. Undoubtedly Renu would be an unflinching ally when it came time for Raj to submit her visa papers to the U.S. Consulate located in Madras.

Trained as an engineer and who ran his own water drilling business, Fiaz Quader frequently came by B4F4 to play chess with Raj's dad, and to entertain the Sebastian household with his never-ending yarns and wit. Like cousin Roy, Fiaz was fond of hunting and fishing, and over the years, the Sebastians became his second family. There also was the "Auntie Mame" of Hyderabad – Marie Charles. Energetic and fearless, Marie was the "go to" person if something needed to be done or someone contacted. While a school teacher by profession,

Marie seemed to know just about everyone in Hyderabad; her gift of gab and guile was legendary. During the time of India's Independence in 1947, Marie's dad served Nehru's fledgling government as a staff photographer. Through him Marie began to learn at a young age where all the bodies were buried in India's coming of age after Independence. It was Marie who arranged Raj's 'dhoolan' ceremony, where a bride-to-be was decorated on her face, hands and feet with henna by female friends and relatives. It seemed every letter contained one exploit or another of Raj's circle of friendships.

One particular letter had me in tears. Raj had read up on muscular dystrophy and wrote that the disease would not be in our way. Her words of "I love you..." resonated within me to the core, as did her constant encouragement and concern for my welfare. "Don't worry, we'll sort things out" made my heart race with anticipation. With each passing day, I became more consumed if possible with her and our scheduled meeting in May.

A month before her flight to the US, Raj was consumed with farewell dinners, teas, and gifts from relatives, friends, and colleagues. On the work side, Raj was also conducting practical exams for her anatomy class, as well as final exams to be given in June. Even though she would not be at Osmania University in June, Raj's plans were known by her close colleagues who offered support whenever they could. With demands of her time coming from all quarters, Raj exclaimed in one letter: "I hope to survive...I need you to fuss over me in New York City!" Indeed that was my plan. In April, I made plans with Western Union to deliver a dozen roses to Raj in India. In ensuing letters, I had hinted that a surprise would be coming soon; however, a couple of weeks later I was informed that the flowers could not be sent because of the volatility of the dollar/rupee exchange rate. In the end, I would have to save the gesture for our JFK meeting.

# Chapter 11

# Three Roses

Like a child anxiously waiting for Christmas, the day was near at hand for me to leave for New York. With my laundry in tow I went home in late April, and expressed my travel concerns with my parents. As I had hoped, Dad suggested that he and Mom drive together to Syracuse on May 4; the next day Mom and I would head off to Long Island to stay with Karen. I felt very relieved knowing that my strongest ally would be accompanying me. During the last days of April, notes from Raj became infrequent; since we agreed to not press the issue of living together, we kept our latest correspondence as optimistic as possible. Raj's last message however dotted the I and crossed the T – indicating in no uncertain terms that we were finally going to make a 'team' together. Punctuating her last letter she scrolled boldly – "Air India #115 arriving at 3:35 PM May 6 at JFK. Be there!" I had to pinch myself when I read details of her arrival – she was actually coming! What remained for us to ponder was: "What on earth are we like now that three years have passed?"

After my folks arrived in Syracuse we headed to a theater to see the newly-released *Poseidon Adventure*; followed by a quiet dinner at a nearby restaurant – nothing fancy but a relaxed interlude where each of us could be lost in thought. After Dad headed home, mom and me had a few quiet exchanges and an early night. Morning came quickly, and soon Mom and I were navigating the streets out of Syracuse. On route we stopped at a doughnut shop for take-out. Up until now I had been as quiet as a dormouse – completely lost in thought. Coming back to the car with a tray of coffee and doughnuts, Mom broke the ice (or I should say shattered the ice) – "Mike, I know you're concerned about Raj and all, but remember she is a wonderful person, and this is going to be the happiest moment of your life!" Her words proved to be a watershed, an inspirational timely admonition. I was slapped back into reality! Yes you idiot, this is what you have been looking forward to for the past three years! Wake up! You are finally on your way to MEET her!

Leaving the doughnut shop parking lot, the drive to New York became invigorating, effortless and pleasant. We quickly got on Interstate 81 South and headed for Pennsylvania, and with a tour of the southern reaches of the Catskills, we took the Tappan Zee Bridge over the Hudson River, and thereafter shortly met up with the meandering Hutchinson River Parkway. Surviving the heavily trafficked Interstate 95 South, we traversed the Whitestone Bridge and caught the Cross Island Expressway to Sunrise Boulevard. We exited at Long Beach Road which took us to Karen's duplex only a block from the Atlantic Ocean. Leg number one accomplished!

On the morning of May sixth, I called Air India and confirmed Raj's flight status. While she was crossing the Atlantic from London's Heathrow at over thirty thousand feet, I had one important item to accomplish – the purchase of a dozen red roses, which would frame three yellow ones, each one signifying a year we had been apart. With flowers in hand, we arrived at JFK to begin my long awaited vigil. While time seemed to stand still, the colorful, noisy chaos within the International Arrivals terminal was exhilarating. Each arriving jumbo jet disembarked hundreds of passengers later to mingle with awaiting friends causing the reception and luggage hallways to quickly fill up. Oh how I wanted Raj to be among them.

In her last letter, Raj told me there would be a delay after landing before I would see her – she needed to collect her luggage among the hordes and eventually to suffer inspections by the US Customs and Immigration Services. Just when I thought I had counted over a thousand Indian passengers, along came Raj walking resolutely down the hallway: decked in a colorful printed sari and open-toed sandals, Raj was glued to a luggage cart being pushed by an attendant. I tried to shout above the clamor, "Raj, Raj..." but to no avail. After several attempts, Karen and Bob finally got Raj's attention, and our reunion commenced. Beaming yet weary, Raj greeted each one of us. When my turn came, I presented her with my bouquet. In the midst of our joyous gathering, Raj kept an eagle's eye on her luggage which contained the sum total of all her earthly belongings. With the luggage cart safely in our hands, we all moved outside for pictures. Posing with smiles a mile wide, and three yellow roses presented *and* accepted at JFK, Raj and I exhaled almost in unison – what a day! Leg number two accomplished!

After a sleepless night and breakfast, we left for Massachusetts to stay with Greg and Joann. With Raj now in the passenger seat and Mom in back, I wanted to ask Raj so many delicate questions, but in the end, I kept to safe topics of how her flight went, how she felt, her send-off back home, etc. With my AAA map to guide us out of NYC, and through Connecticut, we eventually arrived at the sprawling Fort Devins Army base in Massachusetts; With directions given to us at the gate, we found Greg's one floor ranch. Leg three of the journey now accomplished.

With time to unwind from her long trip and to get her biological clock in order, Raj had a chance to get to know my family more intimately. Dad and my sisters, Steph and Pat, arrived the next day making for a rather packed house; however, I didn't need to worry as the TV was showing the Boston Bruins playing the Montreal Canadians for the Stanley Cup, and the game kept my family hostage for the evening. At one point in a break in the action, Greg, in his inimitable way, paused to ask Raj who was wearing a sari, "Do you have legs under that?" And so it went, East meeting West, Hudecki-style.

Early the next morning, I was awoken by Greg's St. Bernard, who somehow managed to get nearly on top of me. Deciding not to get crushed, and my decision to arise early was an easy one. After bacon and eggs were provided by dad for everyone (whether they were wanted or not), on impulse Dad subsequently decided to trim Greg's outside shrubbery. Before dad trimmed everything to the bone, Greg and Joann rescued the day and took Dad and Mom to the base's golf course for a few holes. Under sunny bright skies, Raj and I also drove to the park-like course, in search for a niche to be finally alone. Nestled among the pine trees, we found a bench to quietly chat about our near future together. Without discussing the subject in so many words, we both knew we were going to Syracuse *together*, and not push on to Buffalo so Raj could stay with Saras. Sitting next to Raj, I lit up every time I cast my eyes upon her – she was here, right next to me! From the moment we first saw each other within the bowels of the JFK terminal, we knew where we were headed, and we liked it very much.

The next day Mom and Dad along with Steph and Pat, headed back to Buffalo, leaving Greg and me to find a place to fish, and Joann and Raj unfettered to get to know each other. The following morning Raj went with Joann to see her second son Gregory Junior, who was confined to a Boston hospital. Most babies die early from Trisomy 18, but the little fellow somehow hung on causing tremendous heartache for his parents.

Later, after the visit to the hospital, Raj and I went sight-seeing. Our excursion took us to the historic Concord and Lexington areas, now heavily populated, leaving how things might have been two hundred years ago to the imagination. Not far away, we went by the ancestral homes of Louisa May Alcott of *Little Women* fame and poet Ralph Waldo Emerson. Moreover, we were able to locate Henry Thoreau's often-written about Walden Pond. Getting to the pond was a little tricky, as we had to inch our way through a dense, tree-lined mud lane. Upon arrival, we were greeted by some crusty locals who were fishing from shore. Raj and I got out of the car and enjoyed firsthand the serenity of the Pond. One could almost picture Thoreau mediating along its banks. During my reverie, I couldn't help staring at prominent 'No Fishing' signs tacked unceremoniously to the nearby trees. When I brought the signs to the attention of the locals who were fishing quietly and contently, they just laughed and said "So?" Thoreau would have been proud of these native sons.

Before we knew it, Raj and I were back on the road together; alone on our way to Syracuse! As we cruised along the Mass Turnpike on past Albany, the two of us chatted away; it seemed like old times again. The formalities of our earlier exchanges since her arrival softened considerably, if not entirely. By the time we reached the Syracuse exit, we had a rough draft of the guest list, who would be maid of honor and best man, and some idea about when we needed to get to Buffalo to sort out the particulars of the reception. We were going to make a "team" together after all!

It didn't take us very long to settle in our apartment together. The first item was to acquire a queen size bed to replace the twins which Raj joined together our first night. An auspicious beginning to say the least. Raj loved the new stereo system and eagerly played music we both enjoyed. Eating together after three years was foreign territory as we had very little idea of what we each ate. I certainly had no clue of her routine back home with morning chappatis, pickle, etc. I had much to learn. In a day or so, I introduced Raj to my colleagues at SU. On the way to the campus, we passed an Indian walking along the road. As I began to slow down figuring that Raj would want to say hello to a fellow Indian, she adamantly had me continue driving. It was then and there that I learned that there was a huge spectrum of backgrounds which constituted Indians studying or living in the US. Naively, I had lumped all Indians together which was a mistake, but a correctable one. Leg number four accomplished in rousing fashion.

Since we only had a month before the wedding, we needed to go to Buffalo and sort out several details – blood tests, meet Father Trautman, wedding cake, etc. During a whirlwind weekend, we stayed at my parents' home as our base of operations. Not incidentally, one evening as Raj and I were about to see Saras, my dad beckoned Raj to come into his lair, the den. As they chatted together, I got more and more uncomfortable as Dad began pressing his concerns: "What do your parents do? Some people come to this country only to get married!" Ouch, where was he going with this? If things got too heavy, I was ready to bolt. I should have had more confidence in Raj and she checked and counter-checked Dad at every turn. "My parents are teachers, my dad had a stroke and couldn't travel, I plan to work here and earn, your son will have a permanent dowry, a working wife." So it went, at every turn Dad was fed straight talk, which he delighted in. Before we knew it, Dad announced that he would erect a large tent in the backyard so the reception could be held here at home – complete with food and beverages catered by Brookfield Country Club. Moreover, Dad fired off the names of people who should (and should not) be invited, who the photographer would be, etc. As we left to see Saras, I said "What the hell did you say to Dad? It looks like we're going to have one hell of a reception!" Raj described how she broke the ice with him with plain and simple straight talk. Her ploy was to be diplomatic, respectful, and earnest in her dealings with my clan, and not take personal umbrage. In this area I indeed had much to learn from Raj.

On the previous day, we went to see Saras so Raj could personally break the news that she wanted her as maid of honor. Because Saras was still at work teaching, we let ourselves into her ground floor flat. Reaching the kitchen and dining areas, Raj chuckled when she saw the same old black and white TV that she and Saras had to watch programs, like, *I Love Lucy*. The flat was a time capsule for Raj where memories were now frozen in time. After speculating about when Saras might return, we found ourselves in raj's old bedroom – here the 'charmer' was in very good form, and suffice to say, we closed the deal on our future life together. At this magical moment, Raj's return air ticket evaporated, maybe to be used as bookmark some day.

On June 7th we returned to Buffalo where Raj stayed with Saras and I was in Kenmore. My house was bustled with activity. A big pink tent was going up in the backyard, tables and chairs were being delivered along with the cake, beverages, tableware, and flowers. The next day I woke up to an eerie silence. After the chaos yesterday, it was strange not to hear a soul. With the kitchen free I took the opportunity to make myself a hearty breakfast of bacon and eggs; however, shortly thereafter I was bombarded with a call to nature as well as the thought of throwing up – what? As I grabbed hold of myself, I focused on the day ahead and how fortunate I was to marry the girl of my dreams.

The ploy worked! Thereafter, I was able to happily greet the family as they began to trickle in from God knows where. I even had several kind words for Sister Catherine who came from Toronto, and had insisted on asking my approval for everything she was doing to help in the wedding preparations.

In the evening Greg threw me a small bachelor party in the basement. I had done the same thing for Greg when he married in 1968; however, unlike Greg who thoroughly celebrated the event with his former classmates, thankfully mine was much more subdued. Prior to playing poker with the boys, I phoned Raj at Saras's, and we exchanged our love for each other; in addition, I made a pitch to go with the shorter version of the exchange of vows. Afraid I'd make a mishmash of things at the altar, Raj agreed. Just before I made it an early night, my best man Greg gave me a hearty hug, which was followed by short but sincere wishes from both Dad and Mom. I went to sleep knowing all was in place for the big day tomorrow – a day Raj and I had envisioned for three long years.

While the morning was wet from the previous night's rain, the day was bathed in sunshine to warm my bones and my heart. I arrived at the chapel early to review the ceremony with Father Trautman and Greg, and to greet several out-of-town guests. Rosalind drove from Atlanta in her trusty VW bug and was set for the first reading. Accompanied by his entire family, Carm Privitera would give the second reading. Bob Beall drove up from Cleveland, and later we would stay with him and his wife Mimi during our honeymoon travels. Also invited were a number of friends and classmates from our UB days, as well as several friends and colleagues of my parents, which in the end quite pleased my dad. Because Dad was pleased, Mom was pleased.

When it came to inviting relatives, for the sake of harmony, I elected to follow my parents' lead; hence, my god-mother Pauline and husband Ray came from nearby Orchard Park, and representatives from Canada consisted of Sister Catherine, and my god-father Uncle Stan and wife Leona, plus their entire brood of nine kids. All told we'd have nearly a hundred souls attending giving the small chapel an 'over-flowing' impression. And last but not least Raj's mentor Phil Miles and his wife Eleanor, and their three children were prominent invitees as Phil would be standing in for Raj's dad and escort Raj down the aisle. With a final word from Father Trautman and a pat on the back from Greg, all was in readiness as the 'bride' arrived at the front door.

On the arm of Phil, Raj came down the aisle beaming and looking magnificent. Wearing a gorgeous yellow-gold silk sari festooned with a vermillion border instilled with gold filigree, Raj joined me at the front altar. She certainly looked nothing like the 'fruit salad' I kidded her about earlier. Greg situated himself to the right of me while maid of honor Saras stood to the left of Raj. Without much delay Father Trautman opened the ceremony by greeting everyone, and then he pointed out that he would also be addressing an audience very far away in India. Equipped with a tape recorder on the altar, the proceedings of the wedding were being taped so that Raj's parents and friends would later be able to hear the ceremony for themselves. It was noteworthy that Raj's parents had arranged a church service in Hyderabad in our honor to be held simultaneously with ours.

With my chewing gum getting a vigorous workout (Raj nearly fainted from the sight of me), the Mass proceeded and we were on our way to officially becoming husband and wife. After our exchange of vows and Father Trautman's invocation that we all go in peace, I left the safely of Greg's shoulder and gently touched Raj's; now it would be she who would assist me down the few steps from the altar and down the aisle. We were now on our way to embark on life's journey together. From now on Raj would be my life-line to balance and equilibrium, both physically and mental – Raj would accomplish this feat in many more ways than I could ever imagine.

After several formal photos taken by Bob Smith in front of the chapel, Greg drove us home Fran Hornung's white Cadillac. All was abuzz as a makeshift receiving line was set up in the front hallway, with guests subsequently filtering out to the backyard for beverages under a big pink tent. Amid the sunshine, more pictures were taken for our wedding album. Notable snaps included: Raj with her buddies Clarice Giampaola, Wei-Li Lee and Linda Carter; Raj precariously hanging out the upstairs bathroom window tossing her bouquet; Raj and I posing over the cake as dad snapped our picture through a window (only later did we know he was trying to frame us by simultaneously capturing outside window reflections); and a shot taken of Carm as he gave the toast – "I don't know where it all started," he began. To which I added with accompanying laughter – "Sure you do!" Later Raj changed into a pastel pink sari with delicate silver embroidery; with her shimmering black hair, accented with a most welcoming smile, Raj was the most beautiful woman on earth. The day was pure fun as family and guests ate and drank, and mingled with one another.

**Raj and I Cut Our Wedding Cake)**

Later in the afternoon, we began our preparation for the drive back to Syracuse. After packing a few gifts, we were soon on the highway listening to a radio broadcast of the Belmont Stakes. I noted to Raj that if Secretariat wins today, June 9, 1973, would be etched in history, not necessarily because of us but because of Secretariat and the Triple Crown. Sure enough, history was made, at Aqueduct Raceway as well as St. John the Baptist Church.

Decompressing from all the energy we spent in finally getting together, we didn't pay too much attention to a honeymoon after the "I dos." Fortunately (or unfortunately depending on who reads this), I learned that the US Open would be played outside of Pittsburgh. While, in retrospect, it was not one of my best decisions, Raj played along and agreed to mingle among the other Arnold Palmer-wannabes for five days staying at a nearby Best Western Motel. Armed with press credentials from family friend and TV sportscaster Van Miller, my first business in the parking lot of the Oakmont course was to take a photo of Raj decked out in a floppy hat, binoculars, program, and a folding chair. She must have wondered "what the hell have I gotten myself into with this fanatic?" While we were spectators for a couple of days, we drove to a nearby town and took in the lovely scenery of the hills and valleys, which epitomize central Pennsylvania. We stopped at a nearby park where I took pictures of my new bride. In one sequence, I asked Raj to step toward the edge of a pond – unknown to me that her labored grin hid the fact she was about to tumble into the pond! A steady rain on the final round kept us in our motel room where we relaxed and wrote postcards, and where we watched on TV Johnny Miller shoot a record 63 to win the tourney. Another Secretariat moment!

Saying good bye to Pennsylvania, we drove to Cleveland, Ohio to visit Bob and Mimi Beall for a couple of days; Bob was a postdoc at Case Western Reserve working in a lab once occupied by Nobel Laureate Earl Sutherland of cyclic AMP fame. During our stay, we also had dinner with Freddie and Judy Isaacs; Freddie was Aunt Elsie's nephew, originally from Nagpur, India. Unfortunately, my main recollection of the evening centered on getting ill from some accidentally over-spiced curry. While the meal tasted good, I had hell to pay the next day. Of course, Raj was quick to point out – "I told you not to eat it!"

With Pennsylvania, and now Ohio, in our rear-view mirror, we headed back to Syracuse via a short stop in Buffalo. Getting back to our Syracuse apartment, it was time for the business of being newly christened husband and wife, and especially for Raj, a period of adjustment. While I was rather set in my ways (good and bad), Raj on the other hand was used to working and earning, and now had to contend with handouts from my postdoc stipend. Furthermore, she was used to a hectic life in and out of her Hyderabad home. What the hell was she going to do all day in our claustrophobic apartment? There are only so many letters home, or thank you notes Raj could write in a day.

Raj cooked, but mostly western style foods to please me. A few times she prepared curried dishes, making due without the spectrum of spices normally used in India. While the curries were indeed tasty, they were not up to the standards Raj craved. Hence, we ate out a lot. It didn't take too long for us to realize we needed to find Raj a teaching position. Leads at SU, Onandaga Community College, and even a local technical program looking for English instructors. all turned out to be dead ends. Without a piece of chalk in her hand, Raj was truly a fish out of water. However, one day we saw an ad for a teaching position at Hamilton College just outside of Utica.

Hamilton College was a scenic 45 mile drive away, and upon entering the college grounds our breath was taken away as we moved along the tree-lined roadway, buildings steeped in venerable New England architecture, and old money. Finding the Biology Building, the Chairman took us for a tour, and explained the faculty duties were to teach classical biology courses to small classes. From our conversation, it was clear that Raj had the job if she wanted it. Driving home we discussed the pros and cons of her working (and possibly staying) at Hamilton with us getting together on the weekends. In the end, it wasn't practical to either commute through the snow belt or stay on campus, nor be away from each other soon after our marriage. I know how much Raj was disappointed in declining the offer; she would have prospered at the opportunity.

As the summer wore on, it was clear, however, that we needed to do something before the Fall term' Ironically, the midwife in solving our problem turned out to be Dr. Phil Miles then Chair of the UB Biology Department. During a prior trip to Buffalo, Phil indicated he needed a temporary instructor for Cell Biology. He asked Raj to chew on the possibility. Shortly after declining the Hamilton offer, Raj contacted him and told him that she'd be very interested if I could get my fellowship transferred from SU to UB.

Fortunately, I laid the groundwork before our wedding when I met with active investigators at UB. My selling pitch was two-fold – I would come with my own support money, and secondly, I would be interested in pursuing neuromuscular research carried on by the investigators I visited. I initiated a two-prong approach where I contacted the UB folks, as well as crafting a letter to my MDA sponsor to test the waters of this possibility. Good fortune smiled our way when both UB and the MDA agreed to have me on board. With the pre-approvals in my back pocket, I saw Dr. Florini and broke the news, which under the circumstances took the news quite well. I promised to finish the culture experiments, and in the bargain, continue with the chicken CK work (albeit at a distance of 130 miles).

By the end of August, we had our major ducks in a row: we had found an apartment in suburban Amherst, and while Raj joined our old Biology, I'd be working across campus in the Biochemistry Department. With all the twists and turns over the past three years, Raj and I were coming full circle. We expressed our tearful good-byes in 1970, and now married, returned to Buffalo as a couple of working stiffs. In important ways, Buffalo represented a comfort zone for us – familiar, family, as well as several mutual friends. Now it was time to concentrate on married life, and directing our energies into opportunities again provided by UB. Later, through the encouragement and intercession of her buddy Clarice Giampaola, Raj would acquire a faculty position at Erie Community College. Coincidentally, I would continue research in the neuromuscular disease field, hoping some day to develop my own funded research program. It's no exaggeration that Raj and I had come a long way since our chance meeting in an elevator back in 1967. Q.E.D.

# Chapter 12

# On The Road Together

One morning I listened to NPR radio where Adam Gopnik was being interviewed about his new book titled *Paris to the Moon*. As I listened to the author spin amusing tale after amusing tale of what it was like living in Paris as a writer for the *New Yorker* magazine, I began to think of my own experiences in Paris. Quickly a smile came over me as I began to connect the dots. The more I connected, the broader my smile. Since we were married in 1973, Raj and I had traveled quite a bit throughout North America. Many of our travels were to sites of scientific research meetings held in Montreal, Minneapolis, Anaheim, Washington, DC, and Key Biscayne, while others were for pure pleasure such as to Atlanta, New York, Detroit, Vancouver, and Jasper, Alberta.

**Our Cabin at Jasper Park Lodge**

**The British Library in London, England**

However, our trip in 1984 to Europe remained special. It would be the first time I traveled over 'the pond' so to speak, not a small feat form someone like me who was deathly afraid to fly.

Raj and I had already been in London for a week – the first leg of my initial, long-awaited trip abroad. So far the trip was dizzying. In late July, London is jammed full of tourists all going helter-skelter. In joining the throng, our stops included the British Museum, the Tower, Windsor Castle, Harrods, and the Tate Museum, where we marveled at Sargent's *Lily, Lily, Carnation, Rose.* Each morning, we left our nicely-situated Kensington hotel and, after a good breakfast, we lit out either by cab or tour bus. Our daily venues ranged from museums to cathedrals, castles to universities, and of course the ubiquitous gift shops (we were in shopper's heaven!). By day's end we returned to the hotel totally exhausted. Rejuvenation came in the form of a visit to the hotel pub for what became our routine fare – liver pate, bread, and a pint of London's finest served at room temperature. We became such a familiar fixture that the Filipino waitress came to know us by our first names (no standing in line for us!).

By the time we hit the sack each night, we vowed we shouldn't repeat what we just did that day. "Tomorrow we'll go a little slower, see a little less, and maybe, just maybe we'll survive this trip."

**The Grand Canyon**

**English Sense of Humor For Location
of Handicap Toilet for Men**

Our four-day trip to Paris began with a 4:30 AM wake-up call and room service breakfast. After we had most of our luggage put in hotel storage (most of it gifts, museum guides and dirty laundry), our cabbie picked us up at 6:00 and off we went to Heathrow for our eight o'clock British Airways flight to Charles DeGaulle Airport. Accompanied by dozens of British school children now on holiday, our gleaming Boeing sailed us across the channel to the land of Napoleon, Louis the Fourteenth, and Gaetan Viaris de Lesegne (aka, our guide for the duration!).

After we debarked from the plane, we were greeted by an energetic Libyan who took me in an airport wheelchair, and left Raj to fend for herself with the carry-on bags, plus my own wheelchair (brought to us from the belly of the plane). Oh God, what are we getting ourselves into? The newly-opened DeGaulle terminal is massive and structured with lots of chrome, windows, and high ceilings. As we were on the second floor, we had to navigate an array of escalators to the ground level for our luggage. My porter was quite good at handling me and the wheelchair in the rapidly descending escalator, but, as I turned around, I winced as I saw Raj precariously balancing the carry-ons AND the wheelchair (how do you say Blue Cross and Blue Shield in French?). After what seemed like an eternity, we reached the luggage area. Once our porter left us, Raj and I began to wonder out loud whether our guide, Gaetan, would be able to find us in all of the confusion. Just when we get a feeling of abandonment, out popped Gaetan from the stirring crowd!

"Bon!" says Gaetan. (As it turned out 'bon' is one of the few and only expressions that I will understand during our entire trip – more about this later.)

We responded to Gaetan with smiles, handshakes, luggage stubs, and big time relief. Gaetan was not a big fellow – maybe five feet six or seven, but he appeared wiry. He was wearing an open-collared shirt which contrasted with his well-tanned, weathered complexion. His eyes were sharp and dark and betrayed both an understanding of our plight as well as some needed continental experience and assurance for our trip.

Once our luggage was retrieved, we were soon out the door to his waiting Mercedes limousine – yes, limousine! (More about that later too.) Safely seated in the front seat (with Raj occupying a rather spacious read compartment), I attempted to break into a conversation with Gaetan. For example, "My dad was once here during World War Two" and "I believe Lindbergh landed his 'Spirit of Saint Louis' not too far from here? Right?" And so it went, I asked questions, and Gaetan responded in Parisienne English to which I had no idea what he was saying. On the other hand, Raj, from the back seat would yell out, "Mike, he said he is going to take us the hotel first", or "Mike, he said that he had escorted Jimmy Carter during his visit to Paris after he had lost the election to Reagan." While I 'thought' I knew textbook French, Raj knew dialect, and as it turned out Raj became the interpreter. We quickly followed a simple system. I asked Gaetan a question, Gaetan would respond, and Raj would translate. Conversely, Gaetan would say something, and I in turn waited for Raj to tell me what the hell he just said! As we motored through the hectic traffic, I got the feeling that this was going to be quite an interesting trip.

After we arrived at our hotel in Courbevoie (modern suburb of Paris), we quickly checked in, found our room, and once the door closed, panicked! It seemed Gaetan was expecting $200 per day in U.S. Dollars. Here we were, emptying our pockets (and purse) to see if we could afford being chauffeured around Paris for four days. After some nifty arithmetic, I proclaimed to Raj: "We can do it IF he takes us to the airport on our return at no charge." Now that the World Bank had sorted things out, we went to see Gaetan who had been waiting for us in the lobby. He understood the deal and quickly proclaimed – "bon!" Immediately, I got the feeling Gaetan just stepped out of Rick's American Bar in the movie *Casablanca*. My imagination was really kick-started and now humming along at a rapid pace. What's next?

With no particular itinerary or sight in mind, we left it to Gaetan to show us Paris – I sat in the front seat with my Nikon SLR, and my translator Raj sat in the rear (don't leave home without her!). After departing from our hotel, we sped east quickly and hooked up with the famous Champs Elysee. This grand avenue repeatedly took us over the Seine River as it winds back and forth like an undulating snake. Filled with excitement, we saw the Arc de Triomphe in the distance. When we came to one of the stoplights, Gaetan was completely immersed in a political discourse which I could barely understand. Oblivious to the honking of horns surrounding us (as well as the green light), the animated Gaetan continued to carry on, accentuating his points with flailing head and arms. Simply amazing! Here we were in the middle of eight lanes of traffic and we were dead in the water! Like a fuse that's been lit, it has to go the distance before the dynamite explodes (or before Gaetan came to his senses and we could quickly leave the intersection).

As described in our tour maps, Paris is structured like an onion with outer concentric circles of very modern (almost gaudy) architecture. Older and older more classical elements became visible as we continued east on the Champs toward the city center. We craned our necks this way and that until we caught glimpse of the Eiffel Tower, the Royal Palace and its fountains, and countless other sites our guide rattled off as he whizzed us by the impressive Arc de Triomphe. Here, I couldn't help thinking of the black and white newsreel images of the Arc showing those wonderful, fun-loving Nazis goose-stepping their way through Paris, only 40 plus years earlier.

Our exhilarating ride took us to our initial destination – a park-like setting called the Tuilleries for lunch, which was to be followed by a visit to the Jeu de Paume gallery which is only a short stroll away. After we parked, we went to an outdoor café which specialized in something called the "mixed sandwich." Layered inside a freshly slice baquette were an assortment of cold-cuts, cheese, lettuce, tomato, and Dijon-style mustard. The combination was an outstanding treat. With full tummies, Raj pushed me in the wheelchair through the grounds of the park, which got its name from the fact it was the location of a long-gone tile factory. Once we reached the end of the path, we came to the busy Place de Concorde and the mecca for anyone interested in French Impressionist painting – the Jeu de Paume.

After reaching the gallery entrance, we were struck by the building's simplicity and lack of pretension. The present building was once part of a palace complex called the Orangerie where fruit trees like orange trees were grown in a hothouse-like environment; later the facility was converted into an indoor tennis court. We joined a small assembly moving toward the entrance. Once inside, we got our tickets at the counter and quickly entered one of France's holiest of holies – the realm of Monet, Degas, Manet, Brazille, and Pissaro. My pulse was racing with expectation.

Immediately upon entering the first floor area, we were blinded by the bright sunlight streaming through the windows. Some were even open allowing a little breeze to enter. We were struck by the relaxed informality of the guides who were mostly young college girls. The wooden floors squeaked at every turn, This was to allow everyone to know where everyone else was inside the building. Once we gathered our esthetic balance, we began to focus on the walls which were crammed with a veritable Who's Who of French Impressionism. The assemblage was pure eye candy for those of us who had appreciated these paintings from afar, mainly from coffee table books back home.

What was particularly interesting as we meandered from room to room, was the striking contrast to the National Gallery in London which we had visited only a few days earlier. While the Jeu de Paume seemed to want us to enjoy their artistic heroes en plein aire (like the early rebels might have wanted), the atmosphere within the more austere National Gallery was completely different. Instead of vivacious guides, sunlight, and noisy floors, the National Gallery was equipped with formally-dressed warders spying on your every move, carpeting to muffle movements, and subdued, if not dark, light conditions. Moreover, visitors spoke in hushed whispers, unlike the lusty ooh and ahs we heard at the Jeu de Paume!

At one stage in our visit, Raj climbed to the second floor to see if it might be worth my while to inquire if they had an elevator. Just as

I left a Courbet to examine a Monet, I heard Raj clambering down the staircase shouting "Mike, you must come upstairs!"

Raj ignored by lukewarm protestations and went off to see if there was a way to get me upstairs to the second floor gallery. Shortly, Raj returned with a short, curt fellow in jacket and tie, holding a large ring of keys. We were instructed to follow him. He took us to the front ticket counter area where he unlocked what appeared to be a freight elevator. With a noisy ascent we entered a dim storeroom filled on both sides with metal racks, like the ones you might have in your garage to organize garden tools. These racks were filled with paintings! Stacked up like week old magazines, I spot familiar sciences by Monet, Van Gogh, and Pissaro! I couldn't believe what I was seeing. While Raj tried to keep pace with our grumpy guardian, I dropped my feet from the wheelchair foot-rests in a futile effort o slam on the brakes. Ultimately, Raj won out, but not with some exasperating shoving on her part to avoid an international incident. I could just imagine the headlines – Stubborn American Tourist Holds Jeu de Palme Hostage!

After we left the second floor, and a tense return through the storeroom, we bought postcards and guides to add to our endless collection. Once outside, Gaetan greeted us with a smile, "Bon, now where?" We took Gaetan's suggestion and headed for Notre Dame Cathedral. On the way, along the Seine we appreciated the grandeur and immensity of the Louvre. Struck by its sheer size, we deleted Louvre from our to do list; besides we already had bought a Louvre museum guide! In a short time we reached a bridge which would take us to Ile de France and its main attraction. Keeping to form, Gaetan amidst traffic suddenly pulled the Mercedes to a curb. Here I took a photo of the rear perspective of the cathedral, which many painters have favored over the years. Basking in bright sunshine and blue skies, Notre Dame with its flying buttresses was indeed a grand lady.

We reached a parking area in front of the cathedral, where we joined the throng of tourists, most of whom were disembarking from tour buses from all over Europe. However, the noisy chaos couldn't detract from the splendor of the architectural detail of the church's façade. Looking up, my mind unconsciously wandered to a scene from *The Hunchback of Notre Dame* where Anthony Quinn held Gina Lollabrigida over his head. As we got closed to the large wooden door of the entrance, Gaetan pointed out figures within the façade who had had their heads chopped off. Apparently the Parisiennes during the Revolution were less than happy with the Catholic Church's complicity with the royal family. Ironically, beheaded statues would be a common theme seen in many churches we visited on our trip.

Once inside Notre Dame our senses were overwhelmed. Even amidst the hordes, we were amazed at the immensity and intricacies of the gothic interior with its high vaulted ceiling, canyon-like nave, and colorful stained-glass windows. As we moved more deeply into the cathedral, we heard a choir singing in the distance, as well as bells signifying a Mass was in progress. Taking a side aisle, we came to a large stand of candles where we lit two, each one in memory of our recently deceased parents – Raj's father Jaya and my mother Veronica. At that magical moment we were paradoxically filled with tears of happiness.

Outside we witnessed a little mini-drama where a huge Italian motor-coach was trying to extricate itself from the tight parking quarters while dozens of gregarious Italian tourists were simultaneously getting on and off the bus which was still moving. The chaos reminded me of *If Its Tuesday It Must Be Belgium* where life was seen imitating art.

As I folded myself into the Mercedes, I wrestled with a splitting headache. The heat, the sensory overload of seeing so much in so short a time, coupled with the non-stop character of the day which began with an early wake up in London, all conspired to give me a whopping headache. What I thought I needed was some aspirin, a Coke to wash it down, and a cold beer to wash them both down. While Gaetan tried to convince us that we should immediately leave for Montmartre and its star attraction – Sacre Coeur Cathedral, Raj ably cut through the linguistic tangle and got us underway to a nearby café. The Mike to Raj system of translation was now working, thank God.

After driving a short distance, we came to an ornate neighborhood called the Place De Victor Hugo. In his inimitable style, Gaetan jumped the curb in front of the busy café, and with money from us for my headache tonic he went the café. A short time later a handsomely dressed woman came to my window and asked, "Are you looking for me?" Distracted by my headache, I waved her off and returned to my desire for aspirin, a Coke and a beer – in that order. In a moment or two, the scene with the woman was repeated. What am I, an information booth? Again I waved away the woman, but this time I was confused and a bit miffed by her insistence. Soon after that my savior arrived with the beverages and all was quickly forgotten. While I savored my Coke and beer chaser, Raj and Gaetan got into an animated conversation which culminated in an uproar of laughter. As they caught their breath, I was informed that the woman who approached me was a hooker and a well-dressed one at that. While Raj sat hidden in the limo's spacious backseat, she was able to describe the entire mini-drama to Gaetan after he returned from the café. While I too enjoyed the laugh (at my expense), I was much more impressed with the miraculous powers of the Coke/beer combo on a headache.

"Okay, Gaetan what's next?"

It was now late in the afternoon, but there was sufficient time to navigate Montmartre before returning to the hotel. Meandering through back-streets (was there another way with Gaetan?), we climbed the Montmartre section toward the stunning Sacre coeur. He steered his was through tight turns and narrow alleys and somehow reached the white marble steps of the cathedral which was crowded with tourists as well as native artisans. The atmosphere was pure carnival and fun to witness. Now that we were situated on the highest area within Paris, we were able to see much of the city beneath us, including the unmistakable Eiffel Tower off in the distance to the West. After we marveled at the view, we headed back to Courvevoie for dinner. It was late in the afternoon and time to recharge.

After reaching the hotel lobby, we made arrangements with Gaetan to go out into the outskirts of Paris and to stop at notable places, such as Versailles. We had already agreed to visit Claude Monet's old haunt at Giverny the day after. Physically exhausted but spiritually exhilarated, we headed to our room. While in the elevator, we were overwhelmed by the unmistakable aroma of Indian curry. After reaching our floor, we ran into Indians who told us they were with a tourist party accompanied by their own cook. We shook with laughter as we quickly made tracks to our room to clean up and make plans for our dinner.

The dining room in the hotel was spacious and quite comfortable. Greeted in French by a young waiter, we were seated with menus written in French. Without our trusty Gaetan to translate, we were at the mercy or our waiter who was doing his utmost to help us. After a lengthy discourse (mainly between Raj and the waiter), we decided upon a lighter-than-a-feather Bordeaux, appetizers of mussels and prawns, a delicately seasoned salad, and veal filets swimming in a rich brown sauce. The meal was pure magic – tasty, light, and elegantly presented.

During our meal, entertainment was provided by a cantankerous woman from California who was seated a few tables from us, and six American Army chaps seated nearby. The Californian complained loudly about everything – in a needless display of arrogance and ingratitude, she had our waiter jumping through one hoop after another. Concurrently, the GIs on leave from West Germany were not about to experiment with the menu, and ordered cheeseburgers, french fries, and Cokes. All we heard were volleys of complaints – holding a menu one loudly remarked, "Can't even read this thing!" Paying attention to us as well as to the Californian, the waiter did his best Charlie Chaplin routine juggling plates of burgers ("You call this a burger!"), french fries ("You'd think THEY would know how to make fries!"), and gallons of Coke ("This stuff ain't even cold!). While we were enjoying a memorable dinner, we were surrounded by the French chapter of the *Ugly American*. The best Raj and I could do afterwards was to offer the waiter empathy, a handsome tip, as well as several apologies on behalf of our countrymen. However, first things first – dessert!

With rich cups of coffee in hand, we selected a raspberry tart for dessert. Incredible as it may seem, I can still taste the pastry shell filled with a delicate raspberry filling dribbled with fresh chocolate sauce. As a companion to this treat, we experienced Calvados brandy for the first time. Bottled in the apple-growing region of Normandy, the brew has a hint of apples with each sip. For me, Normandy had always conjured up thoughts of D-Day landings, and Claude Monet's home near Rouen, but now I had Calvados to add to the list of associations.

Back in our room, we felt our cup hath truly runneth over – while exhausted by nearly 17 hours of non-stop activity, our senses and spirits were buoyed as rarely seen before. Getting ready for bed, we had another one of our London conversations where we contemplated (or feared) the next three days in France - "How on earth are we going to get through tomorrow?"

Our itinerary over the next three days was mixed. On one day we traveled the countryside adjacent to the Seine and made our way to Monet's home in Giverny. To actually browse through Monet's gardens and water lily pond was surreal. The estate of Monet had made a remarkable effort in renovating both his home and grounds ensuring that this treasure would be available to the public. With Raj valiantly pushing me in the wheelchair, I had my Nikon firing non-stop, capturing several scenes which I would later use as subject-matter for my own oils.

**Claude Monet's Home at Giverny**

Later at the suggestion of Gaetan, we lunched at a nearby restaurant called Vieux Moulon (translation, Old Mill). Tabled outside we began our lunch with a fine vintage of Bordeaux white and an outsized platter of mussels dripping in butter and herbs. Our main course featured mixed cold cuts and cheese sandwiches made with a fresh baquette. Many months later back home, we came across a magazine article describing Monet's refurbished gardens with a strong recommendation to eat at the nearby Vieux Moulon. The author of the article gave the restaurant an unqualified five stars, as did we.

After lunch we continued driving west to Rouen and visited the Joan of Arc Church. Because of our interest in art and history, Gaetan correctly thought we'd enjoy an exhibition of ecclesiastical paintings held within this cavernous gothic structure. Afterwards we drove in front of the Rouen Cathedral made famous by Monet's series of paintings where he experimented with light captured at different times of the day. It was at this stage that Raj informed Gaetan that she needed to find a ladies room, but because it was Sunday not too many establishments were open. Using his ingenuity Gaetan found a small inn and somehow convinced the staff to let a non-guest use its restroom facilities. Needless to say, Raj now thought Gaetan was capable of walking on water.

An interesting thing happened on our journey back to Paris. Rather than taking the back roads as we did in the morning, Gaetan took the turnpike for what would normally be a two hour drive back to Paris. After no more than an hour, Gaetan suddenly pulled the car over to a grassy shoulder, parked, and with a quick "bon" lay down under a nearby tree. Stretched out he promptly went to sleep. In our perplexed state all we could think was that he was ill or dying and how would we get back to Paris? Our imaginations were in high gear, as we shuffled through travel brochures and maps, all the while contemplating our state of abandonment. After what seemed an eternity, Gaetan suddenly returned with his characteristic "bon", and off we went. Back at the hotel we conjectured that the heavy lunch (plus the fine Bordeaux) finally had caught up with our intrepid leader, and he needed a little lie down. Bon!

The day before we jetted back to London, we visited the suburban Versailles Palace. While the Palace was closed to visitors, we were able to get out into the magnificent grounds and view the gardens, fountains, and the grandeur that was once regal France. Before we left, we peeked through the windows of the Palace to get a passing glimpse of the famous Hall of Mirrors. Even from the outside, the Hall could be seen in all its reflective brilliance. Subsequently, we made a lunch stop within the Bois de Boulonge district. This plush area still contains remnants of what was the grandeur of the reign of King Louis the Fourteenth. While the palace was destroyed after the revolution, many stately structures remain, including Marie Antoinette's home called the Trianon. Adjacent to this magnificent marble mini-palace are lakes, highly sculptured fountains, formal gardens, and long boulevards lined with towering trees. Visiting this area gave us a glimpse of what regal France was like over 200 hundred years ago, and why there was a revolt in the first place.

Interestingly, the night before we went to Versailles, we made plans to meet my cousin Mark Muldoon the following afternoon at the Eiffel Tower. Mark who was in Belgium studying for his PhD in Philosophy, decided to take the morning train to meet us along a road which goes through a large park adjacent to the Tower. Around two-thirty, Gaetan dropped us off at the agreed-upon location for our three o'clock rendezvous with Mark. However, we spent three hours meandering around the park, and no Mark – I watched a hotly contested bocce ball game played by some local fellows, and Raj got plenty of exercise walking back and forth in the shadows of the Tower looking for any sign of my cousin. "Mike, if he's here, we'll find him", Raj huffed with confidence, but she also added this aside to me, "I don't think this is the right location!"

No sooner had we entered our room than the phone rang. I answered with "Hi, Mark! Where are you?" He was calling after his return to Belgium. Through laughter-filled interludes, we discovered that Mark had waited for us at the Royal Fountains which was located north of the Tower; we on the other hand waited in the exact, opposite location. While we would have thoroughly enjoyed ourselves with Mark at the Tower had we met as planned, our misadventure was something we'd never forget. To this day, Raj still thinks I was the one who mishandled the plans for the rendezvous. Who am I to argue with history, nor with Raj, who in effect made the entire European trip possible in the first place. Bon!

# Chapter 13

# Meena Kumari

As I went to get the newspaper at the front door, I saw her lying in the living room in her characteristic pose – curled, content, and her right foot sticking out.

Slow, steady breathing...the rhythm belied Meena's time-bomb potential. Named after a famous Indian actress, Meena Kumari, I just sixty minutes earlier concluded our usual evening circuit with me in my electric scooter hanging on for dear life to her leash. After a dinner of Special Formula K plus bits of bologna (precisely shredded by Raj's mother Olivia, Meena's 79 year old guardian), the two of us embarked across the street to the leaf-strewn alley. Sniff. Sniff. With great resolve the spinal arch began. Still walking, sniffing some more, she accomplished the deed (to my delight).

Rather than return hastily to the house as the weather was gentle for a late October evening, we snaked our way to the backyard for a double-time, quick walk. Up the path, past the deck, garden beds, maple, poplar...beds again, and across the lawn. Not staggering, her attention not wandering, she was up to the hunt... the run...the fun!

**Meena Kumari**

Once around the yard was good, but the second circuit came even easier and then again. I saw her determination, her sheer will. If possible, perpetual motion was her role in life. Going for a fourth time, she was on-track with almost lightness to her mechanical pace, almost a gallop. God, what a beautiful sight! Her tongue hanging and flopping from delight, she paced with head high and true. Born to run!

As we went for a fifth circuit we branched off to the neighbor's lawn. No stride was broken, just a wider arc. We came back to the flower beds and the tall trees; we zig-zagged a little but continued unabated. Go! Go! Go! I said to myself only one more time, but I could sense that Meena wanted this one, plus one more round-trip.

After we completed our journey, we headed for the ramp next to the house. When we rounded the path, inertia took her into the concrete foundation – she stopped, shook a little, then gathered herself for the trot up the ramp and the rear entrance of the house. Once inside, she relinquished the leash with ease – no tug or crippled backward tilt of her hindquarters. No, she surrendered the tether with ease, and, with a quick little turn-around, she gathered her bearings.

In the meantime, Raj and Olivia were readying themselves for an evening outing to a church sing-along. I went to heat up coffee and catch the political news on TV, and – where's the newspaper?

This is where we began this story. While I felt Meena would be fast asleep somewhere, I didn't count on her being in the living room at the foot of Olivia's chair! Though the chair was vacant, old habits were tough to break. The chair was a port-in-the-storm. Security. Comfort, Resting at the feet of Olivia.

The passing days were wringing out memories of Meena. Eighteen years to be compressed into twenty-one days. She was not dead as yet, but in some strange way she seemed long gone from us.

Frail, fragile, gimpy, blind, and unhearing, except for a special high-pitched "click" sound I could make by contorting my cheek. Meena was our geriatric pet, special in all ways. A year after we were married, eighteen years ago, Raj and I answered a newspaper ad for a "cock-a-poo." After our university work one evening in October, with checkbook in hand, we headed for an address in Cheektowaga. After we pulled into the driveway, we were greeted at the door by a somewhat skeptical, but otherwise a pleasant enough couple. Through a light rain falling, I guess we both looked a bit of a sight – me hobbling along in my casual laboratory togs, and Raj in her colorful sari. Not the typical looking couple you'd expect to find in this part of town. Shortly after we arrived, the couple went to the basement and retrieved a small, beige, quivering bundle of canine fur.

"Female?" we asked.

"Yes" came a quick reply.

"We'll take her!"

Fifty-five dollars was the advertised price, and out came the checkbook. The gesture was met with a bit of suspicion from the couple. It was at this point that Raj tried to assure the couple that the check is good.

"He works at the University at Buffalo! Raj chirped.

After the couple rather reluctantly took our check, we gathered our purchase into the car. Wet and shivering, she shared the front seat on the ride home. Oh God, what have we done!

That night the pooch would have nothing to do with the cardboard box we installed for her in the kitchen. Nor would she accustom herself to the kitchen floor complete with blankets, pillows, and yes, a ticking alarm clock. After we bracketed the kitchen with the backs of high wooden chairs, fiber-board, and an expandable children's gate, we finally headed for the bedroom to go to sleep. Soon as the lights went out – rustle, rustle. With a leap, a tug, and one of the most determined grasps a small dog could possibly make, she was able to surmount a height 3 to 4 times her size! From that first night on, the pattern was set:

Raj initiated her own brand of "paper training" which consisted of blanket and sheets covering the floors of our two bedroom condo.

Nextly, the population of our bed went from 2 to 3. When Olivia came to stay with us, her bed population during the interim went from one to two. This arrangement lasted for several years up to the time when Olivia could no longer hoist her up on her own, and

Meena herself was unable to jump up onto the bed. During this time, however, the early "blanket days" returned with the floor of Olivia's room being covered with a blanket, accented with a nice fluffy pillow.

Inside our condo, and later within our house, Meena ran and ran. Room to room, hall to hall…under and around the dining room table…cornering, sliding, and collisions were common. One day, Meena squarely hit the top of a coffee table head-on when she was on one of her jaunts. Unbeknownst to her, she failed to clear the table because she had grown two inches in height. Bang!

Outside, Meena had her favorite routes in which to run. Up and down the slopes contained within the grounds of our condo complex. An imaginary course was staked out by Meena as a puppy and held onto for several years. If rain and mud were available, so much the better. We had an old friend Sylvia come to visit us from Australia, and she jumped at the chance to take Meena for a jaunt in some rather foul weather. Gone for half an hour or so, they both returned to our condo very happy, winded, and nearly unrecognizable because of the head to foot mud. On another occasion, my lab assistant Cathy Pollina came to take us to the airport for our flight to Atlanta. Before we left, Cathy volunteered to retrieve Meena after she got loose from her leash, chasing dozens of ducks into a scum-coated pond. Like Sylvia, Cathy returned with Meena very exhausted, filthy, and with the exception of Cathy, very happy.

When we could, we took Meena to a nearby park to allow her to run to her heart's content. Once released, it was 200 yards at full speed. In reaching some far away bushes, she'd turn around and sprint back at full tilt. After a few sniff, sniffs, Meena would head out again for another lap. This pattern would continue until she got tired (which happened occasionally), or until we did which was more frequent. For someone like me weakened from muscular dystrophy, it was pure joy to witness Meena fly with the wind in these outings.

While Meena couldn't wait to get inside a car, however, she went bonkers once inside and the car was driven. Panting took on a whole new dimension when Meena let go with her non-stop hyper-ventilating. Whether 85 degrees under sunny skies, or a wind chill factor of minus 20, the window of our Meena-laden auto had to be lowered so that she could stick out her head with ears flapping in the wind. It seemed at times like this Meena had an innate desire to become either a weathervane or a hood ornament. While business as usual for Raj and me, passing motorists were always a bit bewildered at Meena's antics trying to climb out the window. Interestingly, my brother-in-law Bob once remarked, "How bad can it be?" After a trip around the corner with Meena, he returned saying: "Mike, you're right, wow!"

Haircuts – battle, battle…non-stop strain, fidgeting, crying, and big time hyper-ventilation. Man against man, dog against man. For what should have taken maybe 60 minutes, our combat always took three hours and sometimes longer. After the battle and weapons were put back into their respective sheathes, Meena went her way to lick her wounds, and I was left to ponder in each case why I did it in the first place. If the haircut was not enough, getting her hair combed and free from gnarls made me a candidate for the Medal of Honor. Bathing Meena was just as much fun. Assuming I could corner her into the bathroom in the first place, then it was a matter of getting her into the shower stall where behind curtains I could only hope for the best. As I sat on a bench wearing only my birthday suit, I needed to have a death grip on Meena as I watered and lathered her down. Once done, Meena would bolt from the bathroom as if she were just shot from a cannon. Lastly, there was the business of Meena's toenails – being careful not to cause injury, my first snips would elicit high pitched shrills sufficient to stop traffic 10 miles away. Sufficient to say, personal hygiene was not one of Meena's favorite things in life.

One afternoon in 1977, I badly strained my ankle tendons when doing a few aggressive stretching exercises. As I sat on the living room sofa in pain and feeling quite miserable, out of the blue, Meena came up to me and in some way shared my agony. Quietly, she offered me her head so I could pet it, as well her ears to scratch. I wouldn't forget Meena's gesture to provide me with no small measure of comfort and assurance at that time. As much as Meena might have wanted to, there was no running around the apartment that night.

Meena was the best companion one could possibly have in the garden. She was, however, absolutely of no help. Tangling me with her lease in every way imaginable, she gave me support by eating every weed in sight as I dug them up. Bored after a while with the weeds, Meena would turn her attention to the annuals I was actually planting. Biting off a flower or two, we quickly reverted to our shower stall combat positions. Usually by now, Raj would come outside and ask how we were doing. My response would be something like – "Fine Raj, for every three plants I got in the ground, Meena ate one, dug up a second, and under duress left a third one undisturbed."

With resolve and a quiet demeanor, Meena lay coiled near the sliding door of our condo living room. She watched the snow fall, not wishing for anything except for a little space for herself, she continued to heal. Recuperating from a spaying operation, her abdomen was checkered with metal clips. On day two, Meena walked about a little bit. On day three, she attempted to do a little running, but each time she halted after feeling catches of pain. On day four, Meena was ready to go, back to her jumping and running.

Canned food, forget it! Dry and bagged, don't even think about it! Meena had quite specific tastes when it came to food. By human standards the food had to be interesting and gingered up with something to make eating worth her while. Meena's vet said she was a 'self-regulator', meaning she ate what and an amount she really needed to maintain a healthy body weight. That might be so, but give Meena Indian rice and lamb curry, she'd inflate like Jumbo. If you gave her a Snickers bar like my dad did at every opportunity, Meena was yours for life. The simple crackling of the wrapper was enough to get Meena's attention from 100 years away.

Lettuce?...yes. Peas?...no way. You couldn't hide them either by encasing them in tasty ground beef, nor anything else for that matter. Fruit?...yes. Bread?...yes if layered with butter. Nuts?...all kinds, especially enshrouded in a Snickers bar. Egg?...no, unless gingered up with onions and the like. Bacon?...move over. Its aroma stopped her in her tracks no matter what the age. Pizza?...yes, especially with pepperoni topping.

"Who's here?" It was four o'clock in the morning in July when I heard a clicking sound coming from our bedroom window. Roused from sleep, I spotted a moving shadow through the curtains. O God! Frozen, I whispered to Raj that someone was outside. Next, I shouted toward Meena who was lying on the floor next to the curtains. "Who's there!" Awakened, Meena saw the figure at the window face-to-face and immediately responded with enough GRRRRRRRRRRRRRRRRRRRR to scare away the fellow. The rest was history. With Meena running to the living room barking up a storm, I called the police who came in only ten minutes. With the crisis now over, I told Raj – "Meena, you've got yourself a condominium!"

Over the years, both Raj and I have had our share of pet pooches; Raj with her Pip and Tino back in India, and I with Holiday, Spanky, Kingston, Rookie, etc…Each pet was special to us in some personal way. However, Meena was indeed extra-special to us. In a way Meena served as a surrogate child – full of life, trainable to some degree, a companion through thick and thin, a spoiled brat, and a critter we enjoyed terribly.

Three weeks after I wrote this little essay, we took Meena, then over 17 years old, to the vet to be put to sleep. Our friends Harshad and Prem gathered Raj and me – and the freshly shampooed Meena on a Saturday morning in October. As the car backed up from the house, a tearful Olivia was seen at the door waving good-bye to her buddy and companion. At the vet's parking lot, I kissed and hugged Meena for the last time. To this day, I can still recall the distinctive smell of her freshly washed coat, as well as the tears flooding my eyes as Meena walked (not ran) from me for the very last time.

A couple of weeks later Raj and I had an eight-foot spruce planted in the backyard in her honor. After which we buried Meena's ashes at the trees' base. Should this tree ever draw nourishment from Meena's remains, there was always the possibility the tree might acquire the ability to run, jump, and dance into someone's heart, as Meena did during her life.

# Chapter 14

# Christmas and
# Hyderabadi Biryani

Since my marriage to Raj in 1973, I have shared wonderful Christmases with her which most times have centered around our annual carol singing party – a gathering where school colleagues, friends and family are treated to food, drink, and an opportunity to sing like a kid again. We seem to be doing something right, as most of our friends circle their calendars each December even before we do. However, I fondly recall two very special Christmases in 1985 and 1987 spent in Raj's home in India. In a country where Christians are very much in the minority, and the 'Only 20 shopping days left til Christmas' mentality is nonexistent, it was truly refreshing and spiritual for me to be swept up in celebrations primarily focused on church and family. Amidst the daily hubbub of Hyderabadi life, Raj and her family and friends carry on a long-standing tradition of going to services at St. George's Church followed with a gathering at the home of Raj's mother, Olivia. One by one, two by two, folks arrived at B4F4 Vigyanpuri in an array of conveyances full of laughter with women in new saris, and men in suits and ties. All had in common heartfelt joy of the season and cutting-edge appetites. On my second visit to Hyderabad, I decided to stay at home and not go to church. I had attended a Christmas Eve party and jet-lag was getting the best of me, so I stayed put and became a "fly on the wall" as the 'downstairs' crew did their unsupervised bit. While the loyal churchgoers were gaily singing homage to the birth of baby Jesus, the domestic staff would quietly and efficiently prepare the Christmas feast.

**Raj and Her Mother Olivia Ready for Church
While Lunch is being Prepared at Home**

Ah...the preparations! How should I describe them when so much was going on simultaneously? Let me start by looking in at the food preparations. Petite Anamma was chopping onions while squatting in a dining room corner. Periodically she had to move to make way for the reshuffling of table and chair positions. In spite of all the relocations, the onion chopping went on and on. Once mounds of onions were obtained, Anamma would slice and squeeze dozens of fresh limes needed for the biryani. This duty was followed by the cleaning, stripping, and chopping of immense shafts of fresh, pungent coriander. Sturdily built Balama with her sari wrapped tightly around her waist arrived at the backdoor having gone to the corner market to fetch freshly killed chicken and chunks of mutton. These were washed down with a backyard faucet. The meats were then carefully sectioned and readied for marinating with masala. Raj's aunt Elsie slowed down by a recent stroke oversaw the preparations from a strategically placed chair in the dining room. Elsie's culinary talents were legend in the Sebastian household. Among all the activity and chatter, at intervals each of the staff came by to seek Elsie's nodding approval as to what they were doing.

As I looked into the kitchen, I spied tomatoes, eggplant, and all sorts of pots and pans sizzling away. It was evident that the spice cabinet affectionately called 'Fort Knox' had been broken into, as Posama could be found in the corner rhythmically pounding away at assorted spices using a large mortar and pestle, a holdover from the Stone Age. Aromas emerged and filled the air as curries in various stages expressed themselves in earnest. Just as things appeared to be taking shape in the kitchen, a spindly milkman arrived at the rear door riding a bicycle. Strapped to each side were large metal containers. From one the man carefully ladled out milk to a number of jugs. This procedure was very carefully inspected by Elsie and the others to be sure no milk was wasted. After all were in agreement that the milk purchased was accurately accounted for, the man was paid and sent on his way.

The scene now shifted to the backyard as a large, colorful tent was being systematically erected by Jawahar and his construction *team* consisting of his sister, Anamma and Ashok, a wiry, agile, quick-witted threat to Jawahar's realm (there were all sorts of dramatic side bars to the domestic staff if one paid attention). As he matched the wits of a civil engineer, Jawahar precariously stacked up folding chairs one on top of another, as he strung up the tent poles and canvas. How he didn't hurt himself in the process was a mystery to me. Once the tent was in place, large tables and accompanying chairs were set up. As she took a break from the kitchen, Balama was joined by a rather lean and forlorn woman, Barathi, and together the tables were set with plates, utensils, and small vases of flowers. Jawahar moved to a corner of the yard to oversee the building of a wood fire which would soon be home to a very large pot or dekshi soon to contain the Mughlai *piece de resistance* – lamb biryani! Later Jawahar moved indoors and added festive color to the living room by nailing strings of bright lights directly into the plaster wall. Sparks coming from the 220 volt outlet also provided a nice touch not intentionally created, but were quite effective in scaring the hell out of me. Jawahar and *aide de camp* Anamma just giggled at the ruckus they had created and began to blow up several colorful balloons to be hung within the living room light show.

About midmorning Olivia and Raj arrived from church and quickly began the supervision of the preparation of a *light* breakfast consisting of eggs, toast, cakes, tea and coffee. An outsider might look upon the simultaneous preparations of breakfast and lunch as total chaos, but surprisingly the domestic staff never blinked as the extra tennis balls are tossed in the air to juggle. Soon the churchgoers arrived and many pitched in to assist the morning vittles, some made the toast, others scrambled eggs or helped prepare coffee and tea. Once the dining table was set with food, plates, etc., Raj's aunt Lena led the group in prayers and hymns of thanksgiving. Lena easily accomplished her task as if she had done it a hundred times (which she has). With everyone munching away inside and out in the backyard, Olivia quietly moved about the house checking on coffee and tea pots to be sure there were sufficient quantities. While Olivia was quick to smile and greet each guest, she appeared to be in her own spiritual world paying particular attention that no one has been left out.

After an interlude of maybe an hour or two and with much commotion the focus shifted to the biryani-laden dekshi in the yard. Amidst steam, fire, and smoke, the dekshi was surrounded by the domestic staff busy harvesting the biryani. Heaped upon large serving plates, the biryani was brought to the backyard tables with great fanfare – no dinner bell was needed in getting the guests to start feasting. My own plate filled to overflowing contained a generous amount of biryani and curds, the Hyderabadi eggplant specialty called bagara bangain, and a polite amount of chicken curry and potato. Wow! It looked so good I took still and video shots of my plate before I went to town. Soon the backyard was filled with the sounds of eating, contentment, and occasional shouts to the domestic staff for one thing or another. In their time Shah Jahan nor Henry the 8th never, *never* had it this good.

After lunch the guests began to depart each one made a special effort to offer personal thanks and holiday wishes to Olivia. Gracious as always, she made each one feel welcomed and important regardless of who or what they were. However, I soon found out it was *after* the lunch that the true festivities would begin. Olivia now opened up her heart and kitchen to the domestic staff and their extended families. With tables cleared now, it was time to reset them. Out came more plates and utensils, and of course the food. With giggling and laughter it was now time for *downstairs* to take over the backyard. After 7 to 8 hours of continued effort, the gang was to be treated just as the guests before them. Olivia took great delight as biryani was parceled out to Posama and her children, Jawahar and Anamma, Balama, Barathi and her son Ashok, and many more who previously were out of sight. A few of Olivia's old and trusted friends and relatives like Marie, Malathi, Usha and Narsing stayed on to help or otherwise enjoy the fun, each one knowing that the Sebastians always had a soft spot for servants and their extended families. I took a few more photos and I began to think what a big hit the day had been, especially for the small children with filled tummies who just began an impromptu game of tag. Upstairs children ran after downstairs children, and vise versa — for a moment at least, the world was in perfect balance.

Later in the evening as I was sitting in the front room and happily recalling the events of the day, Olivia entered with a rather large tray filled with cakes, each brightly decorated with Christmas wrapping paper. With Jawahar in tow Olivia went to the gate fronting Vigyanpuri and began to hand out the wrapped goodies to the street children. There were several displaced families who made shanty homes along the adjacent railroad tracks. In no time the street was alive with children's loud, boisterous voices as word got around that Olivia of B4F4 was handing out Christmas cheer at the gate. While Olivia expected the kids to line up one by one, Jawahar knew better and quickly distributed the cakes with tosses to and fro. Beaming from the effort Olivia collapsed in a chair next to me. I told her what a wonderful thing she had just done only to be told that "They won't stand in line!" Like Santa, or the Baby Jesus for that matter, Olivia was a dreamer — a wonderful dreamer. As I got ready to call it quits for the day I passed Olivia's bedroom, the room with the television. As a fitting conclusion to a most remarkable day, I saw the entire domestic staff and their children sitting on the floor watching Christmas carols being sung in Telugu, the local language in this part of India. I wished everyone a Merry Christmas, and in Olivia's house the greeting truly meant everyone: Christian, Hindu, Moslem or Parsi – it didn't really matter at B4F4.

**Side-trip to Our Stay in Hyderabad
took us to the Taj Mahal**

# Chapter 15

# Fishing – Later Years

To listen to me you'd think I fished every day. While certainly not true, I do dwell on snagging the little critters quite a bit. When I close my eyes and relax with my secret mantra, I transcend into envisioning a bobber gently floating with the breeze on a glassine surface. Quiet joy envelopes me as I'm transfixed upon the float looking for some hint of action below. Time is unimportant. I'm now one with the little red and white orb as it lazes adrift, seeking its place among the shimmering reflections of sunlight. As I sharpen my focus again, I look for anomalous movements. Was that the wind, the current, or bottom giving the float a gentle tug? Then it happens. First a slight, almost hesitant motion to one side followed by a wiggly submersion. Fish on!

What is it that makes grown men patiently do nothing while holding a rod and reel in their hands? I've learned over many years that those who do not fish (and they're in the majority) simply do not understand what makes us tick. Quizzically, Greg recently told me it's an illness…maybe so. On the other hand, I'd like to think that fishing is a noble art – a pursuit that freshens the soul and one's appreciation of nature, as well as an activity stimulating and cementing companionship. Not bad stuff considering the alternatives in life. One of the several books on fishing that my friend Chris Loretz has given me is Izaak Walton's 17th century volume *The Compleat Angler*, or *The Contemplative Man's Recreation*. Within the pages, Walton attempts to provide a guide of sorts on fish and how best to catch them. Yet with all his research, observation and tips, Walton himself came to the indelible conclusion that: "For angling may be said to be so like the mathematics, that it can never be fully learnt; at least not so fully, but that there will still be more new experiments left for the trial of other men that succeed us." Three hundred years later, Greg and I have been eager to provide our own contributions in support of Walton's sage admonition.

Throughout high school and college, fishing became erratic; regrettably, Greg and me outgrew our little niches at Scholfield's. One memorable excursion however made in our teens involved a trip to Lake Kabinkabami, Ontario. Located 20 miles from a tiny town called Oba, the lake was situated in pristine wilderness north of Lake Superior. This was country fitting for the magnificent brush-strokes of Canada's hallowed artists *Group of Seven*! Dad and his buddies Jerry Grace, Lon Wilcox and a few fellows from National Gypsum, decided that we had come of age and they let us join one of their annual outings. Early in June we accompanied a small convoy of packed cars which traveled on the QEW to Toronto for an over-night stay at the plush Royal York Hotel. After checking into our rooms, we were soon engulfed with room service food, booze and the set-up of a large card table. Into the wee hours of the night, poker would be interspersed with one fishing story after another along with continuous laughter and cigar smoke. While we had a few beers ourselves, Greg and I soon realized that these guys were in a different league when it came to putting away the booze. Maybe one of the upsides for me, with all the Crown Royal partying, was that I started a string of winning poker hands which continued into the 18 hours train trip the next day. Morning came early with the room a bit like a scene from *All's Quiet on the Western Front*.

Without much fanfare, we were soon crossing the street to the train station and our departure north. Ensconced in our club cars, I figured that we'd have a quiet leisurely journey where I could spend some time browsing the fishing magazines I had brought along. Nope! Royal York Hotel volume two soon took hold of the gang. Every conceivable flat surface of the largest and most centrally located roomette was filled to overflowing with cards, ashtrays, food, and drinks. Looking back, I'm sure someone paid off the conductor handsomely to put up with all the commotion. It might have been 3:00 or 4:00 in the morning when things started to abate. Thank God that the boys were finally running out of steam. For me, however, I clearly remember the last round of cards. I held six cards in a seven card stud game (nothing wild) and I needed a six to complete a winning straight. With the pot the biggest of the day, including an unopened bottle of Crown Royal, I successfully drew the six! No gun was drawn, but Dad took good-hearted heat for inviting these young bastards along on the trip. Back in our rooms which we had seen fleetingly many hours ago, we catnapped until an announcement was made that we were only an hour from Oba. Oba? What or where is that? We soon found out as we began to gather our gear and to take a crack at some breakfast eggs and toast. It seemed at this stage that sleep could only be desired, a goal hopefully to be attained down the road.

When the train reached the platform, we were greeted by someone from the lodge that we'd be staying at. With me in the front seat of a small truck, the driver gathered our gear while the rest hoofed the two blocks to the river and our awaiting boats. Two boats equipped with outboard Mercs navigated us through some of the most beautiful, untouched scenery I've ever seen. With the boats all loaded up, we looked like Lewis and Clark rejects as we started our 20 mile journey through the pine and fir lined river.

**The Start of Our 20 Mile River Journey**

Along the route, we encountered evidence of beaver activity with freshly gnawed trees littering the banks. Occasionally, we'd spot hawks, eagles, and the omnipresent loon. My camera was kept very busy trying to capture the awesome beauty before our eyes. Both boats held high spirits, especially the one carrying Gerry Grace who made a point of taking a full bottle of whiskey for the journey. All we could do was laugh and shake our heads as they sped by us en route to our landing and short portage to the lodge. With only a small lake left to navigate, we soon reached the docking area and another pick-up truck was at our disposal. After loading our gear into the truck, we began the up-hill trek to the lodge. Midway up the hill, we saw a grinning Gerry Grace sitting on the side of the road with a couple of inches left in his bottle. Greg later told me he thought he might have been invited along on the trip as Greg was the only one fit enough to get Gerry onto the back of the truck and to keep him there for the next quarter mile to the lodge property.

When we reached the summit of the portage, we saw an immense lake before us, and as we descended the hill, we viewed a series of log cabins which would be our homes for the next five days. It all looked too wonderful for words. After we checked into the main lodge and ate dinner in its family style dining area, we found our own cabin. No sooner than you can say 'walleye!', Greg was out the door to see what he could catch before sundown. You have to love Greg's focus. The first night we slept in our clothes because of the frigid temperature and our inability to get a fire started in the pot-belly stove. At day-break we were rousted by Gerry! Like Lazarus from the dead he had sheepishly trundled up to our cabin bearing a tray of hot coffee. We were not too sure about what we might be most surprised to see at this early hour – steaming coffee or a ready-or-not, here I come, Gerry Grace, and so began our Lake Kabinkabami fishing excursion.

The daily pattern for the week involved a hearty breakfast, pairing off into guided boats, trolling for shore lunch (usually consisting of freshly caught walleye), afternoons spent trying to snag a trophy like a northern pike or a musky, dinner of more fish, and an early shut-eye. Usually, everyone was too pooped to do any serious poker playing and/or drinking as sundown approached. Thank God! While the routine was the same each day, there were several incidents worth noting. One day after lunch at a hut deserted by a beaver-trapper, Greg came rushing in all excited that he had just spotted several trophy northern pike near shore. Quickly gathering his rod and reel he began casting a lure, first to the side of the lunkers, then behind, and then right in front of their snouts. There was nothing, not even a tail wiggle from the submerged creatures. Exasperated and yet bemused from what we had just seen, we got back into the boats for our afternoon rounds of trophy hunting. On another afternoon, I was paired with Dad when we encountered a small island filled with loon nests. Being a bit frisky, Dad had the idea of substituting an empty Labatts bottle for an egg in the nest. After the deed was done, we drifted nearby to see what the hen might do. Without beating an eyelash, the loon knocked over the bottle and settled back down on the next as if nothing had happened. These were 'Canadian' loons after all. Looking back at this trip, I remember idyllic beauty coupled with folks who worked damned hard in their everyday life as well as in their pursuit of fun and adventure. I was grateful to have been aboard.

Up to now, it certainly seems that Greg is inextricably linked to my many early fishing adventures. There is, however, on episode in which Greg played a major role, yet we did not share a rod and reel together. In 1967, prior to joining the University at Buffalo graduate program, I was enrolled in a summer research apprentice program at Roswell Park Cancer Institute. Participants like my buddy Peter Gunther from Niagara University, and me, were matched together with established investigators. In our case we were matched with an Australian named Donald Metcalf, who was a world authority on hemopoetic growth factors, along with surgeon Steven Foster, who was doing research as a way to avoid service in Vietnam. We made an eclectic research team. During the summer months, we had the opportunity to meet other grad students and teachers from near and far, including a single guy from the outskirts of New York City. One weekend, I invited him to go fishing along the banks of the Niagara River. In an area where I have frequented many times, we soaked up the sun, caught a few sheephead, and otherwise had a pleasant afternoon. As we drove back to my home in Kenmore, I suggested that we grill a steak for dinner and call it a day. When we reached home, I found Greg preparing for a big date with his bride-to-be Joann *and* in need on money. Greg could not have been more obliging as he smoothly relieved me of whatever money I had in my wallet. In addition, Greg grilled the steaks, threw a salad together, and happily replenished our beers. Soon he was gone, and this fellow and I were left to languish away the evening eating and drinking. Later that night I found that we both had drifted off to sleep with the TV still on at which point I suggested to him that we hit my parent's king-size bed and he could leave the next morning.

Sometime around three AM, I found that the fellow was making advances toward me from his side of the bed. Petrified I stared at the nearby clock radio wondering if Greg had come home yet. Just when I was about to panic, I heard the tell-tale sounds of Greg attempting to find the key hole of the front door. The click, click sounds were soon replaced by the door swinging open and crashing into the adjacent door chimes. Greg obviously had had a good time. While Greg was late in catching the moving door when he opened it, he certainly wasn't when he loudly slammed the door shut. As I heard all this, it made me feel as if the Marines have landed – never mind that Greg was not exactly in any condition to hurt a fly. He stumbled up the stairs, went down the hall for an interminable pee, and once reaching his bed off came the shoes thunderously hitting the floor. With courage, now fortified by the Marine invasion, I told the guy to get back to his side or I would have by brother down here pronto. Pure subterfuge, of course, but effective as the bastard quickly returned to neutral territory. Around six, I got up and went to the bathroom only to spot him from the corner of my eye taking a quick gander. I returned to the bedroom and told him to quickly get dressed and leave. Feigning ignorance of the night he obliged and left. Suffice it to say that was one fishing adventure I'd sooner forget, but not Greg's inadvertent rescue.

I've frequented local tributaries feeding Lake Ontario where migratory fish like salmon and trout abound in the Spring and Fall, and where more residential varieties like panfish and bass are there for the asking all year-round. At Olcott and Wilson, I've shared great experiences with Greg, of course. One spring Greg thundered at the top of his lungs after catching a hefty pre-season smallmouth: "It's a bass!" So much for coolness under fire. Later, I'd be joined in these outings by Greg's sons, Jim and Peter. Each was as different as night and day, but they both approached fishing with passion and gusto. Many former students have accompanied me on these favorite haunts. Foremost of these is Jim Pilc, who shares not only my pure joy of fishing but the simple patient act itself. Of course we're always counting as to who catches the most fish in any given outing. For us it's been wonderful times of reflection and companionship. Today Jim is a successful physician, yet still enthralled with fishing, of days past as well as the present. Then there's Chuck Mack – nurse anesthesiologist, Vietnam vet, and good friend. Fishing with Chuck has not only taken me back to the Ontario tributaries but to Tonawanda Creek in the shadows of DeGraff Hospital and the banks of the Niagara River. Whether basking in the simple pleasures of snagging tiny bluegills or one pound bass (or nothing at all for that matter), Chuck shares my love of doing nothing while holding onto a baited lines.

I might add that sometimes my baited line is fraught with danger. On occasion, I've caught both a mallard and a seagull with my trusty bobber and worm combo. In the mallard scenario, the swimming bird got too nosy and snarled itself with my bobber and line. Once entangled, it raced across Wilson Harbor channel with about 50 yards of my monofilament in tow. A year or two later, I snagged a seagull in the air during one of my casts. Again, as with the mallard, the bird headed out to the far side of the harbor leaving gasps and laughter from some of my accompanying students in its wake. Fortunately, the bird was rescued by the quick thinking and action of a student who was once a lifeguard in Long Island and knew exactly what to do to prevent harm to the startled critter. Reeling the squawking gull close to shore, the bird was gently swaddled by the student who waded out from shore to disentangle yards and yards of six-pound test.

On many sorties, Raj has been good-natured enough to accompany and assist me (what price love?) In addition to Olcott and Wilson, we've traveled together to the Thousand Island area at Alexandria Bay. In the early 1980's, we hired a guide for a two-day exploration of the

St. Lawrence River. After checking into our motel, I thought we'd
get a jump on things and go down to the shoreline and try our luck.
Using Raj's shoulder as my trusty cane, we ambled over the rocks and
got settled into some folding chairs – Raj with a novel in her hands
and I with poles, worms, bobbers and hooks (including my favorite
lure call Phoebe). In no time, small fish were latching on to any size
worm I tossed out. It got to be so busy that I never had a chance to
cast out my lure with the other pole. After seeing this, Raj had all she
could take and put down her book and asked me for a pole. For the
next half hour or so Raj hauled in one perch or rock bass after another.
No sooner had I a worm on her hook than bang another one and
another. Eventually, she took pity and went back to her book. Early
the next morning, we met our guide at the motel dock. Day one was
spent in and around the nearby channels and inlets and resulted in
several rock and smallmouth bass, however, day two belonged to Raj.

Our guide thought that we'd enjoy going after northern pike
and had us leave early so we could travel to the Canadian side of the
river where all the enticing weed beds were located. After securing
our Canadian licenses at a Customs dock, we headed down the river
in hopes of a trophy. As we moved along the shore, we encountered
several weedy areas, but our knowledgeable guide had a particular
area in mind. Just when we thought that he was never going to find a
parking space in this shopping center, he abruptly slowed down to a
crawl and inched the boat toward a small weed–lined inlet. He looked
for just the right orientation of the boat with the drift and he put an
anchor overboard. However, the anchor slipped and the process was
repeated again, and then again. Finally, after meticulous attention to
our anchorage, we were ready for some serious pike hunting. Using
worms, spoons, jigs, and even a minnow or two, Raj and I began to
snag a number of small northern pike which are affectionately called
snakes. The wind picked up a little, rocking the boat to and fro, but
the fishing continued unabated. Raj, who had fished continuously
for an hour or so signaled to me that she'd like to take a break. Our
discussion was cut off by the fact that she had hooked a big one. While
Raj was reeling hard and the drag was doing its thing, I put away my
pole and took out my Nikon. For what seemed an eternity, Raj told
the guide that she'd had enough, and that: "It's too hard. I don't want

to do it anymore!" The guide in disbelief looked at me but I could only laugh and respond: "She's all yours!" As she strained with each revolution of the reel, Raj finally brought the northern close enough to the boat for the guide to slip a net underneath it. With a whoop, the 6 to 7 pound pike was brought aboard for photos and plans for a shore lunch. Unable to top this catch, we headed back across the main channel and into American waters looked for a suitable place to have lunch. After rejecting a couple of small islands, the guide found a quiet little lagoon of one of the biggest islands and we went ashore for our *catch du jour.*

Deftly our guide gathered a cooler containing the pike, a huge slab of bacon, butter, bread, baked beans and a six-pack of beer. After he got a fire started, he took a large iron skillet and began to melt down the bacon. Nearby, on a sun-bleached log, he carefully filleted the northern as if he'd done it a thousand times (which he has). Raj and I, with cold beers in hand, easily took on our roles as guests. With the bacon removed from the pan, the floured pike fillets were added with a sizzling crescendo; in no time we were feasting over the sweet meats of our catch and voicing to each other: "Can it get any better than this?" After lunch we lazily got back on board for another hour or two of fishing – a black bass here, a smallmouth there.

**Me and My 1000 Island Smallmouth Bass**

We soon headed back to our hotel dock with lovely memories of the day and of Raj's fish that did not want to be caught. To this day when speaking of our trip, Raj always chimes in with: "Who caught the biggest fish?"

While I have evidence that Raj actually doesn't mind fishing, she primarily likes it when I get out and fish. On a trip to Vancouver, Canada in 1978, she encouraged me to hire a captain to take us out into English Bay and to try our hand at salmon fishing; however, because of rough weather we ended up cruising the safety of Vancouver harbor and the neighboring tributaries. A few days later and an overnight train ride to Jasper Park Lodge in the Canadian Rockies, I had arranged for a trout outing with a guide over the phone.

**Getting Ready to Trout Fish the Canadian Rockies**

While the weather was sunny and crisp the first few days, the temperatures took a dive the day I had scheduled for trout fishing. Upon waking up that morning we were greeted with a layer of late August snow. During our breakfast the guide called to tell me that the road to his trout stream was impassable due to the snow. Scratch another potential fishing odyssey from the list; however, there were three other trips with Raj which were quite notable from a fishing standpoint as well as for its venue and complications.

The relatively painless outing occurred when our friend Rosalind drove us through the highlands of North Carolina where we came upon a good ol' boy trout farm. Previously Rosalind whose home is in Georgia had been driving us back from a sortie to the Carolina and Tennessee Appalachians when on our return we happened upon this hole in the ground dressed up with a gaudy hand-painted sign: "Last chance to fish for trout for 100 miles." Of course, that was a bald faced lie but sweet music to a fisherman like me. Without much coaxing, I was quickly out of the car and got my line baited with popcorn – yes popcorn! When in Rome and so on, I quickly tossed out my line being careful to get the kernel to float near the middle of the pond. In no time, I had 3 or 4 rainbow trout for our journey back to Tucker and the waiting frying pan of Georgia's gift to Southern cooking, Miz Van, Rosalind's mother.

On another excursion, Raj and I drove up to Bayville, Ontario, at the invitation of a neighbor couple who were retired and owned a lake-side cabin. When she visited us a year after we were married, my mother-in-law, Olivia, also came along. After travelling 100 miles or so north of Toronto, we wound our way through beautiful conifer-lined scenery, and after a few hours we reached a remote cabin, which can only be described as equal to the setting for *On Golden Pond*. After breakfast the next day the three of us headed to nearby Bayville. As we came up to the cabin the previous day, I noticed an expansive river with an accessible shoreline which would be ideal to fish from. We parked along the river and gathered up our fishing equipment while Olivia stayed in the car very contented to be able to read one of the many books she brought for the trip. Still able to walk in those days I had a grasp of Raj's shoulder as we began to amble down the rocks and gravel which made up the shoreline. Just when we were within casting distance, Raj and I took an unscheduled tumble. After we disentangled ourselves from the stuff we were carrying, we were left sitting on our fannies looking at each other. Now what? Without much encouragement, I shimmied on my fanny toward the shoreline getting ready to fish amidst Raj's concern of how the hell we were going to get me back on my feet again and back up to the car. Satisfied that I was okay yet a bit crazy, Raj got the rest of the gear from the car and assured Olivia that things were just fine. With my first cast of sparkling, silver Phoebe, I nailed a small rainbow trout. While only a few inches in length, the pull on the ultra-light rig was a joy to behold. Gently retrieving the line after each cast was so much fun to watch the Phoebe bob and weave likes it's supposed to – imitating an injured baitfish. Nearly every cast brought activity. As I began to get comfortable in this idyllic setting, we were besieged by mosquitoes. If that wasn't annoying enough, a light rain began to fall. With these circumstances Raj and I entered into a short spirited conversation which ended with her taking a walk a few blocks into town for repellent and something to cover our heads. For me, however, bugs and rain couldn't spoil the moment. I was in my glory as I nabbed one small fish after another and took in spectacular sights, such as an air-born heron gliding aloft doing some fishing on his own. We spent only two nights at the cabin choosing instead to move on to a Holiday Inn and its amenities as well as its proximity to Algonquin Provincial Park. While Raj and her mom have their own distinctive memories of this trip, I for one have never forgotten the few hours of shore-side tantalizing year-old trout. How did I get back to the car you might ask? My short answer is – not by my feet.

Lastly, there was the time Raj and I and very good friend Nimmi Mudalier traveled to my parent's condo in Florida. Prior to our trip, my brother and his wife Joann enthusiastically convinced us that we must go out in a party boat called the *Lady Stewart*. "You'll love the big boat with seats and they do everything for you." After recovering from our day long flights from Buffalo to West Palm Beach via JFK and Atlanta, and waiting for lost luggage which didn't arrive til midnight, we gathered our thoughts as to what we might be doing for the week. "Mike, you need to book reservations for the *Lady Stewart*" jumped in Raj. I still couldn't believe my ears. Both ardent land-lubbers, Raj and Nimmi were still interested in going out in a boat! The next morning, with a rising sun in our faces, we arrived dockside along with other snowbirds from the north. We ambled onto the 60 footer and we took our seats facing starboard. As the boat quietly left the dock and entered the protective calm of Florida's Inland Waterway, the girls had their purses open to enter the daily betting pools of first, biggest, and so forth. All were in high spirits. Cameras were out and snapping away, I thought to myself that this might not be a bad day after all. As we slowly and serenely glided through the Waterway, I looked ahead toward our immediate destination – the Stewart Inlet. Like all inlets along the eastern shore of the United States, this is where the Atlantic and the Inland Waterway meet – sometimes quietly and uneventful and sometimes with a brisk on-shore breeze causing chaos.

As we bucked first to the left, followed by a wild slide to the right, the *Lady Stewart* came to grips with the Atlantic. As we rocked back and forth, I could see that the boat was more than sea-worthy, and I quickly drifted into thoughts of loading up my gear for some serious fishing. The last time I was out in a party boat was out of Freeport, Long Island, along with my brother-in-law Bob and his young son Matt. On that occasion we were accompanied by quite an assortment of boisterous yahoos, each intent on cashing in on the day's pool. My *Lady Stewart* companions were no different, except as the boat freed itself from the inlet turbulence and entered into a rhythmic roll, I could see the Nimmi sitting next to me began to feel squeamish. In about a half hour, we mercifully reached a small marker buoy which signaled that the crew was ready to anchor. In no time a bell was rung and down went our lines en masse. If you've never been on a party boat, it's quite a sight to witness all the activity and chatter. With help from one of the crew, my little party also had baited lines overboard. After panning the line, I waited til my bait hit bottom and then brought it up a few turns of the reel. Under a bright blue sky and with a crisp breeze in my face, I was psyched. It reminded me of times out in Lake Erie or a time years ago I accompanied my dad and some of his doctor friends fishing for sailfish out of Pampano Beach. Upon settling in on board the *Lady Stewart*, it didn't take long before I had a bite. Excitedly, I began to reel in the little fellow. However, during my reverie my attention immediately went to Nimmi, who leaned over the rail and lost her breakfast. Concerned that she might be unstable, I put my rod between my legs and hung on to the waistband of her slacks. Shortly, Raj stood up to assist but took a detour herself to the rail. With my fish-laden rod secure between my legs, I now had waistbands in the grasp of both hands. Alternatively, Nimmi and Raj mixed railing visits and sitting contrary to admonitions from a crewman, who insisted that they use the bait bucket. The merrymakers immediately downwind of us cooperated by getting into a rhythm of their own, and they moved back from the rail each time one of the ladies stood up. I know that my active fishing was over for the day, and I quickly retrieved my little sea robin and put away the rod.

"Mike, when are we going back?" Raj asked plaintively. I conveyed the bad news that it was only nine-thirty and we had the boat til noon. My response seemed like a death sentence to the girls. For the next two hours, each of us somehow struggled on. Nimmi, below deck, was periodically inspected by her soulmate Raj. As for me, I got into a lengthy chat with a fellow from Long Island (all the while staring at the horizon hoping to allay my own seasickness). Mercifully, around eleven-thirty the gong sounded and we were soon underway for homeport. When we reached the dock, Raj and Nimmi slowly regained their balance as we quietly trod our way to the waiting car. A few miles later Raj pulled the car in front of our condo, at which time I innocently asked: "Shall I make reservations for dinner?" Even though it was New Year's Eve, my question was greeted with steely-eyed daggers from the girls who quickly slipped into their separate bedrooms. Leaving well enough alone (they didn't hit me), I went to work on an oil painting on the dining table. However, an hour's worth of solitude was broken by a knock on the door. It was an exterminator who had been contracted by my dad. At this point I was perplexed as to whom I should please or displease – have the fellow come back another time and irritate dear old dad, or face the wrath immediately within. Choosing the latter, I let the fellow in with his canister of foul insecticide spray causing Nimmi to bolt from the condo and an awakened Raj to contemplate some form of medieval torture on someone close to her. As a closure of sorts to the day, the three of us did go out to dinner later that night – as I recall, the ladies skipped the seafood on the menu.

There were a few other instances where I've been out fishing in less than calm conditions. Many years ago after my paternal grandfather died, Dad bundled up the family along with his mother for a trip to the East Coast. After a day or two in the Boston area, we headed south to Hyannisport where Dad chartered a fishing boat. Out beyond the harbor inlet into open seas, we began to catch blowfish which amazed us all with their reflex capacity to inflate. Part of the fun, of course, was to catch the little buggers, but in hindsight we most enjoyed them bouncing over the waves as we tossed them back into the sea. Our enjoyment, however, was rather short-lived as the winds picked up and began to toss our 40-footer to and fro. No one got sick but the episode gave us a pretty good scare.

Years later I would come in contact with an old patient of my Dad who ran a charter service out of Wilson, located on the southern shore of Lake Ontario. Blinded by my zeal to catch salmon and trout in Lake Ontario, I booked the guide for an outing with my nephew Jim, also a student working in my lab, Jim Pilc, and Darrell Doyle then the Chair of our Bio Department. Once we were out a few miles from the mouth of the lower Niagara River, Jim snared a very respectable brown trout. The wind from the northeast began to freshen and soon we were embroiled in some serious rock and roll. As we went bow first into growing white caps, it became apparent that we needed to turn back and head back to port. All on the boat thought the idea was a no-brainer except for the guide, who was an old US Navy hand from the Korean War days. He was thrilled with the conditions but rather than risk a mutiny he slowly got the message and got us back to the relative calm of the Niagara River.

Not learning an iota from my past mistake, I booked the guide again to take Greg and my Canadian cousins John, Paul, Stephen, and Kerry. We followed a similar game plan and we exited the Niagara River and headed northeast; only this time the wind was worse than before. In the bucking and weaving through the deep swells, the cousins one by one hit the head to lose their respective morning doughnuts. Occasionally, the head was by-passed in favor of the rail and aiming downwind, thank God. Periodically, Greg and I would look at each other wondering if we would be next. For what seemed like an eternity, our terror soon ended; for the sake of hygiene at least, our captain aborted further fishing, and with the wind at our back he soon got us back to the protection of the river.

It's important to note, however, how memories of fishing companions can be highly selective. When I shared this story with cousin Paul, he had a different spin on things. With apologies to Ernest Hemingway's "Old Man and the Sea," excerpts from a letter Paul wrote me are quoted here. After he correctly mentions that the batting order for the first fish was selected lottery, Paul stated that it was HE who caught and landed the only fish – a 15-pound King Salmon! Fasten your seatbelts, the Gospel according to cousin Paul follows here:

"...Soooooooooo out in the lake on either the first excursion into the raging seas or the second, sure enough a fish took one on the lures and I, after just finishing my jumping jacks routine on the deck...a practice I've perfected to keep myself ready just for such a strike... bound forward and grabbed the rod from its mounting and set the hook and proceeded to begin to reel in the prize. It soon became apparent that it was a prize indeed because I'd no longer bring in 20 feet of line and 'the fish' would take out 30. As this pattern repeated itself the captain commanded John to take the helm and just keep the boat facing into the waves as he was required to bring in the other three lines so 'the fish' would not get all up in them. Controlling the boat was a difficult task because we were not traveling at a fast speed and the waters were very, very rough. The boat was tossing from side to side. It was further complicated because John was not an experienced helmsman and with his soaked glasses and somewhat chartreuse complexion was having trouble fulfilling his duties. The battle with 'the fish' continued for at least 10 minutes as I would bring the line in – he would take the line out' routine continued. On more than one of these trials Stephen was heard to say 'just cut the damn line and let's get out of here.'

At one point as I was finally getting 'the fish' close to the boat then the ridiculous happened. You know how the angler's task is to keep the fish in front of you, rod tip in the air so the captain could make a successful netting…well remember John was also trying to keep the boat facing the waves and was having difficulty in doing so. Well as I was getting 'the fish' close and captain poised with the net to scoop what we had glimpses of being a truly large fish, the boat shifted on the waters and was now facing the other direction. John looked out on this side of the boat and proclaimed in his proclamation voice that 'Hey…there's another one on this side of the boat.' My fish, the one that I was bringing in close to the edge for the captain was now under the boat on the other side. I yelled at John that it was my fish and to turn the boat away. After a few tense maneuvers by all of us we were able to do so and finally the captain was able to net 'the fish.' A beauty, a 15-pound King Salmon, which I kept and eventually sliced into salmon steaks and enjoyed n the barbeque. I'm exhausted now…I need a rest…or a few jumping jacks to re-energize."

Now whether the reader succumbs to Paul's tale hook, line, and sinker, the fact remained that we did return to the safety of the Niagara River where we quickly ran into a school of white bass. With a few beers and quieting waters, the fishing party began to take on a festive atmosphere. We spent the remainder of the morning trolling up the river towards Lewiston and beyond. At one point we were within shouting distance of the magnificent Niagara Power Dam. We turned around and let the current take us peacefully and slowly back down river towards our port-of-call, Youngstown. No more fish were caught on our final leg but the journey was relaxing. Just when we thought we were about to head to the dock and call it quits for the day, intrepid our guide started out toward Lake Ontario again! If that wasn't enough, he started to assemble the down-riggers complete with rods, lines, hooks and even the heavy ball weights. Incredulously, I looked at Greg who had the same look that I did – he's going to kill us! Apparently the little flask coddled by our captain during the day had more than mouthwash in it. As it smashed up against 5 to 6 foot breakers where the river meets the lake, the boat held its own but shook everyone to the core. Undeterred the guide continued on until we reached a point where we were in apparent jeopardy of crashing up against rocks and tourists dotting the Canadian shoreline of Niagara-on-the-Lake. Fortunately, common-sense took hold or more likely the fear of losing his precious little craft got us turned around and heading back to the river. With the wind and waves at our back, we quickly got back to the shelter of the lower Niagara. As we were meandering our way back to the dock, I couldn't help but think about all those lovely shows on TV where guys are pulling up one salmon or trout after another under clear skies and placid waters. No northeasterlies and no crazy ex-Navy man at the helm, just me and my remote.

A few other outings worth mentioning include an ice fishing endeavor arranged by Wayne Hadley, a fish biologist at the University at Buffalo. Early one February I found myself sitting on a stool in front of a six inch hole cut in the ice of an impoundment located within the nearby Iroquois Wildlife Refuge. Suspiciously hanging on to my rod and fearing the worst (crashing through the ice), I felt a tug and then another. Before I knew it, I had reined in a two-foot Northern Pike! Others in our party were equally successful, such as Carm Privitera and his young son Frank, as well as my dad who came armed with his trusty Nikon. Who'd a thunk it? To which Wayne would keep saying "I told you so." All of us later enjoyed the fine pike fillets for dinner except for the heads which were carefully kept for grad school and Taiwanese native Wei-Li (we became heroes in her eyes). Later that spring, still invigorated by the winter trip to the refuge, I was able to convince Greg and his sons to take a crack at Oak Orchard Creek which ran through the expansive series of impoundments initially created for migratory birds. After several hours in the rain and trying every conceivable rig in the tackle box, we came up empty – not even a hint of a bite. My reputation took a well-deserved nosedive. On the other hand, there was another outing soon after which took the four of us to of all places – Niagara Falls. Tapping into the local rumor mill we were led to believe that there were fish to be caught along the shores of the rapids leading to the American Falls. Our primary evidence came from seeing some fellows fishing along the banks – what other evidence do you need? First, we naively took a shot at fishing near the water intake which transports huge volumes of water to the Niagara Power Dam. We soon learned that fish would be crazy to be near this area as the thrashing current was enough to rip the skin off any fish. Our next stop was Goat Island, which separates the American from the Canadian Falls. We parked the car near the helicopter landing pad and transported our gear to the shore of the

American Falls Rapids. I sat in my wheelchair a few feet from the current and loaded up my line with my sure-fire Phoebe and made my first cast. When I reel in, I quickly learned the immense rate and power of the current. Not dissuaded, I tossed the lure far up-stream and quickly reeled in – bam! No sooner had the lure hit the water than I hauled in a scrappy nine-inch rainbow trout. My only thought at the moment was directed at the fish. What the hell are you doing here! Immensely satisfied, I became a spectator and spent the rest of the time fretting over nephews Jim and Peter, who scared me silly each time they climbed on top of one boulder after another to get closer to the rapids and one of the Modern wonders of the World.

Blessed with friends and relatives, I've managed to haul in one time or another smallmouths, perch, brown and rainbow trout, and every conceivable panfish known to a taxonomist. Whether it was chilly or hot, clear skies or raining, calm or windy, each fish brought me pleasure. That's the way it is with fishing for me and untold numbers of fisherman I've encountered. Because my residence has been mainly in Western New York, my angling has focused on freshwater species, however, there were two special times where I could easily have taken to salt water fishing. The first time occurred in October, 1972, when my brother-in-law Bob and my sister Karen rented a small boat and we took off for the inland bays of southern Long Island. Equipped with warm jackets and a hearty supply of bloodworms, we jigged the bottom silt for flounder. First Karen, then Bob, then I in the cycle that kept repeating itself til sundown – catching a flounder nearly every time reminded me of the time Dad and I ran into our evening school of smallmouth bass at the cottage described earlier.

On another special occasion I had traveled to Maine via Montreal with friends Harshad and Prem Thacore and their young son Harshu while Raj was in India visiting her mother and aunts for the summer. One day after a waterside lobster lunch in Bar Harbor, I found an adjacent US Coast Guard Station with plenty of open dock space. I quickly retrieved my fishing gear from the car trunk, and I found myself situated fifteen feet above the water surface where I had an eagle's eye view of young mackerel hitting my Phoebe and racing like hell. What fun it was throwing an arcing cast far below and soon after it hit the water – bang! While each catch was only a pound of two, the strain on my ultra-light rig was pure joy. By setting the drag, I was able to play each fish for a few minutes. The fish would dart to and fro until they eventually got tuckered out and I could land them safely. I bagged four and promptly gave them to Prem's brother Jay Sundaram and family who accompanied us from Boucherville, Quebec (ourside of Montreal). They had set up camp and were eager to fry up the fish with plenty of spicy masala over an open fire. Bon appétit mon amie! As a side note, we returned home by again going through Boucherville, which is located opposite Montreal on the banks of the St. Lawrence River. After lunch at the Sundaram's, I seized the opportunity to try my hand casting from a dock near a children's park. While the kids ran and played, I found an opening between stands of tall reeds lining the river bank. The water was clear and calm and my aim with the Phoebe was precision-like. By tossing the lure out seventy feet or so into open water beyond the reeds, I teasingly retrieved the line to be sure to let the Phoebe do its thing, which is to sparkle and imitate a wounded baitfish. Once, twice, then vary the speed even more. Slow the retrieve almost to a halt. Cast again but speed it up. After repeating this routine for nearly an hour, I was sure something was lurking about within the reed cover. Just as Jay came by to see how I was doing, a wild splash occurred as I was reeling in. I was not sure if it was musky or a northern, but I had apparently pissed off the old boy sufficiently to take a crack at my Phoebe, which I purposely dangled in front of him as often as I could. No fish but a thrill all the same.

This humble piece of fishing literature began with a description of my first outing with Greg as kids, when Dad finally succumbed to our cajoling and pleading. Many years later, Greg and I would find ourselves at a venue under quite different circumstances. During the winter of 1986, Greg needed to have an angioplasty procedure sending a shock-wave through us all. With rehab and meds over several weeks, however, Greg started to get his sea legs back again and resumed most of his normal activities, one of which was to discover trout fishing. During early spring, Greg ventured either alone or with one of his sons southeast of Buffalo, out where the landscape becomes hilly and laced with many small creeks and streams. After these outings, I'd get a report from Greg on how a snappy rainbow either was snagged or got away. As spring-like weather descended upon us, I of course was a bit envious but also aware that the spoken-about terrain was not fit for me nor my wheelchair. Wistfully I thought – keep those stories coming, Greg!

One day out of the blue I got a call from Greg who had just returned from the Arcade area. "Mike, I've got to get you down there. There's this Clear Creek, and I think I can get you there with the wheelchair." Needing no encouragement, we fixed a date for a morning in April. Armed with my gear, Greg picked me up in his new bright yellow Datsun and off we went to trout country. We zig-zagged through hill and dale, and we eventually found Arcade and the large stream running through it. It is interesting to note that Arcade is snuggled in a small valley and usually holds the record for Western New York's coldest spot in the winter. Many years ago the Arcade Hotel had been the site of our parent's annual Lions Club Halloween party – a bawdy affair from some of the pictures I secretly viewed as a kid. After leaving Arcade Greg headed along a road which seemed to parallel the stream for a couple of miles. As we crossed a small bridge, Greg excitedly pulled over into some knee deep grass. "See, over there that's Clear Creek!" What I saw was an idyllic stream meandering against a steep hillside, and if my quick calculation was correct there was about 70 yards of tall grasses and bushes to navigate. Undeterred, Greg got the gear from the trunk, including my folding wheelchair, assisted me into the chair and loaded everything into my grasp. Greg started to push the chair, then he pulled it, and, after a few yards through recalcitrant terrain, he changed his travel plans. "Shit Mike, enough of this!" Before I knew it, I was piggy backed to the creek after which he returned to the car to gather the rest of our gear and the chair. I was situated on a stony bank just below a small dam improvised and maintained by the local Trout Unlimited folks. Within a minute or two I nailed a 9-inch rainbow using a worm or a spinner. What a thrill it was to be actually fishing in the wild. The scenery was beautiful and I promptly took out my Nikon for several pictures. The morning turned sunny which highlighted the creek with sparkle, and this brought out the muted tones of the early spring foliage. As Greg had been here before he systemically worked the creek catching a fish every few minutes. After fishing a while behind the small dam, he walked up stream along the pebbly bank being careful to always have his line in the water. He was doing his 'Scholfield' thing.

A number of oil paintings stemmed from this particular trip. Photos taken on site were used as ideas for painting. However, my favorite one shows Greg fishing from shore about 50 yards from me. Intent on his line which was cast to the far bank, Greg was deep in concentration trying to bag a really big one in the shadows. Framing him were the pastels of the trees just beginning to bud after a long winter's rest. The foreground is filled with the creek, itself alive with reflections amongst the ambers and blues. I was happy years later to give Greg the painting and to share with him a very special day fishing. Like our early years as kids, when I sat in one spot and Greg roamed about like a springer spaniel after a quarry, we renewed again that special bond and love of fishing.

As a postscript, I should mention that I was honored with a couple of dinners and some gifts upon my University retirement in 2006. I guess you could say it was a testimony to my not-so-oblique preoccupations with angling that I was given a gift certificate to a local tackle store (together with a sapling outfitted with string and bobber ceremoniously presented to me at one of the dinners). The gift which blew me away, however, was a framed photo given to me by Greg. I am pictured in the photo sitting in my wheelchair fishing along the banks of Clear Creek and the inscription – *"Always be on the stream – Greg."*

Fishing for Trout at Clear Creek with Greg

# Chapter 16

# The Creative Process In Oils

One day after work, I looked outside to see the progress being made on a brick facing of a condo unit opposite ours. In 1974, Raj and I moved into a new condo complex, parts of which were still under construction. While taking our dog Meena out through the patio door, I was greeted by the on-site construction foreman who was out surveying the progress of the day. The foreman was a big, brusque fellow who gave the appearance of Burl Ives; he was the type who was easy to like, or dislike, depending on the nature of your complaints. In our case, we struck up a bond with him because our post-occupancy demands were reasonable and because he found us college professor types intriguing. On this particular afternoon, the foreman accepted our offer of a cup of tea and joined us in the living room for a little chat. After we exchanged pleasantries on the progress of the condo complex, the foreman began to tell us of the high regard he had for our work. Raj was teaching several allied health classes at Erie Community College, and I was at the University at Buffalo conducting research. However, it didn't take too long for both Raj and me to interject that our respective work had plenty of inherent pitfalls and frustrations – not the least of which was the snail-like slowness in seeing the results of our labor. Raj's students blossomed only later on after leaving the school; and, my research, if it ever sees the light of day in the form of a publication, will eventually become a ripple in the maelstrom of research data achieved by scientists the world over. On the other hand, I pointed to the brick wall just completed that day and I told the foreman: "Now, that's progress!"

Unlike Raj and me, the foreman had something to see and feel at the end of a day's labor. He had the satisfaction of accomplishing something in real concrete terms. Ironically, the foreman never looked at his work in quite those terms; however, I did. For me, oil painting provides that satisfaction. After I have finished a painting, whether I've spent an hour or so or several months on it, looking at the end results makes me pause as if I had just completed that condo brick wall. In the beginning there is only a bare white canvas, and now there is an image to be savored or critiqued. Something has been created, good or bad. My satisfaction not only comes from the finished product, but as I soon discovered the process of painting. The prep work with sketches, the pigment selections, the mixing of oils on a palette, as well as on the canvas, placing a dab here, and a dab there, until the rough imagery gradually is replaced with more and more color intensity and detail. The process goes on and on. I am in my 'creative sandbox.'

**In My "Creative Sndbox" at an Early Age**

With practice, I eventually learned when to quit working on a painting in order to not overdo it, which was my early inclination. By continually nipping around the edges, I tended to lose focus of the image I wanted as well as the artistic freshness which I had appreciated in several European and American masters. If I really wanted a photo representation of a scene, I should simply take a photo and be done with it!

It has been quite a revelation to me in looking back at paintings I've done over the years. I either skim through a chronological listing I have kept for a dozen years, or I pause to look at paintings hanging at home. Each canvas has a story. Each one is highly personal in some way. There are portraits, as well as scenes of flowers and places traveled. Encrusted in oil are my efforts to reproduce something and to capture a moment or a person, as well as to learn something new about the process of painting. I dare say that overall my body of paintings represents something more personal about me than my fingerprint or for that matter DNA! For obvious reasons, I never knew Claude Monet, but his impressions reveal otherwise. Winslow Homer? Mary Cassatt? John Singer Sargent? Andrew Wyeth? I think the casual observer would agree contained within their collective work rests beauty in all its form. In addition, their paintings reveal much about each artist. They attempt to capture the intrinsic nature of people, experimentation with light, shade, color and detail, exploration of the world around us and afar, and an unabashed celebration of what it is to be alive! I see some of these same qualities in my own paintings. Like writing, painting more often than not takes you in different directions, and a journey into the unknown. I hope to take you along my own journey using brush and canvas as my chariot.

Like most kids I was a doodler, and filled margins of my class notebooks with all sorts of cartoon figures. My dad was a doodler too. As a kid, Dad used a notebook for a stamp collection, and within it he penned various drawings in India ink. In grammar school I was exposed to a real "artist." As I sat in class as Sister Dorothy worked at her easel, I was in awe of her. With surgeon-like fingers and deftness, she navigated a shard of charcoal into a figure. While she may have tried to instruct us, her words had no impact on us kids. Our eyes were operational, not our ears. After carefully ripping out the page containing the sketch, Sister drew our attention to a small vase with flowers on her desk and began to sketch. Again, I was dumbfounded. I could doodle like my dad, but what Sister was doing was inspirational. Here was my first real experience of seeing an artist at work. Not only was she technically good, but Sister enjoyed what she was doing and was very happy to share the experience. Many years later Raj and I bought a watercolor from Charlotte Barnard, a Rochester artist who had exhibited her wares at our local Allentown Art Festival.

**My Presentation at the Allentown Art Festival)**

A gregarious, fun-loving sort, Charlotte explained that the still-life we bought was one which was used in her art class at Rochester Institute of Technology to illustrate what one could accomplish using only the three primary colors of yellow, red, and blue. She went on to explain that before going to class, she quickly gathered a few items at home and grouped them together for a quick pencil sketch. By using the sketch and only three pigments, she created a masterpiece for her class, and, ironically one for us to enjoy for all time. Sister Dorothy redux!

As for myself, I continued to doodle. I fill up class notebooks with faces, arrows and geometric figures, and occasionally a scene or two containing a boat, a car or a building of some sort. It seemed my left brain was always in charge, and careful to keep things linear and exact. Or was it? When I tried to sketch from actual objects or scenes, I'd hit a brick wall, and the outcome was lop-sided and contorted. In effect, I was not sketching what I was seeing but something else. What this was I don't know. Like most kids, my dabbling was just that – dabbling. Whatever came from the recesses of my brain spilled out on paper.

My dad on the other hand could loosely sketch away and capture the essence of a form or scene. I envied his talent – his ability to flip-flop from his right to left brain thinking and then back again. A precise, detailed sketch immersed within a holistic framework.

My artistic achievements in grammar school were confined to class projects like an early Pilgrim village and a heart-shaped entrance for a Valentine's Day dance. At St. Joe's High School, my artistic reach extended to the design of a float for our annual football game against arch-rival Canisius High School. We used classmate Mike Batt's convertible to erect a goalpost from the hood of the car, and we also used cardboard and aluminum foil to fashion a rocket pointed at the goalpost. A large sign on the car read: "Send Canisius to the moon!"

As sports editor of our senior yearbook, I had license to cut and paste photographs into all sorts of shapes and sizes as well as on the lettering. My approach to art was rather stochastic, more befitting someone interested in architecture. Thanks to my knack for things linear, and to my mother who bought me a biography of Frank Lloyd Wright, I was seriously considering a college program in architecture. I marveled at Wright's ability to harmonize geometric formations within their surroundings.

As I mentioned earlier, Dad was the resident Rembrandt at home. He dabbled with poster paints for his annual Christmas tableaux on the living room mirror. He made sketches of us kids in pastel and there were even a few oil paintings tossed in for good measure. While I was intimidated by the various media, Dad usually jumped in with both feet. Call it talent, or just an I don't give a damn attitude, Dad was unique to me in that he could take on a project and fearlessly work with whatever medium he fancied at the time. There were four oil paintings which he did during the war when he was stationed near Sens, France. After he died in 1996, I had each of his paintings framed to hang in my home office. Each one shows a varying aspect of Dad's talent. The Sens Cathedral was painted from a black and white postcard and exhibits his knack for accuracy, verite and color.

He used oil for the surrounding country-side. Painted in plein aire style, it shows influences of Gauguin with its patchwork, linear quality. The other two paintings are portraits of women. One is an exacting depiction of my mother taken from a photograph, while the other is of a provocative woman holding a cigarette with her arms folded, an illustration from a magazine advertisement.

Dad also introduced me to painting-by-number kits. While I was okay in filling colors within each allotted space, Dad always took the extra step of not following instructions and mixed and matched colors to his heart's content. His results were always better than the painting represented on the kit box. Later when I was in college, I gave him a cutout from a whiskey ad depicting a golfer blasting out of a sand trap from Troon, Scotland. "What do you think Dad? Can you paint this for me?" In a week or so he surprised me with an oil. It was beautiful and fresh with bold colorful strokes accomplished in true alla prima fashion. One day I hoped to be able to do that. For the time being, I was contented in drawing up caricatures of friends and family for special occasions. I used a magazine cover format. I drew a figure and connected it to cartoons and lettering appropriate to the person and occasion. In this way, I was able to artistically celebrate a special event, such as a birthday, graduation, or anniversary. Things changed after I married Raj and we began to take vacation trips together. Equipped with my trusty SLR, I fired away hoping to capture that one, perfect, National Geographic cover photograph. Before long, we had albums full of mountains, lakes, gardens, and everything in between. It was in the early 1980's when I began to think about painting some of the photographed scenes in oil! If my dad could do it, if my sisters Steph and Pat who took actual art classes could do it, and if my aunt Sister Catherine and her sisters Mary and Vicky could do it – why shouldn't I give it a go.

My initiation started with a couple of 5 x 7 panels of scenes from our trip to the 1000 Island area. Quite tentatively I sketched two water scenes from photos taken on board a boat piloted by our fishing guide. The first painting showed the shoreline of our hotel and the other of a small island jutting out into the St. Lawrence River. This was not an ambitious start but a start nonetheless in oils. I soon found oils to be a forgiving medium – mixing and blending can occur on the palette as well as on the canvas itself; and, importantly, a wet painting could be left alone until the next day without any change. Since both scenes had prominent water elements, I soon became infatuated with the surface reflections made by trees, buildings, etc., and how to best capture them. This was a start.

By using the photo albums, I painted more out of town scenes – e.g., Jasper Park Lodge, fishing boats moored on Long Island, our Canadian cottage, and a coastal road near Bar Harbor, Maine. The more I painted the more I enjoyed the process and challenge, and importantly derived the satisfaction of completing something unique and satisfying. With my confidence growing, I focused on painting a portrait of my mother the year after she died. I used an engaging photo of her taken in 1981 at the cottage. She was suntanned and happy, and the photo had all the elements I wished to capture on canvas. Equipped with back issues of *American Artist* magazines, some of which took me through portrait procedures, I jumped into the project. I worked on and off for a month until I reached a stage where I was satisfied. Once the painting was varnished and framed, I hung it on the wall as a daily reminder of what a special person she had been.

Over the years, I've done several other portraits, including ones of Raj's father and mother after each had died. For Jaya, I used a photo of him sitting in a chair wearing a fire red sweater that I had given him on one of Raj's trips home to India. Work on the painting was under constant scrutiny by both Raj and Olivia, who was visiting us for the summer in 1983. The more I worked on the portrait, the more it became clear that Raj and her mother were looking for something special, and it wasn't there yet. One day they went shopping together leaving me alone to wrestle with "what is missing here?" After further minor changes I found the problem. The eyes were too close together. Recalibrating his eyes and expression, the elements of the portrait fell into place. Once home, Raj and Olivia broke into tears and explained that I had indeed captured the essence of what all who knew Jaya remembered most about him – his loving, gentle eyes.

Capturing my dad on canvas would also be a tricky proposition. After he died in 1997, I set aside a day to work on his portrait. I used as a model a photo I had taken years earlier at a time when my parents were at home celebrating paying off their house mortgage. As Raj and I said our good byes from the car, I shot a picture of the beaming couple. I can still hear my dad's words as I snapped my camera? "Mike, it'll never come out." Working with thin washes, I gradually captured Dad's highlights and expression. After working for only an hour or so at the kitchen table, I placed the painting in the family room so that I could have lunch. The more I stared at the painting, the more I felt I needed to stop. Earlier, I would have kept plugging along with more washes, more color, depth, highlights, background, etc. But no, in this case the painting was done. I had accomplished what I set out to do and captured that moment several years earlier when Dad uttered in his usual needling way: "Mike, it'll never come out." I painted another painting of him which I included in a grouping of small paintings of my fishing companions all hanging together in our family room. The painting I did of Dad was from a photo taken by Greg in the Florida Keys. Like his portrait I only worked for about an hour. The time was sufficient enough to capture Dad's pride and pleasure in catching a fish in the sun-drenched Keys.

Over time I've enjoyed portrait painting. In most cases the paintings were for survivors of someone who had died. A notable example was a portrait I did of the very young daughter of our good friends Prem and Harshad Thacore. These parents were devastated when Sharmila suddenly died from pneumonia. Not too long after the funeral, I set my sights on a portrait I wished to give to the parents in the hopes that it might help assuage their grief. Even after over 30 years, it brings me great pleasure in knowing that a framed oil of Sharmila hangs in the Thacore household, bringing them a daily reminder of the daughter they loved, and who had been prematurely taken from them.

**Self - Portrait at 40**

Watching artists work their magic on PBS to accompany my growing interest in the alla prima ('first go') approach to painting, I started to experiment with wet-on-wet. Using myself as the guinea pig, I set up my gear in the bathroom to paint a self-portrait on the occasion of my 40th birthday. As I stared at myself in the mirror, I jumped into the project. I was tentative at first, but soon my strokes were all over the place – a dab here, a scrape there. It was an evolutionary process where refinements were constant. As I worked, I marveled at the nuances of my face, subtle coloring and shadows, all of which I tried to replicate on my canvas. The bathroom soon turned into my creative sandbox where I was free to dabble and explore. Thirty years later I can look over my shoulder and see my framed face which seems to have withstood the test of time. I have tried a few self-portraits since then, but nothing compared to my first outing into wet-on-wet.

As I looked for other alla prima projects, I cornered my nephew Peter while he watched TV. Decked out in his GI Joe camouflaged shirt, he turned out to be an ideal model, as were other kids, including Harshad

Thacore, Jr., and Julie Gardner, daughter of Diane, a colleague of Raj's. Freezing these kids in front of the TV turned out to be the perfect ploy to hold their interest while I painted away. Soon I was outside exploring what I could do in our garden (e.g., marigolds, poppies, lilacs) and elsewhere, such as my old fishing hole at Sixteen Mile Creek, an apple orchard in full Spring blossom in Niagara County, and a Fall excursion to Akron State Park to capture brilliant maples at their peak. In each case, I had Raj by my side to both encourage me and, importantly, to help me set up my easel. Many of these paintings were later framed and exhibited (some sold) at our local Allentown Art Festival in Buffalo.

I was now in my forties and circumstances with my disability forced me to come to grips with what energy I had to allocate for my day to day life. A severe ankle sprain in 1977 brought my ability to drive a car to a halt. I could have worked out some mechanism to let me drive using my hands, but in practical terms it was better to leave the driving to Raj. As it was, I needed my bodily resources to keep up with my research and teaching activities which were expanding with each succeeding year. Any extra time I had I was happy to spend with Raj, and, as it turned out, an hour here and an hour there to painting. Often I felt like the clock was ticking on what time was left for me to continue to paint. In this regard Raj was my inspiration and the one encouraging me at every turn. As time went on, we began a collection of art books. Many were purchased at galleries we had visited. Within the US, we started with the Buffalo Albright-Knox and later extended our range to include the renowned galleries of Washington, DC, New York City, Boston, Detroit, Atlanta, Minneapolis, and Toronto. As our repertoire of galleries and exposure to the masters increased so did my passion for painting. I particularly loved the impressionists, as well as those who performed highly detailed work. It's one thing to ponder at a painting within a coffee table book, but it is quite another to examine a painting up close where each stroke of a brush can be seen and appreciated. For me the experiences were nearly religious in nature, and they still are today.

In 1984, I finally summoned enough courage to take a trip overseas to England. Staying at home while Raj went a couple of times to India to see her family, I always regretted not going with her. My fear of flying and, I guess, other factors with my health, kept me put. With Raj's encouragement, I finally bit the bullet and we flew to London out of Toronto. During our stay, we visited one gallery and museum after another; so much so, that we had to mail our weighty collection of books, cards, and pamphlets to our address back home. In particular, we enjoyed the National Gallery, British Museum, Victoria & Albert, and the Tate. Our minds were abuzz each day as we freely commuted to and from our hotel seeking more and more art, history and culture. The National Gallery was all one could expect from this venerable institution – quiet rooms, dimly lit, and warders over your shoulder to prevent you from even thinking of shooting a picture of the masterpieces. The collections represented a "Who's Who" of art the world over – all contained in hushed almost reverent silence. As we were leaving, the gallery had a number of educational exhibits set up. While the emphasis was for school age kids, we adults learned much as well. For example, there was one exhibit where two paintings were situated side-by-side and you were asked a simple question. "Which one is real?" One painting was a colorful impressionistic rendition of an English countryside. I found it quite appealing. The other painting was a bold, colorful abstract – dots, dashes, lines and geometric figures jumbled together. As I turned the question pad looking for the right answer, I had to laugh as I was told the abstract was the appropriate answer. "What you are looking at is red paint, black, blue, yellow, and so forth. What could be more real than that? What I saw in the impression was not the paints but the artist's allusion to something real." Touche!

On another day we visited the Tate gallery which was situated along the Thames River. Buzzing with activity, the Tate is much more laid back compared to the National. Visitors scamper around from room to room catching a glimpse of a Turner here, and Sargent there. It was wonderful seeing so many works from European artists all under one roof. There was one painting in particular that we wanted to see – Sargent's *Carnation, Lily, Lily, Rose*. Not knowing quite what to expect as we didn't know its size nor where it might be situated within the Tate, we went from room to room on the lookout. Our quest was short-lived as I spotted it from two rooms away as the painting was so large and prominent. After seeing the masterpiece for ourselves, Raj and I knew we had to get a life-size print of it in the gallery gift shop (another addition to our growing mail bag). While Raj and I have vivid memories of the Tate, there is one episode which stands out. It was early afternoon when we decided to leave and get something to eat. When we were about to depart, I told Raj that one of our guides to London highly recommended the Tate restaurant. As luck would have it, the entrance to the eatery was just down the hall, but as we started down the hall, I read that reservations were needed. Throwing caution to the wind, I spoke with the hostess and explained our desire to eat if at all possible. After telling us to stay put, she disappeared, only to return shortly to escort us to our table. With Raj pushing me in the wheelchair, our first barrier was a large circular table inhabited by ten diners. Without batting an eye, the hostess explained that they needed to move the table a bit to allow these two to pass. With Raj and me apologizing left and right, the diners graciously stood up each gripping a bit of the table delighted to be of help. Once we got by the table, it was downhill as we simply had to zigzag a bit more until we reached our own table for two. As we gathered ourselves together with menus in hand, Raj and I marveled, not so much for the art we had just witnessed, but for the 'can do' spirit of the Brits. It would be the same throughout our trip in the British Isles where we daily encountered people only too happy to assist us. Whether it was getting us into the inner bowels of the physically challenging British Museum, bus rides to Windsor, Cambridge, and Oxford, or commandeering a food lift to get me on and off a British Airways 747 when not tethered to a flyway, the British measured up to my image of them as they withstood the Blitz during WW II.

During our trip, we made a four day excursion to Paris where we took in the French impressionists at the historical Jeu d'Paume. Within the hallowed walls of the gallery, we leisurely savored the likes of Monet, Manet, Pissaro, Renoir, Van Gogh, Carot, and Cassatt. Our joy at seeing firsthand the handiwork of these artistic geniuses had no bounds. Later in our journey, our guide drove us to Giverny, where we visited the last home of Claude Monet. It gave us great pleasure to retrace areas within Monet's garden, as well as his famous lily pond. During this particular leg of our European trip, my Nikon clicked away as never before. As I fired in all directions, I made mental notes of scenes that I would love to paint myself once we got home. Some of the paintings I accomplished included scenes along Monet's garden paths, the Japanese bridge, and the lily pond, where I was able to highlight an adjacent rose arbor, reflective willow trees, and, of course, the signature water lilies in bloom. With a photo as my guide, each time I painted a scene I happily relived our trip abroad.

Because I had gathered enough gumption to fly over 'the pond' to see Europe, I was now eager to take the trip of my life – India! In 1985 and 1987, with Nikon in hand, Raj and I made successive trips to Raj's homeland. For the photographer and for any artist worth his salt, India represented the *crème de la crème* of opportunities. People, animals, plants, color, sun, and shade are all thrown together in a maelstrom of wonderful activities called India. I reveled at one scene after another. As I aimed my camera this way and that, I knew at once that I couldn't wait to get back home and paint. One scene in particular jumped at me. After we visited some friends, Raj and I were returning home by car from suburban Banjara Hills. As we came down a small hill at twilight, we were about to enter a busy street filled with buses, lorries, carts, ox carts, motorbikes, and several walkers. When I first spotted the glow of waning sunlight illuminating an ox cart just up ahead, I knew I had the picture I wanted. Struck with the interplay of shadowing caused by the fading evening light, I quickly grabbed my Nikon hoping to capture this fleeting moment. As it turned out, the picture was the focus of several oils once I got home.

Even though I had given several paintings away by now, especially the portraits, I was beginning to collect a fair number of them at home. There are only so many paintings that friends and family are willing to hang in their homes! My storage problem was temporarily fixed when, with the encouragement of Raj, Cathy, and my aunt Sister St. Catherine, I entered the Williamsville, NY, Art Show in 1986. With trepidation I gathered and framed most of my oils for the big day. Cathy's father, Ben Pollina, got into the act by constructing a wood frame for chicken wire needed to hang the paintings for showing. Once the day arrived and my exhibit all set up, I thoroughly enjoyed meeting the several passersby who came to the show. I had no "theme" like most of the others showing their wares. Mine was an eclectic mixture of paintings of Monet's garden, lilac trees and assorted flowers from my own garden, a sari shop in Toronto, an ox cart in heavy traffic in India, portraits of my nephews Jimmy and Peter, colorful bottles of water from Edison's Museum in Detroit, Florida scenes, winter snow accumulated outside my bedroom window, blossoming apple trees from nearby Niagara County, still-lifes of copper vases at homes, scenes of the Canadian Rockies, and of course, various fishing scenes. Maybe some might think that what was on exhibit was a time-line of my love affair with painting from slap dash alla prima attempts to more detailed, controlled efforts, such as a large painting of my mother-in-law's school in India call Mahbubia. That effort took over a year and a half to finish, because I needed to see for myself the immensity and grandeur of the stately structure.

With the local art show under my belt, for the following year I decided to take the plunge and enter the competitive Allentown Art Show held each June in downtown Buffalo. As instructed, I submitted slides of four of what I thought were my best paintings for consideration by the judging panel. After what seemed like an eternity, I received a package containing an acceptance letter along with a schematic diagram of where my spot would be on Delaware Avenue. Once the thrill sank in, I soon realized all the work I needed to do to ready myself for the show – more painting, lots of framing, more painting, etc. The frame from the Williamsville Show was destroyed when a gust of wind blew down my exhibit late in the afternoon. To the rescue came Cathy and her dad Ben, who fashioned a much sturdier frame using PVC piping.

With the car packed to the gills, Raj and I headed to the Allentown Section of Buffalo. As we got closer, I found myself getting more and more anxious. What am I doing? I'm not an artist! I'm a researcher, a teacher! Reaching the curb of our reserved 15 feet of Delaware Avenue, we joined the hundreds of other exhibitionists who were busy setting up their wares. Cathy met us and took over setting up the PVC frame as well as helping to hang the dozens of framed paintings of my exhibit. Once ready, Cathy and Raj pushed me in the wheelchair to see other exhibits lining Delaware Avenue to get an early glimpse of the show. As I found out, the serious art aficionados come early when relatively few strollers are up and about, and there are amply opportunities to see the art work up close, as well as to chat with the individual artists. If you didn't come early, about midday the show is transformed into masses of spectators, complete with kids pushed in strollers, dogs on leashes, and a sea of humanity wolfing down Italian sausage. Quite a sight!

Now seated behind my exhibit, the Show officially began at 10 amidst little or no fanfare just the gradual increase in foot traffic and rumbles of voices. Now came the waiting. Would anyone be tempted to buy one of my paintings? Seeing the masses stroll by gave me hope followed by despair. How could they not buy one of my garden irises? A stringer of fish? A scene from exotic India? Or something local like the fall leaves at Akron State Park? What helped were the many friends and colleagues who came by to say hello and chat. That magical moment eventually arrived! Cathy came to me and said a man was interested in my Florida water scene where fishing boats are returning to port after a day's work. I was so nervous and happy that I told the fellow to pay me $55, not the $60 listed on the sticker. "Don't worry," I told the man, "I'll pay the NY State Sales Tax for you!" Hurrah, my first sold painting. It would be a moment never forgotten, and one repeated a dozen times over the weekend. Toward the end of my first day at the Allentown after selling dozen or more paintings, a young man on a bike wanted to buy my colorful autumn scene of Akron State Park. "I bike there all the time, and you captured it perfectly!" he went on. He didn't have any money with him, it was all at home. Cathy, after hearing all this said, "No problem, we're closing down now, and I'll bring the painting to your home." Against the objection of the biker's wife who didn't think spending $60 was such a great idea, the sale went forth as Cathy had suggested!

So it went for the next six years. With the exception of 1989 and 1990, when my painting time was interrupted by a trip to India, I exhibited at the Allentown until 1993, when I had finally had enough.

**Painting of Hyderabad Street
Scene Taken From a Photo**

By then, I realized that all the work and expense necessary to get an exhibit ready, just wasn't worth the effort anymore. Looking back, however, at those years I did exhibit, I'm filled with countless memories. It was fun meeting the artists right next to us – Rip Bodman and his wife, Judith. Rip was a Vietnam Vet who threw his emotional and talented energies into colorful silkscreens, while Judith displayed large format etchings, a craft she learned in Italy. To mark our wedding anniversary, Raj and I purchased "Mill Pond," an ambitious depiction of biological life in and around a pond not far from their New Jersey country home. On another occasion, also another anniversary, we purchased a lovely watercolor from the garrulous Charlotte Barnard, an artist and teacher from the Rochester Institute of Technology. Getting to meet and chat up art with other artists was great fun for me, as well as an inspiration. One time a man came by to talk to me early in the day after we had set up our exhibit. I had seen him before a few times, going from exhibit to exhibit, as if he were some art critic from the New York Times. "You know, you have paintings here which are truly representative of what this show should be about!" he proclaimed. As he left he wished me good luck. Looking back, I was buoyed by his comment, but in retrospect not terribly impressed as he didn't purchase any of my wares.

It is hard to judge what might sell. One year I sold out my inventory of colorful irises. The next year, I purposely came to the Show with extras – only to bring them home unsold. Abstract painting went well. For example, I painted a few watercolors during my lunch break at school. In one called, "It's that time of year," I had a small vase of violets juxtaposed with a soiled baseball. Another was of a bright orange coffee mug with an elephant painted on it. Still another was a painting of one of my luncheon apples, and I labeled it "Mystical Apple." They all sold. I had a series of paintings from Claude Monet in Giverny. I thought for sure they would all go quickly. No. Lilacs were a big hit. Whether in a vase or springing from our garden, people love lilacs. However, one painting called "Lilacs for Olivia" didn't sell, and it turned out to be one of several 'orphans' from the Show that I brought home with me. Generally, the orphans found homes in my closet, the basement, or hung on the wall at home or at school. "Lilacs for Olivia" turned out to have a life of its own. I was approached by the Muscular Dystrophy Association who was initiating a traveling art exhibit as a way of getting out the word that those with neuromuscular disease can have active, artistic lives. After discussing the situation with Raj, we came up with the idea of donating "Lilacs for Olivia." When the painting didn't sell after two times at Allentown, I had given the painting to Raj's mother, Olivia, to take back to India after she had spent the summer with us. When she returned two years later she brought the painting back with her. She was more willing to part with it for the sake of the MDA. As the saying goes, the rest is history. As a component of the MDA's permanent collection, "Lilacs for Olivia" has been shown in over a dozen prominent galleries throughout the country. Not bad for one of the orphans of the Allentown! Maybe that old guy was right after all.

Ego aside, the Allentown experiences were wonderful opportunities to produce art with an end-game in mind. In looking back, I learned to see art appreciation as individual and personal. What I think is worthwhile may not be so for others, and vise versa. At the very least, the experiences opened up new avenues for me to seek. There were more friends and colleagues who were interested in commissioning me to paint scenes for them. Raj's colleagues from ECC were first in line. Carol Mack wanted me to paint a scene of their house with their daughters and pet dogs in the foreground. Bob Cunningham wanted a depiction of Bryce Canyon. Jane Weston and her husband requested a painting of their favorite watermill in Lower Slaughter, England, Clarice Parrag ordered a picture of a Swiss castle to surprise her husband, Mike, and Chandra Basu wanted a large format of my Indian rice planters. Rich Almon from UB wanted a bigger rendition of my ox cart form India. And so it went, more scenes, more portraits, etc…I had more ideas for painting than I had time and energy for.

The *piece de resistance* came one day when my brother Greg described a conversation he had had with a new patient in his dental office. She asked Greg upon meeting him for the first time, "Are you related to the artist?" Greg was dumbfounded hearing this? She continued, "You know, the artist who exhibited at Allentown. I bought a nice painting from him last weekend!" Well, I'm not sure I could truly be called an artist in the professional sense, but one thing is clear to me after these many years. I no longer envy the builder of the condo brick wall as an embodiment of self-content for a job well done. At the end of the day, I too can look at my many walls, only mine have canvases hanging from them.

# Chapter 17

# High Inside Fastball

En route to catch the Sabre's vaunted French Connection on a cold, wintry night in 1976, I turned my head in the direction of the backseat and asked Arvind, "What do you think he's going to do? There's so much speculation."

"Well," said Arvind after a little chuckle. "I really don't know; he might stay here, or he might not. You know the little man. He keeps everything a secret. We'll just have to wait and see." After coming to a stoplight, I added: "Sam told me recently that he has plans to take over some old space at Ridge Lea, and he had even included some area in it for me. It would appear that, if he were going to England, he wouldn't be moving to Ridge Lea, we'll soon find out."

A few weeks later in May, I was home in the evening working on data at my desk when the phone rang. "It's for you. It's the little man," Raj said as she joined me in the spare room now being used as an office. I took the phone and with a bit of apprehension said, "Hi, I'm nearly done with the statistics we talked about."

In a soft, somewhat cautious tone, the little man noted that he was in the lab with the others. He had just broken the news that he had decided to take a position in England. After a short chat about the reasons for the move, the little man came to the main reason for the call. "The facilities there are wonderful, and I'm thinking I can raise my own chickens there." In a manner in which a lawyer synthesizes a brief, the little man spoke of all the convincing reasons why the drug therapy work should be done in his new lab in England. At the end came the clincher. "I've decided to take the chicken project with me."

At that moment I felt both relief and a sense of deep sadness. I was relieved that the little man had finally made a decision, and the confusion in the lab could now be put to rest. On the other hand, a sickening feeling came over me as I thought of the time and energy I had spent on the project since joining the little man's lab two and a half years ago. After Raj and I were married in 1973 and moved from Syracuse to Buffalo, with my Muscular Dystrophy fellowship tucked under my arm, I joined the little man's research lab.

I was initially saddled with some on-going projects and a couple of eager undergraduates. While some of the work had its obvious long-term clinical spin-offs, I found the surgical and radioactive labeling procedures tedious and far removed from my desire to learn more about muscular dystrophy – the scourge of 'Jerry's Kids,' as well as the Hudecki family.

One day I drew the little man into a discussion of how we might utilize the chicken in a drug trial. I had experience working with the noisy beasts at Syracuse, and ever since then I had closely followed the expanding dystrophy literature, including some futile attempts of treating or simulating the disease in animals. In particular, I was attracted to a series of experiments conducted by W. King Engel at the NIH. Based on work using rabbits and rats as models, Engel and his colleagues proposed that dystrophy was a result of a circulatory impairment in muscle. They found by injecting small latex beads together with vasoactive chemicals that muscle lesions appeared that were similar to that found in patients, hence, a 'circulation hypothesis' was born.

More or less to assuage my over-riding interest in dystrophy, the little man relented and said: "Okay Mike, go ahead and get some chicken eggs and see what you can find out." To get things started, we decided initially to test chemical that had vasodilatory properties. If Engel's hypothesis was correct, and our chicken model cooperated, we thought we might be able to reduce muscle weakness through drug intervention. The first drug we tested was methysergide, a drug obtained gratis from some very cooperative folks at the then Sandoz Corporation (which is now part of Novartis). While methysergide's primary application was to relieve migraines, the active ingredient was a powerful inhibitor of serotonin, a chemical transmitter well-known for its vaso-active activities.

As luck would have it, Raj had a student who she thought would be perfect to carry out the trials for me. After one of Raj's evening classes at UB, she greeted me with:"Hey Mike, I think I have someone who might be interested in working with you! His name is Skip Beeler."With long, shaggy hair, Skip first met Raj in 1973 as a premed student in one of her classes.They hit if off immediately. Skip enjoyed and responded to Raj's 'school marm' qualities while Raj liked Skip's blend of eccentricities, youth, and talent. Fortunately for me, a budding research team was hatched.

When he wasn't house-sitting our cock-a-poo or hawking *Rolling Stones* tickets on campus, Skip embraced the project. Concurrent with the daily injections of methysergide, Skip performed the ritual of 'flipping' our chickens every 5 days to determine strength. We toyed with different approaches, but in the end we settled on a manual test where each bird was put on his back, held briefly to calm the little fellow, and then allowed to flap its wings so it could right itself. In each session, the flip test was done five times in succession, with a perfect score recorded as five.

A month or so into the trial, I unexpectedly got a late night call from Skip. "Mike you won't believe it. All the treated birds flipped five out of five! The controls couldn't flip at all!" With that single observation, a chicken test system was born. We continued the trial to where every tiny bit of benefit could be squeezed from the drug. Along with positive flip test results, we also saw a measurable decline in blood

CPK, which is elevated in the muscular dystrophy. With benefits seen in our first trial with methysergide, all systems were 'go' for a confirmatory repeat trial, which we needed if we wanted to publish the work. In the clinical world of dystrophy, where no treatment existed, our study had tremendous potential. With the little man about to pick up his toys and head across the pond to the UK, I regretted each passing day that my pivotal role in the project would soon come to an end.

As Easter approached, Raj and I found temporary distraction by making a Bicentennial trip to Washington, DC. We were accompanied by Leela Masilamoni who was staying with us while she researched writer Bernard Malamud for her PhD thesis back in India. Once inside the Beltway, we eagerly soaked in the sights of the Capitol district. Our ramblings took us to the National Art Gallery, The Smithsonian, Lincoln Memorial, and Mount Vernon. On our way home, like icing on a cake, we made a detour and visited Gettysburg. Throughout the excursion, Raj was simply tireless pushing my wheelchair all over hell's half acre so I wouldn't miss a thing. The sortie to DC was just the antidote needed for a junior scientist who was about to be cut free and finessed into the unknown.

Throughout the summer, the little man's lab was frantic with activity. In spite of tripping over moving boxes, last minute experiments still needed to be wrapped up. Some people were busy tidying up the loose ends of a multi-year study of an enzyme. Others like the garrulous Oliver Dolly, another MDA postdoc, had chromatographs and lyophilizers running overtime separating components of a protein. From time to time, the little man dropped by gulping down a sandwich, not so much from enjoyment, but out of sheer biological necessity. Periodically, I met the little man behind his sound-proofed office door, and among the chaos of papers everywhere we went over the latest chicken results. It was a time the lab would never see again. As was typical of the little man's symphony, there were plenty of instruments and performers, but only *one* conductor. Compartmentalization was the rule with each one busy in their little spheres. Often someone would ask, "Why are you doing that?" The question would be answered by a brief, "I don't know, the little man told me to do it."

During the previous year I was able to replace Skip who had gone on the Med School. Responding to my dilemma, Skip strolled into the lab one day and confidently proclaimed: "Mike, no problem. There's this girl Cathy Pollina who's in my pharmacology class. I've been talking to her about our work and she's very interested in working on the project. She'll be here tomorrow to see you." The next day Cathy came to see me wearing the uniform of the times, long brown hair and wire-rimmed glasses. After a brief chat I found Cathy was ready to jump into the project with both feet. Skip did a great scouting job, and the transition ended up being seamless. We never missed a beat in the methysergide project because of Cathy's ability and eagerness to embrace the research. We kept all tennis balls in the air in spite of a change in key personnel.

Along with the rest of country, we celebrated the nation's bicentennial on July Fourth with a barbecue at my parent's home. It was nice to take a breather from lab and classroom work and play badminton and eat hot dogs, however, as the summer wore on, it was back to reality. Coupled with my fellowship coming to an end, Raj was in imminent danger of being retrenched from Erie Community College. A time for decisions (or panic) was at hand.

Out of the blue in late July, my lab phone rang – "Hey Mike, how's it going?" asked Hal Segal calling from the Biology Department. "Did you ever read Stracher's work on protein turnover?" Immediately recalling the study, I responded with "Oh yeah, I'm very familiar with his work." "What do you think of it?" Hall continued. "How about coming over sometime so we can talk about it?" As I hung up, I pondered the possibilities for future work (and funding) such a meeting might bring. I dialed Raj at home, "Raj, guess what? Hal Segal just called me and asked me if I'd come over and discuss some dystrophy work! It might be nothing but it's worth a try."

The discussion with Segal went better than I had expected. Hal had a long-standing research program involving protein metabolism (albeit using liver tissue), and he told me he was willing to sponsor me in a fellowship application to the NIH. Leaving Hal's office, I began to gather my thoughts on a proposal centered on cultured muscle cells. Once back in the lab, I jumped into my reprint file and began to outline what I'd need for the proposal, such as: background information describing the current state of dystrophy research, where was the field now, and where was it likely to head. In addition, I began to outline specific goals of the project which would rest on using cultured muscle. In this area, my prior experience with Florini in Syracuse proved to be invaluable.

Throughout the summer, written requests for reprints of my first paper with the little man came flowing in on a regular basis. This signaled a fair amount of interest in our methysergide study. While not the sexiest thing on earth, we seemed to have put our foot in the door of a realm dearly in need of a clue towards treatment. There was even some local interest in our study. One of the TV stations came by with a film crew to interview the little man and me. The on-air story was accompanied by some nice shots of our 'flipping' chickens.

In August, I got a call from Dr. Mel Moss of the MDA: "Dr. Hudecki, I wonder if you could do me a favor," inquired Moss. "Can you send me twenty additional copies of your drug paper as I'd like to distribute them to various drug companies." As the Director of Research Development, Moss went on to describe the MDA's effort to encourage pharmaceutical companies to take a much more active role in the search for therapies relevant to neuromuscular disease. In this regard, Moss added, "Also Mike, could you give me the names of the people you deal with at the drug companies? I'll be contacting them soon and it would be very useful to know the people who have helped you in the past."

Toward the end of our conversation, Moss added: "What are you doing now, Mike?" I responded with: "Well, I'm in the process of writing a fellowship application to NIH. As the little man has recently left for a position in England, I'm searching around for some sort of position." With this bit of news, Moss interjected, "Well Mike, why don't you put your thoughts for future work on the drug project on paper and send it to me!" I could hardly believe what I was hearing. I was being offered the opportunity to write a research proposal involving the very work I had immersed myself in for the past three years. Moss went on to describe the MDA's newly-formed 'Task Force on Drug Development,' along with its aims, budget, and progress to date; but I was hardly listening now. I was in a stupor. I was given the green-light somewhere in our conversation to put *my ideas* together in a proposal. *My ideas!* As I hung up the phone, a renewed spirit took over me. With the little man now situated in London, I was on my own to frame my research.

As feared, Raj was retrenched from the community college. Under the strains of a county budget crisis, junior faculty were the first to go. In a word, both of us were now unemployed. As the Fall semester neared, however, things brightened considerably. Again to the rescue, Phil Miles arranged further courses for Raj to teach; and, as if to prove an old adage, if it's raining it's pouring. Raj simultaneously got her old job back at the college! Our Fall term involved morning-duty at the College and night-duty at the University, and the development of a very strong bladder for our stay-at-home dog, Meena. On the other hand, as my time was flexible I used the semester to write research proposals to the MDA and the NIH.

Ironically, I received a letter from the little man, now writing from England. He described the modifications made on the third and final manuscript authored by him and me, as well as with Arvind who remained in Buffalo. In addition, the little man listed several questions regarding previous work done here in Buffalo. As I sat back in my chair, I was bemused by the little man who had all the resources in the world at his finger tips, and here he was asking me the most fundamental questions regarding our drug studies. How were the chicken kept? Were the drug solutions made fresh each day? The questions went on and on. In response I took out sheet of paper and began answering each question in detail.

One of the spin-offs of the drug therapy work was the attention of the local news media. One interview ended up in the *Buffalo Evening News* where our research was cited, along with flattering words about me as a person struggling with the disease every day. There was even a picture of me with Cathy holding one of our celebrated birds. While not intentionally seeking the limelight, it was a time to bask in the warm sunshine of recognition. It doesn't happen often.

The winter of 1976/77 turned out to be one of the snowiest and coldest on record. This statistic was climaxed by our infamous *Blizzard of 1977* when Western New York was smacked in late January with over a foot of snow. Temperatures were in the minus range, and all of this was accompanied by horrifying winds peaking at 70 mph. Fortunately, before the storm hit us, Raj and I had ample time to hunker down in our condo; however, thousands like Cathy were not so lucky, and she ended up stranded for a couple of days at Roswell Park Cancer Institute where she currently worked. Until I was able to get funding to continue our chicken studies, Cathy kept solvent working a number of jobs, ranging from babysitting to serious lab science. She was indeed dedicated, as well as greatly optimistic.

Mercifully, spring arrived early, and our huge snow pack began to melt yielding fears of intermittent flooding. The warmth of the moment was dramatically chilled by a rather innocent looking air letter from England. In it the little man filled the early parts with self-congratulatory comments on the appearance of our second paper in the well-known British journal *Nature*, as well as some pleasantries regarding my fellowship application and Raj's job situation. It didn't take long, however, for the little man to get to the crux of his letter. Someone mailed him a copy of the recent *News* article and the little man wanted a clarification of one of my quotes cited in the interview: "I'm presently looking for support to continue the drug investigations." The little man mentioned he was greatly disturbed that I was trying to follow-up on the dystrophic chicken studies, adding as well a host of reasons why I should not continue with the work. While not stated in so many words, the little man wanted exclusivity.

Raj was furious when she read the letter. She was like a lioness out for blood protecting her cub from a threat, veiled or otherwise. Her quick response was to send a frank and accusatory letter to the little man. On the other hand, I vacillated within my naiveté which was wearing thinner each day. Contrary to Raj's "how dare you" theme, my response was an uneven compromise. While disagreeing in principle, I admitted to the little man that I had sent proposals to both the MDA and the NIH; I even sent him copies of the two proposals. Now that both mailings were safely on their way to England, all we could do now was wait for the other shoe to drop.

In the interim, I started on a small study to see if exercise would be beneficial to our dwindling flock of dystrophic birds. With the help of Dan Schmidt, a dedicated physical therapy student, we attempted to finally put to rest the question of whether or not physical exercise was useful in sustaining strength in those affected with dystrophy. Quantitative research on the matter was sorely lacking. Our initial study was encouraging. Dystrophic birds which were 'flipped' daily maintained righting ability longer than the 'unflipped' controls; however, more study would be needed before we could submit the work for publication. This repeat study could only be made possible pending the outcome of my proposals for MDA and NIH funding. For now we were on a holding pattern.

Fortunately, I didn't have to wait too long to continue my chicken studies, as I received work from the NIH awarding me a two-year research fellowship. I was on the phone with Raj, "I hope you're sitting down. I got the fellowship!" True to her practical nature Raj responded with, "Now Mike, you've got to get busy!"

A little later Ethel Cosmos from McMaster University in Hamilton, Canada came to our Department to give a seminar on a topic which she was a world authority – animal models of muscular dystrophy. Prior to her taking a position at McMaster, Ethel spent many productive years at the MDA's flagship research facility called The Institute of Muscle Disease. Located in New York City, the Institute was long known as the premier breeding ground for scientists dedicated to the cause and cure of neuromuscular diseases; however, because of escalating cost of doing business in New York, the facility had to fold, and its best and brightest were recruited elsewhere by leading universities and research centers. In Ethel's case, I first met her the preceding year when I went to McMaster to be on the receiving end of neurologic testing by Alan McComas. An eminent scholar, Alan had perfected a method to quantify motor units of muscle by applying his technique on scores of patients; he came up with his controversial "sick neuron" hypothesis as the root cause of weakness expressed in patients with muscular dystrophy. Once I showed up in his lab, I prepared to be one of his future data points.

While I was at McMaster, I also took the opportunity to give an impromptu seminar to Ethel and a small gathering of faculty and students. The seminar went well. While informally delivered, my talk was laden with specifics of my chicken trials carried on earlier with the little man. It was also an opportunity to get to know Ethel at a personal level. Later in Buffalo, when she gave her seminar, Ethel's knowledge and experience of the dystrophy problem was very impressive. Throughout my talk, I had the sense that Ethel took a genuine interest in our work; she liked the detailed conditions in which our chickens were tested for strength. Moreover, she resonated with the kinds of research questions we were asking. It was not wedded to only one approach to solving the dystrophy riddle. Unless disproven, all ideas were welcome. Research-wise it was a heady time for me where a proven figure in the field respected me and my research. I seemed to be the real deal in Ethel's eyes.

The proposals to the MDA and NIH were going through normal peer review processes. Dystrophic chickens were being exercised by Dan and Cathy. Muscle culture experiments were initiated with Hal. After dusting off my lab notebook from my Syracuse days, I had muscle cells growing in flasks in no time at all. Using a radioactive labeling procedure, we would see if there were any defects in protein synthesis in our dystrophic cultures. We had high expectations that the answer would be yes. Periodically, Hal would pop by and ask, "Heard anything yet?" After hearing more of the same old reply, he'd say, "Why don't you give them a call? At least you'll know one way or the other."

One day a strange thing happened. Carm Privitera, my graduate advisor now co-investigator, received an intriguing phone call from someone at the NIH. Carm was asked whether he had full knowledge of his name (along with Arvind) being included on my grant application. Furthermore, Carm was probed about my physical ability to carry out the proposed research. Afterwards, Carm and I scratched our collected heads looking for whatever sense we could make of the call. "What do you think, Mike?" asked Carm. All I could say was, "Well, I can only guess that the little man is up to his old tricks again. The NIH is presently weighing the relative merits of his *and* our proposals. It's the same situation that the MDA is in." When I called Arvind, he confirmed that he too got a call from NIH. By days end, I had this dead feeling in my gut that the other shoe was about to come tumbling down.

At the end of March, a voice on the phone requested, "Dr. Hudecki, would you hold please for Dr. Moss?" With heart thumping and sweaty palms, I held the phone. It was pep talk time. I kept telling myself, "Relax, take it easy. It won't be the end of the world!" In spite of my inner pep talk, I was full of apprehension. "Hello Mike," Dr. Moss jumped in. "I've got some good news for you. The advisory committee voted unanimously to approve your grant proposal for the entire amount you budgeted." With those words, I left planet earth, or in mortal terms, I joined 'the club' of grant-sponsored investigators. My elation shared only by those fortunate to get outside funding for their research labors. Moreover, I felt finally vindicated that my motives were well-recognized and sound. As Raj and Hal were both fond of telling me, it was a time to get busy, and busy it got!

Cathy was immediately hired as a full-time assistant. Just in time to take up where Dan left off on the exercise trials. Chicken orders had to be made, and new drug trials to plan. With renewed interest, I also continued the muscle culture experiments. I was happy. Raj was happy. Cathy was happy. Hal was happy. Even our dog Meena was happy. Periodically during this time I thought, "Who needs the NIH grant anyway?" As our research progressed into June when decisions in Bethesda are made, I half expected to receive one of those "Dear John" letters from the NIH which would start: "Your proposal…has been approved…but due to great competition for funds…has not been funded." Ironically, my letter did arrive, and it said nearly what I thought it would say. Nice try, but no cigar. Into the file the letter went. Time to forget about the folks at Bethesda.

A week later, I received another letter from NIH. "Could this be? Could they have reconsidered? Would the grant be given after all?" With my mind racing, I carefully opened the official-looking envelope.

"Dear Dr. Hudecki…It has come to our attention that…false representation…bad faith…major sin…don't let it happen again or else…Sincerely yours.

Staring at the official letterhead of the NIH for what seemed a lifetime, I couldn't believe what I was reading. I was being accused of changing the order of the authorship of the last paper submitted with Arvind and the little man. I was charged with including Arvind's name as a co-investigator without his knowledge. I was accused of… "My God!" I exploded: "Every charge in this letter is false!" Without much hesitation I got on the phone to NIH to find out what the hell was going on. My responses from him proved only one thing. Guilty, without much of a chance for an appeal. As I hung up the phone, my mind was reeling with rage, unfounded guilt, and a deep sense of failure.

Raj, Hal, and Carm all agreed that a response was necessary. But what? A short note of indignation? A letter with complete documentation to support my contention that "I'd been had?" Later that night I called an old friend and former classmate, Bob Beall. I needed advice and damage assessment from a trusted friend. Bob was now working at one of the Institutes at the NIH, and he'd be in a good position to give me the perspective I desperately needed. After I read the letter to him, Bob was far from encouraging. "Mike, this is serious. A copy actually went to the head of the NIH?"

As I resolutely hung up the phone, I sat back in my desk chair and soon realized what I had to do. I would have to sift through my file of old and recent correspondence from the little man and dispute the allegations in his own handwriting. I'd also need a supporting letter from Arvind to further refute the charges.

I immediately began to outline a draft of a letter, which in the end would amount to a six-page legal brief. As it turned out, putting the letter together was actually quite easy. I had kept all my correspondence, past and present. My main decisions had to do with selecting which supporting documents to attach. As Raj often remarked, "Mike, you never throw anything out!" In two days I had a draft of the letter completed, as well as my collection of supporting documents. The latter mainly consisted of letters from the little man requesting detailed information on how to set up the chicken test system in England. In two more sleepless days I had the letter in final type. With Raj's help, I copied the file, collated the documents, and prepared the mailing envelope. With an uncertainty that I never had experienced before, I reached for my worn-out Bic ball-point and signed the letter. Licking the envelope signaled my officially taking on the establishment. In essence I was calling the little man a liar, as well as found guilty of intentional deception and slander. In the bargain, there was the implication that the NIH was a dupe in the process. My heart was pounding as we were off to the post office.

At this fragile time, I was encouraged by Raj to join a one-week summer adult camp run by the MDA. It would give me a chance to re-discover my values and sense of humanity. It would be an opportunity to lose myself for a week in the midst of other "campers." Campers were comprised of young, and not-so-young adults all having one thing in common – some form of neuromuscular disease. We were to be soul-mates for the next seven days.

As the bus pulled up to a suburban pickup point, Raj and I stared at each other hoping that the other would not break down in tears. It was an extremely emotional and difficult time for us. Fortunately, my vulnerability in the whole affair was counter-balanced by Raj's awesome inner strength. As the bus settled into a parking area and its doors flung open, it was now time to let the inertia of the moment take its course. No turning back. I was assisted onto the bus by one of the camp volunteers and situated in a seat next to my sister Pat, who was also making the trip. I peered out the window to get a last glimpse of Raj whose glistening eyes were welling up with long-delayed tears. With my throat choking with emotion, I dared not blink as my eyes were welling up fast. I kept saying to myself: "Keep smiling, keep waving," as the bus finally ambled out of the lot. One final look out the window and the vision of Raj, I was filled with only one thought – "God, I love that girl!" It was truly an indelible moment for us. As we picked up speed, the bus reached the highway, and we campers were finally on our way to Camp Bergamo, wherever that might be.

In the week spent at the camp which was tucked away in the rolling hills east of Rochester, I had the opportunity to salvage my self-respect which was on the verge of disintegrating. I met many folks who were more physically disabled that I. Folks who had difficulty in doing simple things that I myself had taken for granted. Most had a positive view of life and all that it could offer. It was a welcome time for me to reflect, as well as to meet and acquire new friendships. It was a time to be silly and entertained. It was a time to doodle with paints and handicrafts. It was a time to trade stories and take pictures. It was a time to swap addresses and birthdays. The week became a love affair. All in broad daylight!

The camp was essentially run by enthusiastic volunteers who came from high school and college. They all shared two qualities, strong backs and a genuine concern and love for each of the campers. It turned out to be a mutually enjoyable experience for camper and volunteer alike. The morning when the bus arrived to take us back to reality, the scene filled with joyful chatter, loving embraces, and sadness. Tearful good-byes were everywhere you looked. For me the experience was invaluable. It was time to forget the little man, the NIH, and all the useless intrigue they created. I had a chance to pause, reset my priorities, and get my mental feet firmly planted back on the floor. After I said my own good-byes, I lumbered back on the bus for the two hour trip back home. Once all the campers were safely on board, there came a resounding shout, "Come on driver, let's get this thing going."

As I looked behind me over the heads of the now-seated passengers, I couldn't help but reflect. Here was a bus full of people bubbling over with enthusiasm and high spirits. All of them were chatting away like sparrows at a backyard feeder. Only a short week ago the bus resembled a truck laden with quiet weary laborers on route to a work camp. Now amidst all the chatter, I mused to myself, I wasn't the only one who left his problems here; but it was time to go. Time well spent. The bus soon swung out the gates of the camp and down a winding country road. A few miles later we were on the New York Thruway which would first take us to Rochester and then on to Buffalo. Good bye Camp Bergamo!

Once home I sounded like a long-playing record. I recounted all my experiences by chapter and verse. The people met and activities shared. God bless Raj who listened, and listened some more. She was quite pleased that I had actually gone. Back in the wintry days of February, Raj had strongly encouraged me to go to the Camp. She had felt that it would serve as a good break from all of the little man stuff, however, she too was full of mixed emotions about me going. I had been down on myself, and maybe the idea of going to a muscular dystrophy gathering wouldn't be such a good idea after all – my problems mixed in with the problems of others. Maybe not a good mix? Yet in hindsight, Raj's initial instincts were proven correct. She felt I would feel quite comfortable with the other 'campers.' In the bargain I might be able to serve as psychological boost for many of

them. Raj's credo was: "He that gives, receives! But in a different coin."
It was a homecoming neither of us would ever forget.

It didn't take long to hear from the NIH. When I returned to
the lab after my week away, my desk was covered with mail. With a
deep sigh, I quickly sorted through it and came upon a letter from
the wonderful folks from Bethesda. Learning long ago that bad news
was better when dealt quickly, I unceremoniously ripped open the
envelope and began reading. The tip-off that the letter was in my favor
came towards the end of the first paragraph. It read, "…*your response
is most impressive.*" The next paragraph went on to explain that only
a few people knew of the allegations, and that each would be given
a copy of my response. The sweetest, however, was kept for the last
paragraph. "*We are very sorry if we caused you any unnecessary or unjust
concern. However, as I'm sure you can appreciate, when presumably responsible
individuals raise such questions…*" With that, I quit reading; I saw what
I wanted to see. I was vindicated. I breathed new life. I also had a
feeling that I may have over-reacted – maybe, maybe not. In any event,
my camping experience, together with Raj's continued support, had
reacquainted me with the balance I needed to be a productive scientist,
and more importantly, a better person.

Riding home after work with Raj, I thought of a million things.
One particular thought persisted. It was a childhood scene of me
playing baseball with kids either at school or in the neighborhood.
Here I was standing in the batter's box, teetering, and trying to keep
my balance for the initial pitch. Just when I was about to be ready for
the first pitch, the ball had already zipped past me. Strike one! The
quick pitch caused me to inch back from the plate for fear I'd get hit.
Shaken, I readied myself for the next pitch. This time, however, the
pitch came faster than the first one. Nearly losing my balance, I saved
myself from falling by leaning on my bat. Strike two!

Taking inventory of my two strike situation, I realized that the
pitches were indeed fast, but each one was fired directly across the
strike zone, and not at me. Regaining my composure, I slowly stepped

into the batter's box. Only this time I was prepared. The pitch came, faster than the first two. This time I met the pitch with a short, even swing of my 32 inch *Louisville Slugger* (signed by Mickey Mantle, of course). Crack! Game over!

# Chapter 18

# High Inside Fastball
# – An Epilogue

It's been more than 47 years since I got the mea culpa from the NIH – seems like a lifetime ago when I was paralyzed with the thought that my budding research career might come to a crashing end. However, a gullible 'old boy network' had gone askew under the subterfuge of a little man. With Raj's open-ended support, it was time this neophyte moved on. Much had occurred since then, most of it good, if not very good. I began a successive string of annual grants from the MDA, as well as five year funding from (you guessed it) the NIH! Maybe it was the pity vote. Or just maybe the NIH review panel correctly recognized that back in the late 70's there were no viable therapies for the muscular dystrophies on the horizon. In my application I laid out a roadmap 'to look under every stone' for a treatment. Generally, the NIH adage for funding has more to do with focus, focus, focus; but in my case the jack-of-all trades, master-of-none applied. Ready to bombard my chicken model with everything from serotonin inhibitors to vitamins, I kept my approach simple, to look for therapeutic clues no matter where the path took me. Not a bad place to be, as I never thought I'd live to be 20.

Working shoulder-to-shoulder with me was Cathy Pollina. Now married to a valued friend and colleague Chris Loretz, Cathy had been a dogged and loyal friend through thick and thin. She had worked with me since her undergraduate days in 1975. Cathy took over when Skip Beeler graduated and began medical school. The transition was simple on its surface, but in retrospect it was invaluable to me personally as well as to my aspirations to make a dent in the research arena. Cathy made damn sure my university world was accessible and worry-free. In the process, a few toes were trampled upon to accommodate

241

me – neither wind, nor rain, curbs, stairs, double-parked cars, or self-absorbed curmudgeons, kept me from my appointed rounds. Cathy's singular attention, and roll-up-your-sleeves 'can do' attitude, earned her a major share of anything I may have accomplished in my professional life as a researcher, and later as a teacher and an administrator.

**Cathy Pollina Loretz**

Over time our animal test system became 'the' model for investigating dystrophic therapies. The MDA became to rely on us more and more to test the efficacy of selected drugs, even though the entities were experimentally reputed elsewhere. In addition to our highly reproducible strength test, we had other criteria which made our system more comprehensive – we continued to work with Arvind measuring blood enzymes and metabolites, in addition, we joined forced with neuropathologist Reid Heffner of the med school to assess muscle histology. If we had a competitor it was not the little man, but the enthusiastic, chain-smoking investigator Rick Entrikin from the University of California at Davis. Working with Barry Wilson, Rick developed his own series of tests with the dystrophic chicken. A couple of times Rick joined us in Buffalo when we entertained site-visits by the MDA scientific staff, the upshot from each meeting confirmed the notion that a purported therapy had to exhibit itself in controlled animal trials.

Tediously obtained, Cathy's results provided a solid foundation for our philosophical approach to MD therapy, as well as providing data for several research publications and grants – over 25 papers had been published using the chicken system, as well as over a million dollars in direct grant support. In addition to Skip and Cathy, I've had the good fortune of having over 30 undergraduates jump into the chicken project. Some worthy of special note: Dan Schmidt who conducted the exercise trial and found as we had expected that moderate physical activity was beneficial; Carol Gregorio who after obtaining her Masters with me, later worked on spectrin protein as her PhD project at Roswell Park; an avid fisherman like myself, Jim Pilc with his easy smile and blazing red hair took part in several trials; and Steve Povoski who diligently combined drug treatment with the work-intensive electrostimulation procedure. Regarding the latter, it was through the intercession of the late Mary Beth Spina, an enthusiastic science reporter for the UB *Reporter*, that we were fortunate to join forces with physical therapist Al Caffiero. An extremely busy, sought-after clinician, Al came up with the idea of applying high-frequency electrical stimulation to our birds. The procedure superimposed maximum 'use' to muscles which operate the wings of chickens; interestingly we found the treatment in many cases to be equal to or better than drug treatment alone.

**Richard Almon**

While embroiled in our chicken work, we enjoyed fruitful interactions with several colleagues. Lively discussions with Rich Almon and his 'holistic' (aka, metabolic) view of muscle disease, gave us needed insight in the interplay of skeletal muscle with hormones, innervations, nutrients, as well as use and disuse. Rich made his early research mark by blocking acetylcholine receptors with antibodies yielding a rat model for myasthenia gravis. Hal Segal and many others from around the world viewed degenerating muscle as a combination of accelerated breakdown and insufficient synthesis. Because of clashing personalities, Rich and Hal were at loggerheads most of the time; however, I tap danced between the two camps holding each in high esteem. Then there was neurologist Alan McComas of McMaster University. Alan's view of dystrophy was quite simple – dystrophic muscle lost innervations over time not unlike what might be found in aging individuals. Subjecting myself to his motor unit counting techniques, I was a few 'data points' in some of his published works. Also working at McMaster, Ethel Cosmos postulated that dystrophic muscle didn't mature normally, rather than develop adult characteristics, dystrophic muscle was frozen with weaker, embryonic tendencies. While we didn't collaborate on experiments, we communicated frequently.

Other collaborative efforts involved immunological work with good friend Harshad Thacore in the Microbiology Department; ironically Harsh's wife Prem was a friend of Raj's family years ago back in India.

**Harshad Thacore**

Attempting to unravel the chicken's defective calcium-channeling, we teamed up with Paul and Faith Davis from Department of Medicine; their enthusiasm and research skills were contagious. Once Carol Gregorio left us and started her PhD studies under Betsy Repasky at Roswell Park, it didn't take too long for our labs to team up trying to uncover red blood cell anomalies in our dystrophic birds. Looking under every stone for clues toward dystrophic therapy, our chicken work took us far and wide – whether looking for receptor anomalies, defects in protein turnover, chasing down interferon-synthesizing lymphocytes, or defining red cell spectrin defects, we traveled down multiple paths. In the 1980's, our therapeutic findings seemed to agree with *everyone's* interpretations of the disease etiology – our birds responded to use, as well as to drugs which stimulate synthesis, inhibit breakdown, promote circulation, retard inflammation, boost metabolism, protect membranes, inhibit ion channels, etc…All approaches appeared to be in bounds, but where do we go next?

While the chicken trials took up most of my attention, I continued to work with Hal Segal on a series of muscle turnover experiments. Carrying the ball in this work was grad student Barry Wolitzky who first worked with me as an undergraduate. It was through Barry in the early 80's that I was brought up to speed with the rapid advances in molecular genetics. Barry became my 'translator' as well as wheelchair pusher at a 1981 symposium on muscle genetics held at Cold Spring Harbor Laboratory located on the historical north shore of Long Island, NY. For years CSHL had been the mecca for genetic research, especially after Nobel Laureate James Watson took over the reins of the operation. Nestled within a dense forest, a windy road took us to a covey of new and old buildings which housed research labs and a modest auditorium where most of the symposium sessions would be held for the week. Ever since the advent and application of recombinant DNA technology (which was still controversial in some circles), the biological and medical sciences were being redefined as never before – there was a quantum change on how bioscientists of every stripe looked at their problems, given that new techniques to probe into and manipulate genetic material were at hand. At this meeting, I would have been lost without Barry – for one, he pushed me up hill and dale through the physically treacherous Cold Spring Harbor campus, and equally important, he was there to patiently explain Northern, Southern, and Western blotting techniques, and their myriad applications. For the first time in my life I actually visualized genes which coded for key muscle proteins such as actin and myosin. It was a very heady experience for me as well as the majority of attendees who only had a smattering of molecular genetics under their belts. As a result we were a willing audience while for the first few days several 'gene jockeys' provided us with a primer on cutting-edge molecular genetics. Our heads were collectively spinning by the end of each day. However, for those interested in muscular dystrophy, the greatest stir at the meeting came from a presentation which showed a mutant flatworm with an inherited mobility problem. Because little if anything was known about the specific gene responsible for the deadly Duchenne disease, the work had huge clinical significance. Here for the first time a defect in the molecular genetics of an organism (albeit a worm) translated into an overt expression of weakness. With those that I spoke with, it was agreed that while we haven't turned the corner on the molecular pathology of dystrophy, we can at least 'see' the corner now.

Back in Buffalo, we were not equipped to go after the molecular genetic lesions ourselves. Because of the novelty of many of the techniques, and the financial costs involved, only a few faculty in the department had the training to carry on molecular genetic research. Over thirty years later, nearly everyone does it. In our case, we got back to the lab and contented ourselves with the on-going chicken trials, and Barry's protein turnover experiments.

**Me and One of Our Experimental
Chickens Receiving Treatment**

Therapeutically, the muscle culture work gave us little to hang our hat on. Even though we found protease inhibitors and certain amino acids to be beneficial to cultured muscle as well as intact birds, the therapeutic picture became muddier and muddier. After over 300 trials, we still didn't know the molecular genetics behind the disease expression, and as a result our therapeutic target remained elusive as ever – what domino should we try to protect in the cascade of events leading up to the the fall of the final domino (i.e., inability to right). As much as we might have dreamed, manipulating the 'dystrophic' gene and events downstream was not yet on the horizon. Hence, we continued to search for effective targets in our chicken trials. While some scientists were working on non-avian models such as the hamster and mouse, however, like us, no magic therapeutic bullet was to be found. Fortunately, the MDA continued to support our work.

In the mid 80's, X-linked dystrophic mutants began to appear in the scientific literature. Since the Duchenne disease is an X-Chromosome linked disorder, the animals which caused the biggest stir were mutant strains of a Labrador retriever, a cat, and notably a mouse called MDX. After the molecular geneticists got their hands on these critters, the genetic defect was localized within the X-Chromosome. Eureka! Since these animals expressed the X-linked disorder, it was natural to equate their disease expressions with the Duchenne form. Likely there would be a common disease pathway at work in both the animals and young Duchenne boys – if so, therapeutic targeting would be on much firmer ground.

In the annuals of muscular dystrophy research, 1986-1987 became a watershed period. During this time Lou Kunkel and his associates at Boston Children's Hospital discovered the actual gene mutation causing DMD. Through clever molecular genetic manipulations a large segment of the X-Chromosome was found to be missing (or highly mutated) in Duchenne boys. Ballyhooed in the press, this discovery reset as never before the direction of muscle disease research for all time, and opened the flood gates for studies to determine what the missing gene was normally responsible for – what gene product was missing or abnormal? What is the product's function? Soon after

Kunkel's landmark discovery, his lab went to work to answer these questions – and before long they had the answer. Using a simple but comprehensive gel electrophoresis process to separate and identify 'all' proteins made by skeletal muscle, Kunkel and his team focused on one 'spot' in the gel which was missing in Duchenne muscle – as it turned out, the 'spot' corresponded to a large protein which they aptly called 'dystrophin.' Hence, for the first time in history, one could say that DMD was a genetic disease caused by the absence of dystrophin protein. The next critical step was to determine what dystrophin did in muscle – Was it an enzyme? Structural part of muscle? What? In science, answering one question, only leads to more questions.

Buoyed by the work achieved in Boston, I got the okay from our Chair Darrell Doyle to extend an invitation to Kunkel to come to UB and give a research seminar. However, Kunkel was understandably over committed at the time, and he suggested that one of his postdocs, Eric Hoffman, take his place. Before long Eric arrived on campus in his best 'lab rat' clothes – faded jeans, and a very tired shirt. However, it didn't take me long to take a sincere shine to the precocious young investigator – his baby face and outward appearance notwithstanding. Eric impressed all with his keen insight, enthusiasm, and facility in explaining cutting-edge molecular biology. It was a joy to listen to him – one could hear the wheels of his brain grinding away as he took us step-by-step through the procedures used to identify the gene for DMD, and subsequently, the missing protein dystrophin. Before and after his seminar, I got a chance to establish with Eric the seeds of a personal friendship which has lasted to this day. In one of our conversations, I had a chance to review with Eric all that I knew about dystrophy, including what we were doing with the chicken model – he was all ears. And full of questions.

One question which stuck to Eric like a dog with a bone – why do dystrophic muscles become fibrotic – a process which crowds out healthy muscular tissues? This was a question which would hound him (and us) for years to come, especially after Eric later took a faculty position at the University of Pittsburgh. Another question we discussed was whether the chicken (and its autosomal recessive mutation) was a genetically suitable model for achieving the therapeutic end-points we wished. The basis for this question stemmed from recent advances concerning the X-linked disorder expressed in the MDX mouse and the growing likelihood that it would be a better model for the X-linked Duchenne disorder. To answer this question, Eric and Lou Kunkel collaborated with us in a study where dystrophin would be analyzed in muscles from our dystrophic chickens, and comparisons made with the MDX mouse as well as samples from Duchenne boys. Within a few months, we had our answer – our chicken model was 'old news!' Contrary to the absences of dystrophin in the mouse and boys, our chickens expressed normal levels of the muscle protein. After ten plus years working with my winged friends, the findings put a nail in the coffin of any designs we had in continuing to use the bird as a therapeutic model. If we continued doing what we were doing, while scientifically interesting, we were off track in our search for a viable DMD treatment; and as we soon found out, the MDA was less than enthusiastic in continuing our funding. So, it was time to reinvent the wheel. MDX here we come!

With the handwriting on the wall that we needed to make a 180 degree turn in a choice of animal model, I contacted the MDA to request interim funding for Cathy while we familiarized ourselves with the MDX mouse. Fortunately, we learned that there was a small number available at Roswell Park which we used as our initial breeding stock. Knowing that the MDA would no longer fund chicken work (partially based on our joint study with the Boston group), I tried to get up to speed on the MDX literature for a grant application I planned to submit in a few months. Also, in the meantime, Cathy and I put our heads together to best utilize the birds which remained in our basement animal unit. In the end we came up with a KS trial – i.e., let's try everything but the 'kitchen sink.' The trial was composed of the therapies which until now had given us some glimmer of hope, but in this case, each of the therapies would be given simultaneously to the same chicken. Digging into our past studies we came up with: serotonin inhibitor to boost circulation; branched-chain amino acids to boost synthesis; protease inhibitor to reduce endogenous degradation; calcium blocker to stabilize calcium efflux; prednisolone to reduce inflammation; and topping it all off, regular doses of high-frequency electrostimulation. The main conclusion of the KS trial was that electrostimulation given alone was equal to the effect of the drug combination (with or without electrostimulation). So for now, we had a filing cabinet full of chicken data acquired over the years, plus a freezer brimming with muscle which in all likelihood would never be processed and analyzed.

Ironically, many years later I received a phone call from Lou Kunkel who was interested in whether or not I still had any frozen chicken muscle tissues. Regretfully I had to tell him that we didn't, having lost most of the samples through a power failure in the building which impacted our freezer. Lou went on to tell me that he was chasing down the notion that the dsytrophic chicken may be just the model they were looking for a molecular genetic study of limb-girdle muscular dystrophy. They believed a sub-set of muscle proteins called the sarcoglycans were missing or mutated in this specific disorder, and there was a strong likelihood that the chicken had a similar defect. In ironies of ironies, by working with the chicken over several years, it seemed that I had been actually working on my own disease, not the Duchenne form.

In the hope of getting funding from the MDA again, we needed to get preliminary data – in this case from the MDX mouse. Equipped with a few breeding pairs, Cathy set to work with the animal facility caretakers to proliferate the stock. In a few months we had enough to begin some measurements – but what is it that we are going to measure? With the chicken we had our reliable flip test to assess therapeutic benefit, but with the mice we had other hurdles. How would we measure physical ability in the critters? Thanks to colleagues in the neighboring School of Pharmacy, we acquired several 'activity boxes' which allowed us to tabulate vibrations made by mice, any voluntary movement of the mice would show up as a recorded 'event.' More events = more activity. We recruited several dedicated undergraduates to assist us in the tedious work of recording data points, an around the clock procedure since rodents are quite active at night. When we began to plot the data looking for differences between the MDX and their normal counterparts, the resultant graph looked like someone peppered the paper with a shotgun. Because we were seeing high levels of individual variation, as well as significant physical activity in both mouse strains, we were very hard pressed to conclude that the MDX was indeed weak.

In spite of my lack of confidence that we presently had a test system in place, I welcomed an invitation to go to New York City and attend a MDA-sponsored research meeting. The goal of the meeting was to explore various approaches to the treatment of the muscular dystrophies – those in attendance would serve as a virtual 'Who's Who' of dystrophy research. Traveling with Harshad, I nervously waited for my opportunity to give my slide-show of our recent MDX data. While my talk was to focus on the developmental stages of our efforts to set up a mouse test system, not unlike our tried and true chicken system ("Title: Development and implementation of phenotypic monitoring), I also wanted to share my personal feelings as one afflicted with dystrophy, that any potential therapy be rigorously tested first in an animal system. It didn't work out that way. By the time I negotiated my wheelchair to the front of the room, juggled my notes, manipulated the mike and laser pointer, and trying to make eye contact with the audience hidden by bright spot-lights, I nearly froze from anxiety. I did babble on, but I was clearly off my game and my message – mercifully I finished to a smattering of a few handclaps, and returned to the back of the room, both relieved it was over, and greatly disappointed that I couldn't' intelligently repeat what I had been saying for several years in a more relaxed setting. Damn!

Catching my breath, I began to sit back and take notes from the other presentations. Early on I was intrigued by an animated presentation given by Peter Law now working at the University of Vanderbilt. I had first met Peter at McMaster a few years ago when he was doing his PhD work with a mutant mouse strain (dy/dy) that expressed spinal cord degeneration. At the meeting Peter described the benefit of injecting normal muscle cells in to the hindlimbs of dy/dy mice – his flashy videotape showed treated mice able to run within a scaled–down treadmill, whereupon the untreated mice faltered greatly. It was a remarkable study since a good proportion of the audience was interested in determining whether injected myoblasts might be a sound treatment avenue for Duchenne boys. While the study used the dy/dy strain (and not the MDX), Peter's study demonstrated the potential for myoblast recovery of muscular weakness, regardless of etiology. After Peter's spirited follow up Q and A with the audience, I chatted with Peter about the construction of his treadmill. Because he knew me and my desire to develop a MDX test system, Peter hooked me up with his technician who promised to send me blueprints. Thinking I may have turned a corner in our MDX work, I was anxious to get home and build a treadmill. Within days we had our university shop busy constructing a treadmill equipped with multiple lanes and a variable speed motor. After some false starts and much tweaking, we began to acquire data consisting of the duration mice were able to run (at various speeds) until exhausted. Being a labor-intensive enterprise, we needed extra help, and were able to recruit several more enthusiastic undergraduates. Notably, these included Dennis Bennett, Sandy MacAvoy, Katie Daly, Jean Hsiao, John Wang, Liza Chopra, Ryan Bourne, Michelle Barrett, Amy Sikora, Dan Avosso, Deb Enterline, and Jocelyn Lieb. Happily I can report, after graduation these students successfully pursued careers in medicine and veterinarian medicine; after their stints with me I later heard through the campus grapevine I had a laudable reputation for getting students into med school if they diligently worked with me on the dystrophy project. Much of this success came from the initial vetting carried on by Cathy, who like a den mother, paid particular attention to skill meshed with tenacious personality traits. I also heard through the backdoor that Cathy's marching order to each student had been – "If there is a fire drill, find Mike and get him out of the building!" Much to my delight I found out my backside was protected at all times.

We expanded our operation and had another treadmill constructed. With all shoulders to the wheel, we had enough data to make some tentative conclusions – for one, the MDX mice had a remarkable, almost normal capacity to run. However with refinements to the pitch of the treadmill, we began to observe a weakening of the MDX compared to the normal mice. While the study was still in its infancy, we were awarded a much needed two year grant from the MDA. During the interim I kept Cathy salaried with bridge-funding from the university; as for me I kept teaching Basic Biology, and Human Nutrition at night school and during the summer to keep me in the black (at this time I was no longer a funded postdoc but an unsalaried Research Assistant Professor in the Department). Fortunately our research prospects were again looking up as the MDA liked the potential of our neophyte test system, a system geared to yield therapeutic data similar to what we had previously achieved with the chicken model. BUT...the MDX kept running and running. Like the normal mice, the MDX took a liking to the treadmill, and rather than run to exhaustion and give us a useful therapeutic endpoint, the work only exhausted our cadre of undergrad assistants. Somehow I needed to get a handle on these so-called diseased, dystrophin-deficient mice.

One morning over breakfast while watching the Today Show, I heard the hosts making fun of a study where someone measured the strength of lab rats. Yukking it up, Tom Brokaw, Jane Pauley and Gene Shalit described how scientists measured the weakening effect of toxins by tying the tail of a rat to a strain gauge. Yuk, Yuk, Yuk. Listening to their guffaws I became immensely interested – I immediately understood what the scientists were doing and why, and moreover, I knew the strain gauge might be applicable to my 'run to daylight' mice back in the lab. Reaching my desk at school, I did two things – first, I dashed off a letter of NBC with copies to everyone I knew connected to the MDA; and secondly, I chased down the published study which was described on the Today Show's 'happy talk' segment. Within a month I had a fist full of apologies, importantly, our new strain gauge arrived in the mail. In no time, we were able to measure mouse strength by attaching the sensitive gauge to its tail; while relatively crude, we began to see differences in ability of mice to pull away from the gauge after we gave their buttocks a little shock – for the first time we actually saw that MDX mice were weaker than the normal mice. However, the data was too variable to publish. We needed to refine a set of conditions in which we would be able to get reproducible and meaningful results – not only in the strain gauge measurements, but in the treadmill study as well. Enter –Joe Granchelli.

Joe was a disgruntled, sassy, and highly talented first year grad student who lost out trying to get into med school after his degree at

SUNY at Albany. After doing a lab rotation or two in the department, he fell our way – anxious to lock horns with an experimental problem, I gave him one – "Joe, we can't make sense out of our treadmill and strain gauge results with the MDX; what the hell is going on?" It was just the sort of problem Joe was looking for, something to sink his teeth into. With flexibility to do pretty much what he wanted to do (albeit with the goal of fleshing out a mouse test system), Joe set to work out the nitty gritty of our testing parameters. First, Joe tweaked the treadmill – optimized its speed and tilt looking for the best method to run the animals (not necessarily to exhaust them; but in the end they did anyways since he had the mice run downhill, eliciting a form of stressful eccentric exercise). Next, Joe constructed an intricate PVC tube in which to employ the strain gauge; hooked up to a sensitive recording gauge (not the crude spring loaded affair we had bought earlier), each tail was tethered, and after a brief electric shock each mouse would try to hide within the PVC tube. With the treadmill and strength gauge up and running in parallel, the next thing was to marry the two – mice which had a track-record of running were then tested for strength. The first results were highly encouraging – normal mice as one might expect got stronger from a treadmill workout. However, this was not the case with the MDX which got progressively weaker the more they ran on the treadmill. Eureka! It was another 'Skip Beeler' moment! For the first time we had a mouse test system. Rather than have a set of feeble numbers to present to the MDA in a grant renewal, Joe had provided us with the fuel we needed to make our case that we were ready to test therapies. And test we did.

Our first choice was to dose mice with the anti-inflammatory prednisolone – for many reasons, glucosteroids were the only ones selected by most MDA clinics to give their Duchenne boys. If you can make a case to the MDA that prednisolone actually works in our MDX system, we would go a long way in insuring continual funding, as well as getting closer to providing a serious system for routine DMD drug screening. In the ensuing trial, prednisolone was given to treadmilled as well as non-exercised MDX mice; as we had seen previously, strenuous exertion within the treadmill had a weakening effect. If we were to see a beneficial prednisolone effect, treadmilled and drug treated mice would be stronger than control mice which were treadmilled and untreated. And, that was exactly what we saw. While the therapeutic effect lasted only for 4-6 weeks, its significance paved the way for us to collaborate with Robert Griggs at the University of Rochester who was a big proponent of using steroids to treat Duchenne dystrophy. Using our MDX model system we were hoping to get some understanding how the steroid registered its therapeutic effect on dystrophic muscle; even the MDA people were impressed with our study and couldn't wait to renew our grant. Wanting to get the word out, we finally published our results in a lesser known but reliable journal *Research Communications in Chemical Pathology and Pharmacology.*

In parallel to our MDX screening system to screen other drugs, we initiated a collaborative study with Eric Hoffman. Following up on our prior discussion of why dystrophic muscle becomes entrapped within a connective tissue matrix, Eric proposed that mast cells may be the root cause. Like 'smoke detectors,' mast cells act as an early warning system when things go awry within the body; in response to injury and the like, mast cells excrete chemicals which tend to patch things up – thereby protect the integrity of the body. A notable example is scar tissue which is laid down after skin is scrapped or injured; only in the case of muscular dystrophy, the 'wound-repair' cycle occurs within the body, within the muscle tissue itself. Hence, dystrophic muscle which is already missing the key structural protein dystrophin, responds to exertion or usage (like in the case of our treadmilled MDX) by sending out a 'wound' signal thereby activating resident mast cells. In response, various factors are released, including key activators of fibrosis! Ergo, we experimented with approaches to see if we can pin-point a relationship between mast cells and MDX weakness, as well as uncovering a clue or two toward treatment. Towards that end, Joe developed a hybrid MDX mouse which expressed elevated mast cells; and as might be expected the hybrid was weaker that it's MDX counterpart – more like the Duchenne disease. As a follow-up, Joe began trials using mast cell inhibitors which began to give promising results.

It was in the mid 90's, however, that I began to think of winding down my research. For one, Cathy was about to begin a two year residency in Tokyo with husband Chris who would be heading up the National Science Foundation's Tokyo branch. It was a plum appointment which could not be ignored. Secondly, Joe was actively looking for a permanent position. After his PhD and subsequent postdoc with me, it was time for Joe to test the job waters. Without my two stalwarts, the handwriting was on the wall that I could not sustain my dystrophy research program any longer. It had reached the stage that when the Chair of the department called me to see if I would entertain the idea of filling in for the retired executive officer of the department, I immediately called Raj to hear what she had to say. She immediately said to go for it – "You can do it!" In a matter of minutes, my life became transformed. Rather than being preoccupied with dystrophy research, I now embarked on my first 'real' job. I'd be getting a regular salary, rather than the bits and pieces I had been getting over the years from teaching, teaching, and then some more teaching.

At the time my feelings were bittersweet. While looking forward (with trepidation) to assuming my administrative post in 1995, my mind reeled with countless memories of 28 years of muscular disease research. I recalled my trips to Hamilton, Montreal, New York, Washington, Anaheim, Minneapolis, Key Biscayne, Pittsburgh and Tucson where I had contributed to muscle disease conferences. I would miss the interactions with the dedicated folks at the MDA, as well as with those of the Parent's Project. With each face-to-face meeting, I became galvanized anew to fight muscular dystrophy.

Anxious to get the word out as to what we were doing over the years, my lab was always open for tours by science and non-science visitors alike. Notable among the latter were parades of school children such as those from my friend Sharon Minklein's third grade class, periodic visits by those most affected by dystrophy (the parents and friends of Duchenne boys), and 'open house' participants attending various University-wide functions. In addition, we invited high school students each summer to work with us as part of a minority program. They usually required high maintenance at first, but these kids by the end of the summer could walk and talk science, especially in the area of muscle disease. Moreover, for several years I took part in a Western New York 'Science Exploration Day' where more than a thousand local high school students converged on campus each May to learn science from real, practicing scientists. Attempting to recruit these students to the joys of science, everyone from meteorologists to anthropologists put on their best dog and pony show. For my part, I met each class by sharing what we knew of muscular dystrophy, and our research approach to understanding and treating this tragic disease.

I have been blessed with the company of giants who have nurtured me, supported me, and encouraged me in my endeavor – I thank you Raj, Cathy, Skip, Maria, Hans, Gail, Joe, Carm, Ethel, Stan, Alan, Hal, Al, Harsh, Faith, Pepper, Eric, Lew, Louis, Bob, Arvind, Darrell, Carl, Gayle, Luc, Jean, John, Rich, Carol, Jim, Barry, Steve, Katie, Reid, Mike, and Mary Beth. All helped me keep my dream alive to one day understand and successfully treat muscular dystrophy. During this entire time I kept a memory alive of a pencil sketch I did of my sister Patricia as she struggled up the front steps of her grade school. That scene would remain with me over the years as a stimulus to 'move the ball' closer to a treatment. Only now I wish I could substitute the sketch with a colorful video of Patricia bounding up the stairs two and three steps at time. Some things are not meant to be in one's lifetime.

# Chapter 19

# You Know When You Hear It

After nearly four decades in the classroom, I think I might have gotten it right. It wasn't always that way. The mere thought of addressing students in a classroom had sent me into immediate panic. Rapid heartbeat and cold sweat swept over me as I contemplated myself at the lectern - not a pretty sight. Then how did I get in a position in which I actually relished the classroom and all the drama within?

Through my formal schooling prior to my college years, I was subjected like most wet-behind-the-ears students to a steady diet of cookbook lectures. With a few notable exceptions, the faculty spoke, I listened, I wrote down, and I rarely questioned (except maybe to ask if this or that might be on an exam – novel, huh?). When all was said and done, I would sequester myself with my notebooks, and the occasional text, and prepare myself for impending exams. Data in, data out. I guess my memory was pretty good as my grades for the most part were quite good. I was generally okay with objective questions (data in, data out), but when we were asked questions which were outside the box, I usually didn't do as well. For me, I relished grammar and high school for their adherence to the first level of teaching – data in, data out.

In large measure this routine continued in my college years at Niagara, but again with notable exceptions. For example, history professor Daniel McGuire used a case study approach to teaching American History, and while we students still needed to know dates, names, locations, etc., Mr. McGuire had the class role play in acting out key segments of history. We as a class certainly knew the eventual outcome of the American Civil War, but by "role playing" we students had a keener, more lasting view of the stakes involved on both sides of the conflict. Lessons learned in Mr. McGuire's class would ultimately last me a lifetime, both in and out of the classroom. Another example of a college teacher who made a difference in the extrapolation of rote learning to a higher plane was biochemist Wayne Gallagher. His technique was rather simple – the injection of passion. After filling a backboard with a complicated metabolic pathway, he'd stand back and exclaim to the class: "Isn't this neat!" At first, we prehealth majors hadn't a clue as to what he found so neat about the systemic chopping up of a molecule of glucose yielding carbon dioxide, water, and several forms of energy. How's this information going to get us into med school? But, with his infectious enthusiasm, we finally bought into this world of biochemistry and how critical its knowledge was for all of us in the life sciences. He not only gave us details in abundance, but most importantly, he gave us context upon which to build from for future learning.

When grad school, not med school, turned out to be my career move, I was slowly introduced into the realm of "real" higher learning. That is to say, I was still expected to continue with my data in, data out thing, but in addition I was tutored in the hows and whys of the scientific method. I was now on track to take baby steps in the world of scientific research and critical scientific thinking. I entered the Masters Degree Program at Niagara University in 1965 with a teaching assistantship tucked under my arm. Together with Peter Gunther and Bob Sheehan, we TAs were expected to help run undergraduate courses in the Biology Department – grading, proctoring, lab set ups and practicals, as well as to introduce lab exercises and to answer any or all questions from the students during the lab period. For the most part, the actual course lectures were given only by the faculty (thank God!).

It didn't take too long to find my comfort level as a TA as long as I didn't have to do any classroom teaching. In the teaching labs, I found I was good with small groups of students. The atmosphere was informal, and my natural ability to foster Q and A came to the fore. As I did years before, my students were being prepared for data in, data out, only now, I was the data generator and subsequently its receiver. Moreover, I was quite good at animal dissections and microscopic work. Together these proclivities made me a natural in instructing undergraduates in the nuances of cutting and dicing tissues, as well as interpreting microscopic imagery. I was a good match as a TA in courses like histology, embryology, as well as human anatomy and physiology, where cat dissections were commonly used as teaching tools. For me, the textbook charts came alive within the teaching labs with the students. Now it was my job to instill those connections with my own students.

The two years I spent at Niagara as a TA provided me with an opportunity to learn what might be successful elements in the realm of teaching, even though at the time my career aims lay elsewhere. Should I try to get into med school, or as a fall back, more grad work, maybe, toward a PhD? Ironically, it was my medical school interview which pushed me toward a PhD program at the University at Buffalo. Early in the day, I had entered the UB campus thinking about getting an MD and left thinking that a better choice was a PhD and all that it might entail (and it was not necessarily teaching). Within a week from applying, I received a letter notifying me that I was accepted into the UB Biology PhD program along with a teaching assistantship. At the start of the Fall term, because of my prior experience, I was assigned to Gordon Swartz as a TA in his embryology course. In addition, I enrolled in a few graduate biology courses, such as Nucleic Acids, Comparative Biochemistry, and Physiological Ecology.

We grad students at that time also tried to hitch our wagon to a faculty member who would serve as our research advisor toward the holy grail of a PhD diploma. Should I pick someone among the young turks and their growing cadre of engaged grad students? Fred Rosen and his electron microscope used to unravel the inner structure of chloroplasts, or maybe Reed Flickinger and his DNA/RNA hybridizations from tissues of developing amphibians? Then there were David Yphantis and Todd Schuster and their ultracentrifugal separations of molecules and organelles? Others of the molecular breed included: TY Wang who was studying histones as potential regulators of gene activity, Norm Strauss and his *Bacillus* mutations, Larry Berlowitz of nucleolus fame, along with plant biochemists Frank Lowus and Vince Santelli. The foregoing embodied the clarion call for the merits of molecular biology. Within their labs you would be hard-pressed to ever come upon a living, breathing organism, only the unmistakable hum of ultra-low freezers and centrifuges, as well as the omnipresent clink/clank sound of the door to a cold room containing an array of fraction collectors.

Maybe I should sign on with one of the organismal preferences? Since my interest in ecology was recently whetted at Niagara, I took a long, hard look at Ken Stewart, a fresh water limnologist who enthusiastically sampled Western New York's waterways for later lab analyses. Marine ecologist Jack Storr studied invertebrates both in fresh and salt waters, but he had a particular love affair with the Bahamas where he had a second home. Others I looked at were Marge Farnsworth and her genetic studies using the tried and true fruitfly model and Alan Bruce, a biophysicist holdover from the Manhattan Project days who studied genetic mutation using irradiated bacteria. Some senior faculty like Gordon Swartz and Clinton Osborn were not considered since they long ago had quit active research. On the other hand, there were some young faculty recently hired from their postdoctoral stints. Maybe I should choose among Jim Tavares and his plant studies, Kipp Herreid and his physiological ecology work on a wide range of organisms, or fish biologist Wayne Hadley and his cantankerous 'Old Man and the Sea' persona?

Some faculty were middle of the road types who carried on research spanning the chasm between the organismal and molecular spheres. While biochemists Mort Rothstein and Hal Segal carried on lab experimentation and assays, they also implemented a variety of lab animals in their work. Geneticist Phil Miles studied mutational crosses and expressions using a range of fungal species, some of which were collected in the field. Zoologist Carl Gans traveled frequently to the wilds of Central America where he collected living specimens for his studies of locomotion in reptiles. I found out a few years later that Gans kept a backroom hidden from departmental eyes which housed an assortment of venomous snakes, in addition to a feisty young crocodile. Lastly was comparative physiologist Carm Privitera whose lab worked on mitochondrial changes in heart muscle from cold-adapted turtles. Carm had an engaging personality full of wit, enthusiasm, and empathy. His lab too was welcoming by the likes of grad students Jim Kane, Al Rotermund, and Bob Beall, each of whom carried on research of some permutation of the central turtle heart project. For me the choice of Carm as my mentor was an easy decision and one which I highly value today. I followed a different route from the turtle heart project and embarked on studying a wild mouse indigenous to the southwest. Using the pigmy mouse as my model system, I studied the metabolic interplay of tissues during and subsequent arousal from cold-induced torpor. While my research didn't set the world on fire, it did provide me with the tools to prosper later as a principal investigator in my own right (which in essence should be the aim of a quality graduate program).

Interestingly, many departmental faculty weren't really keen on teaching at all, but would rather occupy their time having discussions with their grad students and lab technicians, pouring over recently published journal articles or planning new experiments. While grad students did little lecturing in the classroom, but similar to Niagara most TAs delivered mini lectures in the teaching labs. I found the TAs to be a dedicated lot, where each one took his responsibility as lab instructor quite seriously. I soon found out that most TAs, like myself already had some teaching experience through prior graduate study.

In an effort to lessen the teaching burden of faculty, many undergraduate courses were team taught. The large enrollment Basic Biology course was a particular problem, not only because of its size (and inherent exam administration and grading duties), but because the course was an "entry" level course where not only potential biology majors enrolled, but non-science majors as well. Many of our faculty, especially the molecular biologists felt that they were going to be exposed to leprosy at the mere thought of interacting with non-science majors. A remedy for this came when the department hired Charlie Smith as an instructor from California. Charlie's principal responsibility was the Basic Biology course and the supervision of dozens of lab sections. While I never heard Charlie lecture, I could tell from my frequent hallway chats with him, that he brought competence, curiosity, and enthusiasm to the classroom. One day I rode the elevator with Charlie, and, as we got off to go our separate ways, Charlie stood frozen in thought. I asked "What's up?" Charlie answered not missing a beat: "Mike, I was thinking about the electrical controls of the elevator. You and I got on at different floors yet the elevator stopped to pick one of us up, right? I just got this thought of the parallels of the elevator electronics with the functioning of the nervous system of the grasshopper. Pretty neat huh?" So there we were standing in a busy hallway discussing invertebrate neurology, which not so incidentally was Charlie's graduate research interest back in his California days.

At UB, it became clear that learning was where you found it, whom you spoke with, what you read, and what you did in the lab. Our biological training was like an apprenticeship. We were within a milieu to learn, either in the classroom or research laboratory. Most of the courses I took were geared around published research articles and not some dated text. We students quickly found out that the biological sciences were anything but static, but evolving fields dependent on the tried and true methodology of scientific discovery: problem identification, hypothetical proposals, research plan to address a reigning question, data gathering, and lastly and importantly, a discussion of whether or not the results shed any additional light on the problem. Has new knowledge been advanced? If so, how and why? If not, how and why? We students eventually found out that successful accomplishment of this type of research thinking became the key to whether or not our dissertation would lead us to conferrals of our PhDs, as well as keys to published papers, funding from granting agencies, and later in securing a post graduate position.

An important vehicle to further learning came from outside speakers. The weekly seminars were usually of high caliber and highly technical, occasions where invited speakers from on and off campus extolled the virtues of their own research. As we students found out, however, it was during the Q and A where the real fun in learning began. It was during this period where global questions as well as laboratory minutiae were brought to light. It was a time to see how a healthy exchange of ideas can take place. It was a time for the scientific method to come alive (and for us students to emulate). We thought there will come a day when each of us students will be called upon to deliver our own seminar, our defense-of-thesis exam. In addition, there were well-published visits from noted scientists recognized the world over – scientists such as the Nobel prize winning Christian DeDuve, James Watson, and Sir John Eccles were treated like rock stars. It was like Claude Monet coming to discuss art, Ben Hogan analyzing the intricacies of the golf swing, or Frank Lloyd Wright reviewing his latest architectural wonders. We students were awed by their presence. In addition to their own formal seminar presentations, each distinguished scientist volunteered time with us so we could meet and discuss science – a heady experience for us. Incidentally, the biggest buzz on campus in the late 60's came from the two-time Nobel Prize winner Linus Pauling of Cal Tech. In spite of being blacklisted by the State Department because of his very public anti-war stance, Pauling delivered stirring seminars on his molecular modeling work with proteins, as well as on his new pet projects of Vitamin C and the common cold.

After I put my PhD behind me and joined as a postdoc in the Biology Department of Syracuse University, in many ways it was business as usual, that is, except for a change in focus of my research problem, in my case, muscular dystrophy, I spent most time reading, writing, discussing, and carrying on hands-on research. Not too much different from how I spent 5 years at UB. Oral presentations of my work were pretty much confined to informal lab discussions and a smattering of short talks for the benefit of the local chapter of the Muscular Dystrophy Association, the sponsor of my postdoc support. After my marriage to Raj, this trend continued after I had my postdoc transferred back to Buffalo, first within the Biochemistry Department and 4 years later to the Biology Department.

Looking back, where did I prepare for classroom teaching? Interestingly, it seems I had quite a bit of practice through my grad and postdoc experiences where, in a countless number of venues, I had been called upon to answer this simple question: "Mike, what is it that you do?" Whether it was a question from my mother who wanted an update so she could impress her friends or questions from scientific colleagues, I usually answered with a set recipe. I would identify the over-all problem I was working on, put the problem in an understandable context, and depending upon who asked the question in the first place, I'd explain what I did and why, as well as what I hoped to find. It seemed as though I had by this stage given a vast number of mini-lectures. Whether I was addressing the subjects of depressed metabolism or muscular dystrophy, I attempted to frame my answers in simple understandable terms, not unlike what I'd like to hear within a classroom if I were the student.

In thinking of role models for what I think are successful teaching strategies, I already mentioned a few that I came across in my formal education. Here I can add a few more, which on the surface, may appear a disparate group but in the end a highly effective group. Jim Crockett and his PBS *Victory Garden* series in a way emulated my biochemistry professor Wayne Gallagher with his passion, knowledge, and infectious love of subject. Actress and cook, Madhur Jaffrey explained how complicated Indian curry preparations can be broken down into simple, logical, clear steps for all to replicate and enjoy. Furthermore, I could add to this list many artists appearing on educational TV who again distilled a complicated scene into simple understandable strokes, with each one contributing step-by-step into a highly appealing painting. I could add many scientists to this list of role models, such as: molecular geneticist Eric Hoffman, and scientists of his eminence whom author John Brodmann considered to be members of the *Third Culture* in our society. This group included talented practicing scientists who successfully bridged the gap between what C.P. Snow called the "two cultures of science and non-science thinking". As our classrooms contain students of varying abilities and backgrounds, it behooves us as scientists and educators to make every effort to bridge this gap.

Ironically, one of my earlier and best paradigms of effective teaching was under my nose all along – Raj. After we were married and each of us set in our respective career work with Raj teaching at UB and later at ECC and I ensconced in my dystrophy research, I had several opportunities to give talks to professional organizations interested in muscle disease. In some cases I had been asked by the local Muscular Dystrophy Association to take part in their annual workshop where healthcare workers, as well as parents of dystrophic children, were in attendance. For my part, I was asked to describe recent advances in the research and treatment of muscular dystrophy. In these sessions I would first give a general overview and follow with some specifics of my own research. Because of my empathy for family members in attendance, I tried as much as possible to give a positive spin to where we are in the research realm and where we are headed. In a couple of workshops, I proposed that Raj also join in and give a mini-lecture on the underlying genetics of the muscular dystrophies. The aim here was less for the clinical people in attendance, but, it was for the family members who in spite of the availability of current disease testing continued to rear dystrophic children (in many cases a preventable situation).

Typically the workshop was held at School 84, which provided a teaching venue for handicapped children. The program consisted of addresses by Dr. Joseph Link, medical director of the local MDA-sponsored clinic, a physical therapist, a psychologist, and Raj and me. When Raj's turn came, she pulled out the blackboard riding on wheels, and with chalk and flowing sari she began her lecture. In all its clarity and simplicity, she engaged the audience with her genetic knowledge, the kind of stuff that sticks to your ribs. Reviewing how our genetic information is packed into 23 pairs of chromosomes, Raj described how these structures contain genetic recipes for everything from eye color to digestive enzymes. As she continued, she described how genetic information is passed on from parent to child. Even for college students, the concept of meiosis is not easy, but here Raj made the whole process understandable, adding examples how eye color etc. are transmitted, and why in some cases genetic traits can be hidden in the next generation, hence these genetic traits are described as recessive rather than dominant. After 20 minutes or so, Raj got to the nub of her lecture and reviewed how certain muscle diseases follow a recessive pattern of inheritance, and some are like the devastating Duchenne disease which is an X-linked disorder. Because the Duchenne disease was all too common and prematurely fatal, all ears perked up. Not missing a beat, Raj explained with the aid of the blackboard, how our sex chromosomes, X and Y are disseminated from parent to child, and, if there is a lesion on the X chromosome, how it would always be expressed in baby boys yielding the Duchenne disorder. This is because males have an XY complement, unlike females who have an XX complement. It would not be an over-statement to say Raj enraptured the audience because of her ability to make a complex process simple and accessible, especially for family members who wrestle each day with questions of whether or not to undergo genetic testing and possibly to use some measure of family planning. This was heady stuff to take in, particularly when the other speakers either ignored or soft-pedaled the subject.

During this period I shouldn't have been surprised by Raj's performance. In the early years when I first knew her, Raj always had a knack of explaining things in clear and relevant terms, whether it was something biological or a range of topics we discussed at lunch during our grad school days. Whether it was Indian history, language, or cuisine, or, for that matter, English literature, Raj would be quick to take a tablet of paper and present a mini-lecture on the topic. She didn't need an overhead projector, 2 by 2 slides, or Powerpoint to get her message across. Raj certainly captures the spirit of this chapter. "You know when you hear it." There was a time when Raj came down with a bad cold and I needed to fill in for her in some of her classes in Human Biology. I had trepidations as this would be my first formal bout of classroom teaching. Equipped with Raj's notes on the endocrine system, fresh chalk, and a chair to sit on, I embarked on a journey and never looked back. The experience was invigorating in many aspects – the value of organization and preparation was shown to be priceless, and I was able to bring my own knowledge of the material to the fore; and I was very pleased that my body didn't implode while trying to physically juggle myself in the process.

One day Hal Segal invited me to give some lectures in his Human Nutrition course. Taught mainly to nursing students and other health-related majors, the course navigated the primary constituents of our diet: what they are, how much we need, and what the body does with them in both health and disease. For my part, I was given the set of lectures dealing with vitamins, which seemed to be a topic no one wanted to lecture on, nor listen to, if you were a student. Given my research interest in muscle, however, I was able to spice up the topic a bit by comparing the vitamin needs of elite athletes to the more sedentary population. Gratefully the students reacted positively to my efforts, both in the classroom as well as in the end of semester evaluations. With regard to the latter, I found Hal at his desk pouring over evaluations from the previous semester. "Hal, how did we do?" I asked. Not missing a beat nor looking up from his desk Hal responded curtly, "Many are not so good." I asked how I did and he shot back – "Oh, they loved you!" As I left his office I was quite pleased to hear this. Later in 1985 I taught Human Nutrition all on my own. I found the subject matter interesting from both a scientific point-of-view, as well as for a chance to introduce a bevy of contemporary issues, such as steroid use among athletes and the FDA approval process for supplements (as well as drugs). During these early years of classroom teaching, I found I was most effective when I used pre-prepared overhead transparencies with my notes already written out (as opposed to using the blackboard and chalk). This procedure allowed me to economize my physical effort in front of the class and to keep my lecture on message and not wander off when I got to a topic I found particularly enjoyable.

I ended up teaching the Nutrition course for another seven years. During this time, enrollment grew as I kept adding new topics as well as refining some hands-on exercises in which students jumped in with both feet. Particularly popular was an exercise to keep a two week diary of all foods consumed as well as a profile of energy consumption through physical activities each day. Afterwards I shared totals from the student diary submissions allowing me to make several cogent comments, such as that the average protein intake not surprisingly was nearly three times the recommended daily allowance. In addition to conclusions based on nutrient intake, I was able to illustrate the pluses and minuses of caloric consumption versus expenditure. Those wishing to lose weight were able to profile what it would take: increase physical activity, reduce food calories, or a combination of the two. I found students to be empowered by what they did individually with their diaries and by what I was able to do with their numbers. This was satisfying for the student and instructor alike.

Having been bitten by the teaching bug, I felt I could teach other courses as a source of income. Even though I was Principal Investigator of a grant from the MDA, I couldn't draw any salary from the project. To my rescue came the opportunity to teach Mammalian Biology and Vertebrate Embryology. For the most part these classes were composed of premed students along with a smattering of students in other prehealth fields. While I looked forward to the opportunity to lock horns with the Department's best and brightest, I was personally challenged to put on a good show. In the first instance, I had some familiarity with Mammalian Biology through Raj, who had previously taught the course where she approached the syllabus as nothing more than a "Human Anatomy and Physiology" course. Since our departmental majors are not exposed to much human biology in their curriculum, the class as a whole welcomed my step by step approach to human structure and function. In the second instance, Vertebrate Embryology was a subject in which I was quite familiar from my graduate school days at Niagara University. As in the Mammalian Biology course, I again made every attempt to stress humans when discussing development. In addition, because of the prehealth makeup of the class, I explored various maladies affecting human development, including genetic errors and nutritional deficiencies. Subsequently, I taught other courses, including: Comparative Anatomy, Topics in Physical Therapy, and Freshman Seminar, which introduced me to the use of case studies as an effective teaching tool.

It was also during the 80's when I received two notable honors – an Honorary Doctorate from my alma mater Niagara University and the George Thorn Alumni Award from UB. The former was granted in part because 1981 was the year to recognize achievements made by the handicapped, and the latter made to those under the age of 40 whose career achievements were judged outstanding. To say the least, it was a very heady time for "yours truly". Things, however, were not quite as they seemed to be. I started to experience a number of panic attacks – not knowing the time or place one might occur. Even though on the outside I could not have been more fulfilled from a research or teaching standpoint, within I was suffering. Fortunately, one day I was with Raj in a bookshop and came across a book which greatly attracted my attention – Clair Weekes' *Peace from Nervous Suffering*. The book at the time changed my life. Within its covers, Weekes explained in simple but compelling terms what I was going through and how to accept the "ibby gibbys" in my life, and, importantly, how to move on. The anagram FAFE became my mantra: F – Face, A – Accept, F – Float, E – Endure. I now had a strategy for living in spite of bumps in the road which occurred now as periodic but understandable, self-limiting symptoms. In a real way I became stronger in an area where I was the weakest. For this I need to thank Raj for her cushioning wisdom and to Dr. Clair Weekes for her incisive instruction in book form.

In the 1990's, I was able to transition the department's Mammalian Biology course into a *bona fide* Human Biology course. In this way I was able to attract a range of prehealth majors and get into the nitty gritty of human structure and function. It became a highly successful endeavor for students and lecturer alike. In the meantime, I embarked on something new, devising a course exclusively for first year students called: Origins of Contemporary Biology. Within the aegis of the University's Freshman Seminar Program, my course which met for 3 hours each week offered me free rein to explore any or all topics I felt relevant to understanding the life sciences in our everyday lives. These included such diverse topics as how prescription drugs were developed and approved by the FDA, how inherited diseases like muscular dystrophy are researched, what a field trip into the woods would teach us about biology's five kingdoms, laws of thermodynamics, power of observation, and overall the tried and true scientific method. Filled with high hopes in the beginning that the occasion would be dynamic and discussion filled, I soon found my twenty students were much more at ease if I did all the talking. Trying to get these otherwise bright students to speak up in class was like pulling teeth. Exasperated, one day over breakfast I got the idea of an exercise I would use in class. I copied a very short abstract of

271

a study where scientists used a mouse model to test whether or not beta amyloid protein caused Alzheimer's disease symptoms. Below the abstract were five questions for the students to answer after they read the abstract. Basically the question sequence followed the so-called scientific method of exploration: 1. What was the problem being studied? 2. What was the underlying hypothesis of the study? 3. What was the method of the study? 4. What were the results of the study? 5. What was the significance of the study?

After all were seated, I handed out the single page and got them started, giving them only 20 minutes to finish the exercise. After what seemed an eternity, I began an open-ended discussion of the study by asking, "What was the central problem the scientists were trying to address?" At this stage I asked one of the students to assist me by going to the blackboard and listing each student's response. Although the students were hesitant at first, the answers started to pour in filling up a sizeable chunk of the blackboard. As viewed by the students, the problem of the study ranged from the specific to the general, *i.e.*, cause and/or treatment of Alzheimer's disease (or memory loss), or to more general notions of how the nervous system works in the first place. With me acting as facilitator, remarkably the students opened up freely and filled the first half hour of the class spilling everything they knew about the nervous system – its basic structure and function, as well as several disorders including Alzheimer's. Wow! Next I led the class to the second question which centered on the underlying hypothesis of the study. Again, the blackboard began to fill up with answers ranging from the specific (*e.g.*, Is the buildup of amyloid protein or something like it disrupting the brain causing memory loss?) to more global notions of brain functioning, and the suitability of animal models in the study of human brain disorders. With another half hour filled with spirited discussion and chalk dust everywhere, it was time for a break. Out in the hallway I couldn't believe what had just happened. In previous classes I had to beg, borrow, and steal answers from the students, but in this instance I couldn't shut them up! It was wonderful. What had changed in this class?

After the board was wiped clean because all the space had been used, I jumped into the next questions, which basically asked "What did the scientists do and what was the method of the study?" Amazingly, the class jabbered on non-stop for another 90 minutes filling the board faster than my student assistant could write. Here the students wrestled with the nitty gritty of scientific research and listed several issues associated with using an animal model, such as: controls, how many, gender, and age. In addition, the students proposed an assortment of measures in which to measure loss of memory in mice. For each measure, suitable controls also had to be included. Also thrown into the discussion were the staggering costs of conducting this research in the first place, as well as what ethical issues were at stake in conducting animal research. As things developed, we NEVER got to the results of the study. Three hours simply were not enough time to adequately cover the study. I was blown away!

In retrospect it seems each student comes to a classroom with information gleaned over time from their formal schooling as well as from life experiences. By guiding them through a problem with a series of open-ended questions as I had done in the Alzheimer's case, a group learning dynamic takes over where each student contributes toward a common end. It was inspiring as an instructor to stand back and listen to the students as they learned, not only from the case study problem itself, but from each other. Not soon after this particular class, I participated in a month long summer workshop conducted by our noted teaching colleague, Kipp Herreid. With grant support from the NSF, Kipp gathered a dozen science faculty to investigate the feasibility of applying case studies as a means of teaching science. For the first three weeks we learned the ins and outs of case studies through a series of invited speakers, each of whom were acknowledged leaders in the field. In the last week of the workshop, each participant presented a case study in a real classroom setting, complete with a "dummy" class made up of paid student volunteers. With the success I had with the Alzheimer's case fresh in my mind, I presented it again as I did in the Freshman Seminar class. As I had hoped, the class quickly dissolved into a highly charged group learning dynamic. Again, I never got to the Results of the case. After a faculty discussion of the exercise, I quickly learned the case was a big hit, mainly because of the case's ability to spawn discussion and higher learning. Subsequently, Kipp asked me to present this particular case to his annual case study summer workshop series. Later in other courses, I interjected case studies into the lecture syllabus. Most of the case studies I used were in the form of recent newspaper articles involving the biomedical sciences.

A couple of years before I jumped into the administration arena as Executive Officer of the Department in 1995, I taught two large courses, Basic Biology and Perspectives in Human Biology. Basic Biology's primary audience were science majors while the Perspectives course was populated by non-science majors who needed a science course to graduate. The two semester Basic Biology course served as the gateway for the Department's biology majors, as well as students interested in the health field. Traditionally, the course surveyed the five major Kingdoms in addition to basic concepts of the cell, biochemistry, and physiology. I felt, however, that the course lacked a cohesive thread needed to engage students over the long haul. I kept, therefore, the traditional Five Kingdoms of life, but I gave a human "spin" to each one. For example, the lower Moneran Kingdom, composed primarily of bacteria, was discussed in its own right, but I raised student interest by delving into how bacteria impact us humans – the good, the bad, and the ugly. To increase further student interest I spent two entire lectures reviewing the major human body systems, including the immune response. I found this approach to be highly rewarding for the students as well as for myself.

I found the three years in which I taught Basic Biology to be quite an adventure as I had the daytime class of 430 students and an evening class with 175 students. I left the running of the labs to a colleague Dennis Pietras who had a track-record of wallowing in the minutiae of such an arrangement. Hence, I was able to throw my energies into the lectures. My student ratings were very good and served as a foundation for my friend and colleague Chris Loretz to nominate me for the SUNY Chancellor's Excellence in Teaching Award, which I won in 1995. Through it all, Raj ferried me back and forth to campus where Cathy provided fathomless support at every turn.

In retrospect, I found teaching Basic Biology to be most gratifying. At the time, I felt that I actually belonged to the Department and the University through my tangible contributions to undergraduate education.

I was making a difference in the lives of thousands of students, most of whom had post-graduate plans in the bio-medical sciences. One student in particular comes to mind. He was an enthusiastic male nursing student who also happened to be a member of the US Air Force National Guard. He sat in the front row, and he entertained me with his quick wit and tireless note-taking. One day I planned to devote much of the class time in preparing the class for their first exam. As students got settled in their seats, my nursing friend took out his Bic pen and made a "brrrrr" sound as he pretended to pull a rip-chord to a power lawn mower. A few days after this humorous episode, he told me before class that his National Guard unit had been called up and activated to take part in the first Gulf War with Iraq. With sadness I wished him well, to stay safe, and to get his ass back here to finish the course (which I'm happy to say he did).

Another challenge came my way at the request of colleague Chuck Fourtner who asked me to co-teach a new course called Perspectives in Human Biology. This course would fit within the desire of the College of Arts and Sciences to offer its non-science majors two semester courses (each with a one semester lab). With a revamping of the College's curriculum it was now necessary for non-science majors to pass a science course in order to graduate. Chuck and I met regularly during the summer of 1991 and sketched out what we thought would be an interesting yet challenging course. We both agreed that the primary aim of the Perspectives course was for students to develop and implement scientific thinking. In a way, we wanted the students at the end of the two semesters to not only be comfortable talking about science, but for them to have a good idea how and what scientists actually think.

Our approach with the class was simple. We would start slowly almost in a juvenile way and present exercises in which the class would identify characteristics of living cells, tissues and organisms. From these building blocks, we would move into the complexities of the evolutionary tree, going from the monerans, to protists, fungi, plants, and eventually to animals, highlighting the human organism. Accompanying classroom explorations of what it is to be "alive" and "biological" were hands-on lab exercises in which students utilized the so-called "scientific method." Each lab exercise came equipped with a Problem, Hypothesis, Method, Results, Discussion, and Conclusions - all the elements which are found in real scientific research. From these baby steps Chuck and I began to delete topics which we felt lacked instructional value and interest, and added elements which we deemed more useful in reaching our over-all aim of the course. As the semester wore on, Chuck and I kept adapting to the idea that our students were indeed quite bright, but "different" from the science majors we normally encountered. We faced students who had a dearth of scientific knowledge and were not used to approaching problems in a scientifically analytical manner. Consequently, we drew upon our many years in active research and tapped into our wide reservoir of classroom experience. With this approach, we quickly got the students into thinking scientifically. For example, our first lab exercise got the students out into the wild on a natural setting trip where students took notes on what they saw, heard, smelled – whether it was a visit to a pond, forest, or even in one case to New York City's Central Park. Students learned the valuable lesson that "observation" is the first important key to the solving of a scientific problem. Another exercise involved students breaking up into groups where they researched a fictitious drug of our choosing in order to present a Poster presentation, not unlike the format commonly used in scientific meetings. This exercise provided a great opportunity to demonstrate critical scientific thinking, as the students tried to convince the US Food and Drug Administration that their drug was both safe and effective. We also got our students to scour the University and search out scientists for interviews which could be shared in class. In each case, students told us what a particular scientist was currently studying, what were the methods involved, what had been found, and, lastly, what was the significance of the research.

Within the classroom, movies were shown which dramatized principles highlighted in class, *e.g.*, Fleming's discovery of penicillin, Banting and Best's saga to cure diabetes with newly-discovered insulin, and notably the Double-Helix story where Watson and Crick and others tackled the mystery of the elusive genetic code – DNA. In addition, newspaper articles were again a common feature in each class where topical scientific stories were presented and dissected to reinforce critical scientific thinking. Within a couple of months, we had most of the students walking and talking as scientists. While they didn't have the depth nor breadth of knowledge we might expect from our science majors, our students were well on their way to thinking as we might think as scientists, and, at a minimum, they were becoming highly intelligent citizens capable of asking scientifically-acute questions.

While Chuck and I taught together for only a year, I continued to teach the Perspectives course for another dozen years. During that time the course grew from 50 students to a room capacity of 240 when I finally gave up the reins in 2004 to spend full time as Executive Officer of the Department. At the time I had pangs in the Fall as a new semester began, and, after 25 years, I had no course to prepare for. My angst for the classroom, however, melted away for good after I had to deal with a couple of dissatisfied students from the previous spring semester. Today I have nothing but wonderful, fulfilling memories of my years in the classroom, and I cherish the honor and responsibility of imparting knowledge to students who many years ago, would have filled me with fear and trepidation.

*Chapter 20*

# Fruition

It is not as if I didn't have enough to do in 1995. The Perspectives and General Biology courses were going full bore. Research with the MDX mouse was paying dividends under the scrupulous labor of Cathy and former grad student, now postdoc, Joe Granchelli. On the home front, Raj and I were happily adjusted to my mother-in-law Olivia who had come from India five years earlier to live with us. It was a pleasantly fulfilling time.

When I was working at my desk in August, I got a call from Professor Ed Brody, who was the Chair of the Department. "Mike, as I think you know, Jeff will be retiring as Executive Officer, and, if you're interested, I'd like you to submit your name as a candidate." Even though I knew something was brewing through the Departmental grapevine, I was surprised by Brody's call. I remember telling him initially that I was flattered by the offer, but I was quite tied up with my courses and research. I told him I would get back to him. I called Raj, who immediately implored me to call Brody back and tell him yes! Within a minute or two, I called Ed back. He told me that it is always a good idea to check with your wife! In a matter of minutes, I committed myself to a minefield, called administration. As I look back it was probably the best move I could have made. With my records of classroom teaching and research, I was now ready to tackle the last of academic's trifecta – administration. In a personal sense, by my taking over the Department's administrative controls, I would have an opportunity to apply what I had learned in academia as well as the lessons I had learned in life itself.

*A priori,* I had the impression that the Executive Officer (aka, Assistant to the Chair) was at ground zero of the activities of Departmental affairs. It wouldn't take me too long to find out just how true my impression was. As my appointment wouldn't officially take effect until October, I continued my teaching and research, but just below the surface were all-consuming thoughts of the responsibilities that lay ahead. Because Chuck Jeffrey had been on leave due to earlier surgery, his office was vacant, except for the intimidating piles of paperwork everywhere! I wondered what kind of world I had entered? As the Fall semester continued, Dr. Brody was eager to give me full responsibility, so that he could get on with his own research and not be bothered with day-to-day administration.

One evening after class Cathy and I went to my "soon-to-be-office". After flicking on the lights, I had a chance to take a close up look at some of the paperwork within. Shuffling through one pile after another it became apparent that my first order of business was to get a dumpster. Outdated memos and reports, reams of unanswered requests, bills to pay, deans to call, schedules left hanging. The assortment of yellowing paperwork was indicative that time had frozen in place since Jeffrey had taken leave months earlier.

On the day I officially took over the Executive Officer reins, Brody greeted me as he left for his research lab (and freedom), He wished me good luck, and then he told me to call him if I had to. With a grin on his face, he handed me a snarly-looking piece of paper as if it were the original rosetta stone, and he said: "Here is a letter you should keep carefully for the next Chair whoever that may be. It's an old letter of understanding between the Dean and the former Chair, Om Bahl, regarding the latter's lab space." Brody went on to describe how sensitive Bahl might be if the Dean ever needed to take some lab space away from him in the future, and that this letter of agreement might be needed to adjudicate any possible dispute. After that little nugget, Brody left in a cloud of dust. Before I started to eviscerate my office of paperwork, I had a closed door meeting with my four secretaries. Even though I thought I knew them fairly well, I wanted to get off on the right step and to get an unvarnished insight from each of them as well as their roles in the office. To me the departmental office was where the "rubber met the road". Nearly all academic, as well as research matters, were funneled in and out of its four walls, and I felt that each secretary should take pride from the enterprise. The pep talk was as much for myself as for the ladies.

I empowered Corinne Dusenbury to be the person responsible for the day-to-day operations of the budget, as well as the gate-keeper to my office. Pleased with her newly appointed flexibility and responsibilities, which she did not have previously, soft-spoken Corinne turned out to be a godsend in patiently helping me to understand the financial and operational nuances with which the department dealt on a routine basis. Later, when Corinne stepped down to take a managerial position at Empire State College, Candy Folkerth from the Physiology Department was hired in her place. What Candy didn't know regarding budgetary matters, and her lack of personal finesse, was more than made up for by her positive approach to problems. Candy's outspoken temperament riled many, but in the end she turned into a solid mainstay of office affairs, as well as to me personally.

Rose Stern was a loyal and reliable old hand in the office, distinguished by her red hair. She handled diverse functions ranging from: mail, typing and distributing memos, gathering student timesheets, as well as setting up refreshments for weekly seminars. Another old hand was Donna Wilde, who handled matters associated with the Department's growing graduate program. Personable and gracious, as well as an active golfer, Donna worked as graduate secretary and made sure student files were up-to-date as the students proceeded toward degree conferral. Apprenticing under Donna was a relative newcomer, Linda Mack, who acted as the Department's Undergraduate Secretary. Linda had the unenviable task of serving as the point person near the front door to greet an evolving flux of Biology Majors, as well as wannabees, who hadn't yet been accepted as Majors. In her quiet, patient, and methodical manner, Linda was a boon to the Department's undergraduate mission.

**Intrepid Secretarial And Technical Staff)**

A bonus for me was Linda's ability to translate my hand-written scrawl into typed works of art. Earlier, I had gotten a heads up from colleague Chuck Fourtner that I would be authoring several departmental reports as EO. Within a couple of months on the job, we were directed by the University Provost to prepare an inventory report detailing everything we did as a Department: our mission, who we were, our student stake-holders, teaching accomplishments, research activities and funding, as well as service activities. Instructions for the report took over a dozen pages! After a few days to take it all in, I developed a strategy with our newly-elected Chair, Professor Ron Berezney, to obtain current CVs from our faculty, as well as a listing of teaching and service activities. During this time, I asked Linda and Donna to ferret through our files for relevant information on our undergraduate and graduate course offerings. On the budget side, I asked Corinne to dig into her archives for financial information proving that the Department was indeed doing more over the years in spite of dwindling resources. Once I got all the information together I made my home dining table "ground zero" for the report preparation, and over the next couple of weeks I fed reams of hand-written prose to Linda to type back at the office. In addition, I recruited my good friend and departmental illustrator, Jim Stamos, to prepare one figure after another in his own inimitable artistic manner.

**Departmental Illustrator and
Good Friend Jim Stamos**

While I may have been the primary author and, as well, the conductor of the inventory report, it was all made possible by everyone in the department pitching in some form or fashion. Ironically, when the time came in June for us to submit our Annual Report to the Dean, it would be a simple matter of cutting and trimming our inventory report. In the years to follow, we continued to use the inventory model for succeeding Annual Reports.

When Donna retired from the Department, Linda took over the reins of the Graduate Program, leaving Undergraduate Affairs to newcomer, Sandy Fitzpatrick, who joined us from the Dental School. Now it was Sandy's turn to occupy the "hot seat" next to the office door, positioned to face the steady onslaught of undergraduates hungry for answers. In addition to her Undergraduate work, Sandy grew into being our IT go-to person. As computer skills and the internet became more and more the tools of necessity in the Department, if not the University as a whole, Sandy kept the office staff up to speed as new developments warranted. When I first got on board as EO and all the paperwork involved in the inventory and annual reports,

I'm amazed at how far electronic filing, storage, and transmission have taken us, not only in data composition, but in reciprocal transmissions among interested academic units. Today the Provost or Dean need only to direct their respective IT people to contact us electronically for information they might require

As new EO, I had at one time worn just about all the hats one could wear in the Department: grad student, post-doc, lecturer, and funded principal research investigator. Facing the task of putting together the inventory report, however, opened my eyes considerably to the value of good administration, and of equal importance to the specifics of who we were as an academic unit. Before Brody stepped aside as Chair (and Ron chosen as his successor), much of my early 'Twilight Zone' time was spent consulting with a few dedicated and trusted faculty within the Department, mostly those involved in undergraduate and graduate affairs. To get our administrative house in order, however, I spent considerable time with the Natural Sciences and Mathematics Dean Joe Tufariello and his assistants, Martha Barton (finances), John Ho (graduate and research affairs), and David Cadenhead (undergraduate affairs). I let it be known that I was the new to this situation sought tutoring. It soon became clear that the Dean's people were eager to work with me as they felt our Department of Biological Sciences was a "black hole". Too often, memos were either ignored or lost. Until Ron officially came on board as Chair, I was in charge. To get a handle on the departmental budget, which was my own black hole, I frequently saw Martha Barton. She was patient and astute in helping me to understand the complexities of money flow within our unit, if not the University as a whole. In a matter of weeks, I was able to work with Corinne in the construction of spreadsheets clarifying at one glance where we were financially. For the first time, I was beginning to understand the forest of anagrams facing me – IFR, PS, OPTS, RF, UBF, etc...

As I worked with the Dean's people, I gained an understanding of how the University works as a whole. You could say that the University acts as a large ecological pyramid complete with its own energy flow and food chain. In looking at the University as a freshwater lake, one could say that the ravenous muskellunge would serve as the top carnivore of the pyramid, not unlike the President's office of the University. His office, through its Provost and host of Vice-Presidents, pulls the strings of just about every aspect of the campus. This level is where policy is made, as well as where money is ultimately collected and distributed. Radiating from the fifth floor of the administration building are the Deans of the University's constituent Colleges and Schools. Each could be looked upon as a secondary carnivore within the ecological metaphor, not unlike an array of feisty pike and bass. Here is where we are introduced to the divisions (or neighborhoods) which in summary, make up the University (or lake) as a whole. Whether it concerns biology, chemistry, engineering, fine arts, or medicine, it's at this level where courses are taught and research done. It's up to the Dean and his minions to see that the neighborhoods within his auspices are neat and tidy, and measure up to the standards of excellence set by the President's people. Within this backdrop, there are Chairs (and their Assistants) who strive to keep their own neighborhoods in order, sort of like panfish who do not live in the deep water where the big guys swim stay close to shore where there are plenty of opportunities for productivity (and I may add, for cover).

After a month on the job, the Dean set the wheels in motion to select a replacement for Brody who would step down as Chair at the end of 1995. Since 1967, when I first came to the department as a grad student, there have been a string of Chairs beginning with the capable but out-spoken Hal Segal. Because a successor could not be agreed upon, the faculty defaulted to a triumvirate – Mort Rothstein, David Yphantis, and Phil Miles. A symbol emphasizing this tenuous arrangement was seen in an unused gavel constructed with three handles. The department soon came to its senses and opted for a succession of two, respected senior faculty members – Phil Miles and Om Bahl. Bahl was at the helm when the Department relocated from the older Main Street campus to the newer Amherst in 1977. It was during this transition that mathematician Chuck Jeffrey joined the Department as EO. A few years later, Darrell Doyle, a noted cell biologist from Roswell Park Cancer Center, joined the Department as Chair. Six years later, an outside search yielded Ed Brody from the Pasteur Institute. Against this backdrop, our faculty faced another

Chair selection vote. Candidates ranged from those simply unqualified because of temperament and/or administrative skill or those who disqualified themselves because they didn't want the job in the first place. Fortunately, there were a few who threw their hats in the ring, because they were not only qualified, but in my words "really cared about the department". In the end, three seasoned and highly qualified individuals ran the Department during the 10 years I served as EO: Ron, plant physiologist Mary Bisson, and biochemist Jerry Koudelka. Aside from a few early hiccups, Ron and I got on famously, and the same occurred later with Mary and Jerry.

In addition to our talented secretarial and lab support staff, Dennis Pietras turned out to be a valuable colleague. He wore an assortment of hats from lab technician to classroom lecturer, and Dennis grew to know every square inch of the Department. When it came time to rig up a new phone system, do space inventory, develop a safety program, rehab a lab, etc…most often Dennis was the first person I called. Once he showed up at my office door wearing his usual t-shirt, I just knew that the task at hand would be in good hands. He was our Department's "utility outfielder" at work! It might be added here that Dennis carried on his work in spite of being diagnosed with MS. In a heart-felt confidential discussion we had soon after the diagnosis, I explained to him that the disease would be as big as he let it be. I told him: "Look at me? Do you think I could possibly carry on if it weren't for all those who have helped me?" I explained that with his vast knowledge of the Department, he could accomplish most of his work without ever leaving his desk. To his credit, Dennis changed his work schedule and the department prospered for it.

Sifting through steno pads which I used as my daily calendar of things to do, there were always note threads of items too important and/or too ambitious to be accomplished in a day or two. Most often these protracted items concerned challenges requiring leadership by the Chair. A prominent example can be found in the erupting fields of molecular and evolutionary ecology where the Department found itself as a major player in the retention and/or recruitment of faculty. Every six years or so our Department underwent University-wide peer review, in which every facet of our operation is evaluated, and the subsequent report was being used to compare ourselves with other major public research universities in the country. As we are a Department of Biological SCIENCES, we have a chronic need for faculty (and resources) to help maintain the Department's balance between molecular and organismic-centric faculty. In the case of ecology, as new advances in molecular biology have been made, previous questions regarding biodiversity and distribution could now be answered. As a result the definition and scope of ecology were significantly expanded. Once relegated as one of the 'field' disciplines, ecology was taking on a whole new veneer; an evolving area which the Department needed to address.

Over the past 40 years or so the Department contained faculty who represented research areas within the gamut of ecological interests. For example, Jack Storrs and Howie Lasker and their marine invertebrate biology studies took them and their students to warm climes like the Bahamas and Florida keys. Freshwater biologists Ken Stewart and Wayne Hadley actively studied inland waterways for their chemical milieu as well as their wildlife. Talking with them reminded me of my early interest in ecology nurtured years earlier by Bryan Britten at Niagara University. On the other hand, Peter Gold and Tim Williams came on board and they studied the behavior of various animals, including migratory patterns of birds. Herpetologist Carl Gans traveled far and wide through the rainforests of Central and South America for exotic snakes and crocodiles to accomplish his mechanisms of movement studies. His field studies were landmark, especially since his array of snake anti-venoms were coveted far and wide by zoos and elsewhere. Among these faculty were investigators such as Carm Privitera, Kipp Herreid, Mary Bisson, Chuck Fourtner, and Chris Loretz who gave physiological twists to their studies of adaptation (and in turn distribution). Because these investigators employed many state-of-the-art molecular methods (as well as questions) in their research, it could be said that they as a group formed a bridge between the organismic and molecular wings of the department. Because of this dichotomy, it became difficult for the Department to compete with the over-all rankings of our peer institutions, *i.e.*, we neither had a sufficient critical mass of physiologists nor ecologists, nor molecular biologists for that matter. Things began to change dramatically, however, when the arrival of new comers Ian Baldwin, Mike Webster, Guiyun Yan, Antonia Monteiro, Derek Taylor, and the rediscovery of our own Mary Alice Coffroth (wife of Howie Lasker and who at the time had an untenured research faculty line).

In a story which resembles a pro football team trying to sign and/or retain a talented athlete, our Department found itself in a bidding war with other institutions eager to sign them up. The Department had an unenviable task of trying to retain some gifted faculty who were at the vanguard of redefining ecology, once a step-child in the Department. In the case of Ian Baldwin, he was a bright and enthusiastic assistant professor who more or less took over our greenhouse facility to grow tobacco plants in his insect attraction/repulsion studies. Together with state-of-the-art chromatography equipment, Ian helped to define the field of ecology in 'chemical' terms – hence the term "chemical ecology" subsequently became part of the vernacular world-wide. It wasn't too long before Ian attracted the interest of Cornell, Georgia Tech, and the internationally famous Max Planck Institute in Germany. As a result the Department needed to convince the UB administration to put Ian on the fast track for tenure and promotion to 'Full' professor, and provide him with increases in space and facilities, as well as future faculty hires specializing in chemical ecology. Cornell's offer was attractive because of its reputation in ecology, as well as Georgia Tech's offer to set up Ian in an endowed chair financially underwritten by the Coca Cola Company. In the end, however, Ian opted for the Max Planck Institute with their offer of a Directorship of a new Institute located in the former East Germany. High draft choice lost!

Another case in point was Mike Webster, who brought the study of avian molecular genetics and evolution from field to lab. Supported by a Career Development Award from NIH, Mike in his soft-spoken and engaging manner was hot on the trail of answering many age-old questions of bird parentage and distribution. Like Ian, Mike helped to redefine ecology, but in state-of-the-art molecular genetic terms; and like Ian, Mike was attracting interest from other Institutions eager to capitalize on the burgeoning interest in the chemical and molecular genetic sub-divisions of ecology. Contrary to Departmental counter offers, Mike elected, however, to take a tenured position at Washington State University, which a few years later was parlayed into a professorship at Cornell. Guiyun Yan came to UB from Notre Dame, interrupted by a year's study in Kenya, and he hit the ground running with his ambitious study of a world's curse – malaria. With wide financial support from NIH, NSF, and WHO (among other sources), Guiyun used his chicken model host to fully explore the molecular biology of the host/parasite interactions responsible for malaria. As he commuted back and forth to study locales in Kenya, it didn't take long for Guiyun to develop an international reputation in molecular genetic and evolutionary ecology, Guiyun thus became another eager target of recruitment from sister institutions. In his case, the University of California at Irvine became the winner along with promises of the usual perks which accompany signing a high draft choice. In the last instance, Antonia Monteiro came from Belguim, where she used her lab set-up funds to renovate much of Baldwin's vacated lab space. Once established, Antonia initiated her evolutionary/molecular genetic study of butterfly spots. While results at first were slow in coming, Antonia's accomplishments, together with her husband's evolutionary genomic tree work, made her competitive for a position at Yale, which she eventually took.

As if the above departures weren't enough to blunt the Department's extramural ratings (especially in areas of evolutionary and molecular ecology), another case popped up which needed immediate attention. The spousal team of Howie Lasker and Mary Alice Coffroth were being wooed by the University of Miami with an offer to pick up stakes and establish their coral reef investigations anew in southern Florida. While Howie was a full professor, Mary Alice treaded along as an untenured research assistant professor; however, in her case, her phylogenetic studies began to yield great dividends in extramural funding, as well as international repute. She was becoming a rising star in the business of using molecular genetic markers to help explain coral distribution or the lack thereof. In essence, her pioneering studies translated into sort of a "canary in the mine shaft" for a growing number of international scientists interested in global pollution and warming. Fortunately, Mary Bisson, who was the Chair at the time, convinced the upper administration of what it would take to retain the Lasker team - a tenured faculty track for Mary Alice as well as future faculty hires in evolutionary ecology. Finally, the department was able to get at least one finger in a hole of our leaky dike! A couple of years earlier, the Department retained Derek Taylor, an investigator in the growing field of molecular evolution. Derek came to the Department on half a line as part of a spousal retention arrangement by the Dean as Derek's wife was hired to a full time position in the Sociology Department. In the interim, Derek's field research involving bacteria and protozoa was paying great dividends to the point where he also was a potential recruitment candidate elsewhere. Fortunately, in the wake of Mary Alice's retention and promotion scheme, Derek was promoted and retained.


Working as Executive Officer gave me a unique vantage point in matters of faculty hiring and retention – highly qualified faculty are the life blood of any successful Department. In the 60's the Department enjoyed a surge in hiring when UB tried to establish itself as the "Berkeley of the East". While good faculty came far and wide to the Department, some, like the ecologists described earlier, saw greener pastures elsewhere. For example, the much touted dual of David Yphantis and Todd Shuster were initially hired because of their expertise in macromolecular separation techniques (an area much in demand due to pioneering scientists like Nobelist Christian DeDuve). In addition, Walter Rosen, was hired to establish the Department's new electron microscope facility. Regretfully, the latter three soon took off for senior positions along the Eastern seaboard. Moreover, a little later one of the old guard, herpetologist Carl Gans jumped ship and joined the University of Michigan as Chair of their Biology Department. It was also at this time when the Department was able to successfully pirate Om Bahl from the UB Biochemistry Department. Coming on board as Chair of the Department, Om brought with him his watershed and richly-funded research program of human chorionic gonadotropin (HCG). Subsequently, Om was replaced as Chair by Darrel Doyle, who came from cross-town Roswell Park Cancer Center and he brought with him his well-funded research team concentrating on cell and molecular biology. More recently, the Department lost Bruce Nicholson to the University of Texas Medical

Center at San Antonio, where he became Chair of the Biochemistry Department. Consequently, Bruce continued his research of cellular gap junctions making him one of the notables in an expanding field of signal transduction. On the other hand, the Department has had successes in retaining faculty such as Rich Almon, Paul Gollnick, and Derek Taylor, in spite of being wooed by other universities. Seeing which way the wind blows (and how to adapt to it) is one of the most important matters the Chair needs to face in maintaining the level of excellence expected from the upper administration. A successful department is more than a compilation of bricks and mortar, but it is utterly dependent on dedicated and enlightened faculty bringing passion in their quest for knowledge in the research lab as well as in their instruction. It was fulfilling for me to share in this quest with each Chair I worked with.


At the beginning of this chapter I was not going to focus on our faculty. As it turned out, however, I came to realize that most, if not all, facets of the Department at their core are carried on by faculty. Yes, there are support staff as good as they are, and, yes, there are students, undergraduate and graduate, but in effect it is the faculty member who brings to the Department the true quest for seeking and sharing knowledge. Looking back over the 10 years as Executive Officer (as well as my prior professional years), it seems all along I had been writing about myself and what I myself have become – a faculty member. In essence, I had finally arrived finding fruition in realizing my first real job. Dating back to my childhood years when I tried to help my neighborhood friend Bob Herzog cut grass or deliver the Sunday paper (or several failed attempts at employment thereafter), I always wanted a real job. Now I finally had one!

# Chapter 21

# Footprints, Keys, and a Dinner

It's been over 20 years since I've been able to stand on my own two feet; my earthly imprints have been tire tracks left by my trusty electric scooter. I can vividly recall steps once made during my ambulatory years – faltering ones in my schoolboy years, trip-laden at play, and cautious ones through my adult years (usually with the aid of a long stick or, with gratitude, someone's understanding shoulder). While my ability to make footprints is gone, metaphorically, other impressions of a sort have taken their place, hopefully for the ages and not ephemeral ones smudged long ago and forgotten.

As I wrestled with a conclusion to this tome, many ideas have come and gone. I could highlight those times when I've touched greatness, like the time I met and shook the unmistakably firm, muscular hand of Mother Theresa when she was given an honorary degree by my alma mater, Niagara University. I have met world class scientists at conferences heretofore only read about in journals and books. I have visited Claude Monet's home in Giverny, where I soaked up the beauty of his garden immortalized in his impressionistic oils. I have also contemplated our country's early history while on the grounds of Washington's Mount Vernon Estate and been in awe while within the shadows of the Lincoln Memorial. Maybe it was greatness which I felt when I made repeated trips to "The Wall" of the Vietnam Vets Memorial in search of two of my Niagara University classmates, John Bobo and Jim Hay. I discussed my idea of "greatness" with Raj, and off the top of her head, she added a few more names, like Hugh Huxley and Ralph Nader, to my growing list, along with some places like the Taj Mahal and the Grand Canyon.

**Mother Theresa and Me at Niagara University**

I could also expand my horizon and include those whom I've gotten to know within the pages of a book; such as, the heroic memoir of Vietnam Vet Max Cleland, where in *Strong at the Broken Places* he recants his recovery from paralyzing, life-threatening wounds, only to succeed as Head of the Veteran's Administration under President Carter, and later to serve as a United States Senator from Georgia! Not to be outdone, Raj added one of her personal favorites of long ago, the biography of Sir Douglas Bader called *Reach for the Stars*. Here, details are provided about the Englishman's loss of his two legs in a flying accident, yet, with artificial legs, Bader became group commander for the RAF in World War Two, and he later served as a consultant for handicapped travelers with British Airways. Touching greatness, indeed!

I recently celebrated my 70th birthday, and for the occasion fifty guests were invited to a dinner party at a nearby restaurant. After a couple of hours of eating and drinking, and as the cake was being doled out, our guests were encouraged to say a few poignant words.

Afterwards, I wanted to make a few comments. Because I knew the evening would be getting long, I wanted to keep my words short and to the point, if not meaningful. While I had mentally rehearsed several stories in the days leading up to this moment, three ideas quickly popped into my head as I gazed around the room. The first anecdote had to do with my dad, who asked me at age ten to join him on his monthly pro bono visit to a dental clinic at Buffalo Children's Hospital. As we reached the rear door of the clinic, Dad was enthusiastically greeted by the staff and their young patients readied for their dental exams; only in this case most of the young kids were lying within iron lungs. Aided by a mirror assembly, each kid recognized my dad with open mouths and broad smiles. As I looked at them, I was struck with fear, and my mind blurred as I watched Dad examine each patient. I remember being lost in thought on the ride home. In retrospect, it seems to have been a watershed time for me. A time in which I started to run, to be on the run, to live in more temporal terms. As the saying goes, "If but for the grace of God…" This primal fear instilled 60 years ago returns each time I might fall or trip, or confront some daily physical challenge. While my dinner companions knew me quite well, what they didn't know was that I've been on the run for most of my life; and each one of my guests has been an unwitting accomplice.

Another vignette concerned my extensive research of muscular dystrophy. Early on, as I became familiar with past and on-going studies of the disease, I focused primarily on the prevalent childhood form of the myopathy, Duchenne muscular dystrophy. Mostly by choice, I avoided research works dealing with my own Limb-Girdle disease. My schizoid priorities had less to do with the gravity of the Duchenne disease (extremely serious in its own right), but on the fact that the Limb-Girdle literature was filled with clinical cases, much too real and close to home for me. Remember, I've been on the run since age 10, and I didn't really need to read about the disease's morbidity.

Lastly, I pulled out my trump card. Looking at my guests, I saw in them an array of footprints which have impacted upon my life (and not incidentally upon the life of Raj as well). With each footprint, came a key - a key to opportunities not foreseen by Raj nor me.

This metaphor reminded me of a recent keynote address I gave a couple of years earlier at my department's convocation for graduating seniors. Over the years I have been invited to give talks to various academic functions, each one special in its own way. For example, I was invited by my nephew Jimmy on the occasion of his graduation from Mount St. Joseph's. On the same stage where I once participated in annual spring shows, I used the morning newspaper to highlight how invaluable their education was at the Mount. Then there was the National Honor Society induction ceremony for St. Joe's High School seniors, where I spoke about the specific role that St. Joe's has played as they were about to enter college. At UB, I was asked to provide the keynote address to inductees of the Golden Key Society, a National Honor Fraternity. Here, I focused on the revolution in molecular genetics and how the newly instituted Human Genome Project will impact our lives. For me, the highlight of the talk came at the end when I dramatically bellowed – "Hey, hey, be careful out there!"

When my own department asked me to deliver the keynote talk, I was particularly honored. Not only because I would be speaking in front of my peers, but ever since I was a student myself, I have always felt events associated with academic achievements to be extra special. It was a time to reflect on the past, the present, and what the future may entail. I took these events quite seriously. Having wrestled with what might be a worthy topic for the evening, I came up with notion that our lives can be distilled into ourselves being, in effect, a collection of keys.

I began my talk by asking the audience to think about the keys they had in their pocket or purse. Whether it was a house key, or a car key, they agreed with me about how comforting it was to know that they possessed the key and not lost or misplaced it. It was unnecessary to dwell on how important keys are in our daily lives. On the other hand, we can look upon keys from another angle, such as: sets of keys given to us, as keys made by ourselves, and as keys we have shared with others. In this sense, these are keys to knowledge, opportunity, and self-awareness. In effect, each of us has accumulated through a lifetime a set of keys which defines our capabilities if not our being.

We may ask when and where we had acquired these keys in the first place? In my talk I showed an old photograph of myself at age three being bracketed by my kind, nurturing mother fresh from the Canadian prairies, and my dad in his US Army uniform when at the time he was part of the U.S. Army Airborne. As could be seen in the photo, I looked like a young chap in desperate need of acquiring keys on how to eat, dress, keep clean, and, of course, keys on how to bait a fishhook. In effect, early keys came to me from my parents, guardians, friends, and subsequently my teachers. Interestingly, much of what I learned during my acquisition of childhood keys has remained with me throughout my adult life.

As the old saying goes, "Give a man a fish and he eats for a day. Teach a man how to fish, and he eats for a lifetime." We all know the value of education. In reality, might education in simple terms be the acquisition of more keys? Keys to help us better understand ourselves and the world around us. I'd like to think throughout our formal schooling we become better equipped to succeed in this world because we are not only acquiring better and better keys to understand ourselves, but in the bargain we are learning a host of newer keys toward making us successful in a trade or profession. It's at this stage when we might be capable of making up our own new keys to use, barter, or give out. For example, I often think of my high school teacher and mentor, Brother Anthony, who through his encouragement got me thinking of a career in architecture. He had a key and passed it on to me. I can also think of physiology professor Hugh Van Liew, who in only one 30 minute interview unwittingly redirected me from a medical career to one embracing research and teaching. He had a key and passed it on to me. To this day, I embrace that key, or else I would never have met Raj (who also had an array of keys which she readily shares to this day).

Throughout my life, I recall countless keys which have been passed on to me which I retain to this day. Does a day go by that we don't do something we learned long ago from our family? Our friends? Our teachers? Something we have read or heard? The repertoire of key-linked opportunities is vast: whether it is admiring brush strokes on a canvas, using a case study in the classroom, gathering statistics in an experiment or for an annual report, appreciating the intricacies of our immune system, planting a window box of geraniums, speaking to an audience, learning how to hit a four wood, plucking notes on a 5-string banjo, snapping photos of a natural scene, or metaphase chromosomes, or making a pretty good guess on what we need to know to treat muscular dystrophy or cancer! Looking around the tables at my birthday dinner, I was in awe as to what I might say. Here, within the room were friends and relatives instrumental in my survival and prosperity, as well as that of my dear Rajmohini.

**Rajmohini and Me**

To me the people in the room represented a large palette of keys, each one with a track record of opening doors enabling me to make accomplishments in this life - a palette containing colorful pigments each with its own hue and intensity. A dab here, a dab there, a little mixing, a little more color here or there, a form begins to appear. More paint, more corrections, the form has edges, nooks, and more clarity; more mixing of the blues with the yellows to yield green highlights, or other sets of primary colors. In a day, a week, maybe as long as a year (or two to three or longer), we see a painting develop. Hopefully it's a keeper, maybe even a masterpiece. For Raj and me, the paintings have become a metaphor for our lives:

Life-long friendships and companionships
Physical assistance in a myriad number of ways
Spiritual and sympathetic support when and where needed most
Mutual enjoyment of life's foibles
Support in the realm of teaching, research, and administration
Recreational partnerships to savor.


The interconnections shared with our friends and relatives are something we both dearly behold and cherish, and it was on this note that I concluded my toast by saying:


"Raj and I are truly thankful for your attendance here tonight. As I look around the room, I want you to know that I could easily fill up 60 minutes on each one of you here, on how much you mean to us and why. We are eternally grateful."

Michael S. Hudecki

**No Man is an Island (John Donne,1624)**
No man is an island entire of itself; every man
Is a piece of the continent, a part of the main;
If a clod be washed away by the sea, Europe
Is the less, as well as if a promontory were, as
Well as any manner of thy friends or of thine
Own were; any man's death diminishes me,
Because I am involved in mankind.
And therefore never send to know for whom
The bell tolls; it tolls for thee.